Julian Wilson's 100 GREATEST RACEHORSES

Julian Wilson's
100
GREATEST
RACEHORSES

Macdonald
Queen Anne Press

A *Queen Anne Press* BOOK

© Julian Wilson 1987

First published in Great Britain in 1987 by
Queen Anne Press, a division of
Macdonald & Co (Publishers) Ltd
3rd Floor
Greater London House
Hampstead Road
London NW1 7QX

A BPCC plc Company

Reprinted 1988

British Library Cataloguing in Publication Data

Wilson, Julian
    Julian Wilson's 100 greatest race horses.
    1. Horse-racing—Great Britain—History
    I. Title
    798.4′00941   SF335.G7

    ISBN 0-356-14293-0

Typeset by Clifford-Cooper Ltd, Farnham
Printed and bound in Great Britain by Butler and Tanner Ltd, Frome

Picture Credits

Ackermann Gallery: 61, 159, 175 COLOUR: St Simon
Associated Press: 35
Blood Horse, Kentucky: 70-71, 90, 100, 117, 137, 171, 187
Bridgeman Art Library: COLOUR: Carbine
BBC Hulton Picture Library: 20, 37, 49, 67, 150, 177, 197, 246
Gerry Cranham: 14, 15, 43, 54, 95, 102, 125, 139, 191, 192, 195,
                215, 229, 232, COLOUR: Arkle, Crisp, Mill House, Mill Reef,
                Oh So Sharp, Red Rum
Sue Crawford: COLOUR: Park Top (by kind permission of the Duke of Devonshire),
                Ribot
Illustrated London News: 52, 57, 112, 169
Jockey Club/Colour Laboratory: 154 COLOUR: Eclipse, Nijinsky, Sun Chariot
Jockey Club/Laurie Morton: COLOUR: Sir Ivor
Jockey Club/Tryon Gallery: COLOUR: Touchstone
Keystone, Paris: 26
Mansell Collection: 46, 69, 73, 104, 120, 128
Paddock Studios: Front cover
Peter Ohlson: 45
Photo Source: 163
Popperfoto: 39
W.W. Rouch: 18, 24, 31, 33, 48, 59, 64, 76, 79, 85, 87, 93, 97, 106, 114, 130,
            142, 152, 204, 213, 220, 226, 241, 252, 255 COLOUR: Brigadier
            Gerard
George Selwyn: 235, 249, 251 COLOUR: Night Nurse/Monksfield, Shergar
Sport and General: 12, 22, 28, 56, 63, 80, 109, 123, 133, 147, 156, 160, 165,
             167, 182, 184, 188, 199, 201, 207, 210, 238, 244

CONTENTS

INTRODUCTION

How to compare generations? It remains an ageless argument in sport. Was Dixie Dean a greater goalscorer than Ian Rush? Was Compton a finer batsman than Botham? Was Ormonde a greater racehorse than Mill Reef?

No sport remains static. In football, defences are tighter — through modern coaching, and the game faster. In cricket, bowling is more hostile — and dangerous — thanks to the West Indian influence. In racing there are now 8000 runners on the Flat in Britain each year, many with the finest international pedigrees and costing, as yearlings, up to $10 million. In Ormonde's era there were just 2000 runners, almost all owner-bred by the British landed gentry.

So how to compare the champions of the nineteenth century and the early twentieth century with the multi-million pound 'super-stars' of today? The task has been both intriguing and speculative. Historical 'evidence' is often confusing. The contemporary wordsmith who claimed that Eclipse (1764) could 'run a mile in a minute' had a clearly questionable method of timing. (The present course record at Newmarket is 1 minute 35.8 seconds.)

The style of riding as evidenced by the classic paintings of the nineteenth century was in total contrast to today's 'crouch' and races would usually become a sprint over two or three furlongs. But horses in general were tougher, more durable, and harder-trained. Future generations will have the benefit of television recordings to evaluate the achievements of the champions of today. We can only speculate on the giants of old.

The post-war popularity of National Hunt racing has resulted in the second part of this book being devoted to jumpers. The Grand National apart, top-class hurdle racing and steeplechasing is a relatively modern phenomenon. For instance, the value of the Champion Hurdle and Cheltenham Gold Cup in the 1930s was a mere £670. For this reason there are, in the author's opinion, fewer jumpers worthy of the epithet 'great', than flat-race champions, tracing back to Eclipse. Hence the ratio of 70/30 in favour of Flat racing.

Inevitably there will be criticisms of any personal selection. The Irish will question how Vincent O'Brien's triple Gold Cup winner Cottage Rake can be excluded, and a relatively modest steeplechaser in Aldaniti, be included. The answer is that there is more than one gate to greatness. Modern racegoers would argue that Pebbles, at her peak, would have defeated Oh So Sharp; that Royal Palace was superior to Grundy. Other omissions sure to offend are, on the Flat: Abernant, Blue Peter, Djebel, Fairway, Pinza, Quashed and Tetratema, and under National Hunt Rules: Poethlyn, Freebooter,

Gregalach, Kellsborough Jack and National Spirit.

A further problem for the racing author is 'the deadline'. By the end of 1987 Indian Skimmer, for one, may have qualified for 'greatness'. To paraphrase that famous quote: 'a month is a long time in racing!'

If this book errs on the side of colour entertainment, and popularity on the part of the subject, I can only beg the reader's forebearance.

Although horses from America, Canada, Australia, New Zealand, France, Italy and Hungary are included, the main bulk are from the British Isles. This is easily explained, Britain and Ireland are the cradle of the thoroughbred. Almost all overseas bloodlines — and notably contemporary American thoroughbreds — trace back to British foundations.

And what, you may ask, is Tumbledownwind doing amongst the elite? The answer is in the title of the book. Even the great Alfred Hitchcock allowed himself a modicum of self-indulgence!

And who was 'The Greatest'? It's a question that no mortal being will ever be able to answer.

If God were a racegoer ...

FLAT RACING

ALCIDE

ALCIDE WAS ONE of the best horses this century not to win the Derby. His failure to do so was almost certainly no fault of his own. Fate decreed that he was foaled during the worst era of doping and nobbling since the First World War.

Foaled 1955
Trained in England

Alcide, by Alycidon, was owned and bred by Sir Humphrey de Trafford, a tall and immaculately dressed member of the still hugely autocratic Jockey Club. He was trained by the equally dapper and distinguished Captain (eventually Sir) Cecil Boyd Rochfort.

He was the classic 'high mettled' racehorse. On the gallops he was forever dancing and rearing, so much so that his jockey Harry Carr described him as the most difficult colt to manage and the quickest in his movements that he had ever ridden. Yet on the racecourse, by contrast, he was lazy and lethargic, like his sire Alycidon, until he and no one else decided it was time to go. As a two-year-old Alcide won the Horris Hill Stakes at Newbury by a length and a half, coming from last to first. Inevitably he was much discussed as a Derby prospect during the winter.

I remember vividly his reappearance as a three-year-old. It was my first ever visit to Sandown Park, on what is now Whitbread Gold Cup day. Alcide, already backed for the Derby, was 11-8 on for the Royal Stakes (1¼ miles) but, tenderly ridden by Harry Carr, he was beaten a short head by the pounce of Lester Piggott on the Queen's Snow Cat. It was a touch of typical Piggott genius. Ten days later Alcide won the Chester Vase, although conspicuously unsuited by the course; and then thriving on his racing, he ran away with the Lingfield Derby Trial by 12 lengths.

By now Alcide was a very warm favourite for the Derby and the bookmakers were beginning to quake. There are two conflicting versions of what happened next. According to Harry Carr in his autobiography *Queen's Jockey,* Alcide was so well in himself eight days after Lingfield that he was turning himself inside-out. After playing the fool all morning, he finally gave a violent buck upwards and sideways. That evening at stables there was a large swelling on his near-side back ribs. The Derby was now out of the question. Harry Carr's view was that he must have wrenched himself internally and pulled a muscle.

The opinion of assistant trainer Bruce Hobbs (later a leading trainer himself) was quite different. 'In my view there is no doubt that he was "got at," ' he told me years later. 'He had clearly been given a vicious blow and he was in such pain he could hardly move. He was hot favourite and the nobblers had done for him.' Three months later Alcide reappeared in the Great Voltigeur Stakes and won in brilliant style by twelve lengths.

The St Leger looked to be a formality and so it proved. Starting at 9-4 on, Alcide ran his usual lethargic race, until suddenly in the straight he decided to 'go', and won by a spectacular eight lengths.

As a four-year-old Alcide went from strength to strength — until two weeks before his main target, the Gold Cup. Alcide sustained a rapped joint and missed two or three vital gallops while Harry Carr was admitted to hospital for the removal of kidney stones, a jockey's most painful disability. Following this entirely unsuitable preparation, Alcide was pipped by a short head by the French colt Wallaby II (Freddie Palmer) in a ding-dong finish.

Harry Carr was still in extreme discomfort five weeks later when Alcide reverted to a mile and a half in the King George VI & Queen Elizabeth Stakes. It was to be Alcide's last race, and many doubted the wisdom of 'coming back' a mile with the Leger winner. In the event Alcide proved himself a great champion, coming from last to first in the straight to beat Gladness by two lengths.

Ironically his two main targets, the Derby and the Gold Cup, had eluded him. In every other respect he was a true 'great'.

Alcide's finest hour — from last to first in the straight to beat Gladness (Garnet Bougoure) by two lengths in the 'King George'. Within hours Harry Carr was in hospital with acute kidney trouble.

BIG RACES WON	
St Leger	1958
King George VI & Queen Elizabeth Stakes	1959
Chester Vase	1958
Lingfield Derby Trial	1958
Great Voltigeur Stakes	1958

ALLEGED

Foaled 1974
Trained in Ireland

IN THE YEARS following the Second World War, the Prix de l'Arc de Triomphe gradually became the most prestigious all-aged Flat Race in the world. It is a race that English stables have always found hard to win. With the concentration of top-class racing in England during June, July and August, the 'Arc' tends to come a month too late. Accordingly, it should be no easier for an Irish-trained horse to win the great race. The fact that Alleged did so twice earns him a place amongst the élite.

Alleged possessed an unusual background for a Vincent O'Brien-trained American-bred. Having been bought as a yearling by a certain Monty Roberts for a mere $34,000 at Keeneland in July, he was re-submitted as a two-year-old in training in California six months later. It was here that the egregious Billy McDonald bought the Hoist The Flag colt for $175,000 (a nice profit) for Robert Sangster, initially with a view to his being trained in California. However, close examination of the colt's knees suggested he would be quite unsuited to racing on dirt; so, soon after, Alleged arrived at Ballydoyle.

No one took a great deal of notice. He was weak, backward, unfurnished and rather plain. Even Vincent and his marvellous staff found it difficult to build any condition onto him. Nonetheless, in November Alleged duly won his first and only two-year-old race by eight lengths.

The following season — the year of The Minstrel — Alleged won on his reappearance, but didn't impress. Accordingly, in his next race, the Royal Whip, he started outsider of Vincent's three runners in the race, at 33-1 — and staggered the stable by beating the 5-4 favourite Valinsky — ridden by Lester Piggott!

But still Vincent did not hurry and overface the rather gangly colt. While The Minstrel was winning the Derby, Vincent was 'thinking' an autumn campaign for Alleged. It began in staggering style with a seven-length all-the-way win in the Great Voltigeur Stakes at York. Runner-up was Classic Example, who had run The Minstrel to less than two lengths in the Irish Derby.

Alleged now looked the best three-year-old colt in Europe — and a 'certainty' for the St Leger for which he started 7-4 on. The Leger proved to be the only defeat of Alleged's career. Lester was accused of falling for a 'sucker punch' when Dunfermline's pacemaker 'died' half a mile from home leaving Lester in front. In the event Willie Carson came with a flourish on Dunfermline and Alleged had little time to fight back. As so often was the case, a month later Lester became Dr Jekyll again in the Arc, dictating the race and launching Alleged to a brilliant success in the straight.

Alleged (Lester Piggott) in his first 'Arc' triumph.

Alleged, now valued at $10 million, remained in training as a four-year-old, but again, as so often happens, everything went wrong. The ground was firm; he jarred his knees — and lost his action. Then came the virus that ravaged the yard. All the while the big four-year-old races were slipping away like leaves from a tree.

Finally, in the autumn, he came right. After a brilliant trial in the Prix du Prince d'Orange (track record), Alleged returned for his second Arc. It was easier than the first. Only Tantieme and Ribot, since the war, had won two Arcs. Alleged retired with a syndication value of $13 million. It was Billy McDonald's finest hour!

BIG RACES WON	
Prix de l'Arc de Triomphe (twice)	1977-78
Great Voltigeur Stakes	1977
Royal Whip (twice)	1977-78
Gallinule Stakes	1977

ALLEZ FRANCE

ONE OF THE foremost guidelines in racing is to give a horse a good name. After all you do not find Derby winners called 'Hellcatmudwrestler'! No name could have appealed more to Parisian *turfistes* than 'Allez France' — and like a true patriot the filly came up with the goods.

Foaled 1970
Trained in France

Allez France was a charming filly and most feminine in appearance. Owned by the international art historian M. Daniel Wildenstein, Allez France was trained at Chantilly, first by Albert Klimscha, and latterly by the brilliant Argentinian-born Angel Penna. Penna had a affinity with fillies that was uncanny. If something disturbed him he would sit up all night to study a filly's every move. So it was with Allez France, whom he took over in 1974.

Already handled skilfully by the Scandinavian-born Klimscha, she had won the French 1000 Guineas, French Oaks (beating Dahlia by 2½ lengths) and Prix Vermeille in her Classic season. Inevitably she was a firm favourite for the Prix de l'Arc de Triomphe, but was no match for the Piggott-ridden Rheingold.

Facing the normally difficult task of training a four-year old filly, Penna responded by guiding her through the season unbeaten, an achievement climaxed by the filly's success, by a head at 2-1 on, in the Prix de l'Arc de Triomphe. Yves Saint-Martin, who had injured a foot a week previously, was passed fit only at the twelfth hour. It was an occasion filled with Gallic emotion.

Allez France remained in training as a five-year-old, and continued to prosper although by the autumn her magic was on the wane. In the 'Arc' she could finish only fifth to the 119-1 shot Star Appeal, while in the Champion Stakes she was beaten one-and-a-half lengths by the three-year-old Rose Bowl.

Allez France was certainly one of the best fillies to race in France this century. In thirteen wins from twenty-one races she won £493,000, a figure only exceeded at the time by her great rival Dahlia. However, in six meetings Dahlia never beat Allez France!

She retired to the paddocks in America, but has not proved the best of breeders. Indeed it was ten years before she bred her first winner, a useful colt called Air de France (by Seattle Slew).

BIG RACES WON	
Prix de l'Arc de Triomphe	1974
Prix de Diane	1973
Poule d'Essai des Pouliches	1973
Prix Vermeille	1973
Prix Ganay (twice)	1974-75
Criterium des Pouliches	1972
Prix d'Ispahan	1974
Prix Dollar	1975
Prix d'Harcourt	1974

ALYCIDON

MANY OF THE great stayers of the post-war era have shared the same characteristics — extreme laziness and a quirky nature. Alycidon, according to his jockey the five-times champion Doug Smith, was 'the greatest stayer I have ever seen and probably one of the greatest stayers of all time'.

Foaled 1945
Trained in England

Like so many eventual winners of the Ascot Gold Cup, Alycidon showed no inkling of ability as a two-year-old. Bred by the 17th Earl of Derby, who sadly died before his ability became apparent, Alycidon was an idle, backward 'slob'. Indeed his trainer Walter Earl found it extremely difficult to make him race-fit. In the end he devised a two-fold plan. He would work Alycidon over six or seven furlongs on the Limekilns (Newmarket's famous Summer Gallop, with wonderful spring in the turf), between two other horses leading them by a neck or half a length. If Alycidon fell behind, even by a length, he would drop everything and pull himself up. Alternatively, he would work on Lord Derby's private peat moss gallop, which ended going in the direction of the Stanley House Stables — i.e. home! With his manger in mind, Alycidon would gallop with unaccustomed enthusiasm! On the racecourse his idle nature was overcome by the fitting of blinkers, and eventually by the use of not one but two pacemakers. Thus equipped he became the first horse since Isonomy in 1879 to win the Cup 'Triple Crown' — the Gold Cup, Goodwood Cup and Doncaster Cup.

The Gold Cup in 1949 was his most evocative win. The previous autumn he had been trounced by Black Tarquin in the St Leger, after the intended pacemaker whipped round at the start leaving Alycidon to make his own running. Now, Alycidon went to battle with his two pacemakers: Stockbridge, who led for a mile and a quarter, and Benny Lynch who took over for the next five furlongs. Alycidon was cruising, but Black Tarquin was cantering on his heels. Doug Smith decided to go for home, gave Alycidon a back-hander and, in the words of Edgar Britt on Black Tarquin, Alycidon's quarters expanded and exploded. Alycidon won by five lengths in the most popular Gold Cup triumph since the Prince of Wales's Persimmon in 1897.

Black Tarquin, destroyed by the power of Alycidon, was never the same horse again. Five years later Chris Brasher and Chris Chataway used similar pacemaking tactics to enable Roger Bannister to run the first four-minute mile!

Alycidon was a successful stallion, but latterly a shy breeder. Alcide and Meld were his most brilliant offspring. He was destroyed painlessly in 1963. Ironically, one of his best sons, Twilight Alley, who won the Gold Cup in 1963, had identical characteristics.

Alycidon, the first stayer since Isonomy in 1879 to win the Ascot, Goodwood and Doncaster Cup.

A bemused Sir Noel Murless telephoned Doug Smith one evening: 'Doug — how on earth did you get that Alycidon fit? I can't get this horse to do a tap!' Doug explained the three-horse gallops on the Limekilns and suggested Sir Noel try the same system. He did: Twilight Alley won the Gold Cup and Doug was presented with a case of the finest champagne!

BIG RACES WON	
Gold Cup	1949
Goodwood Cup	1949
Doncaster Cup	1949
Jockey Club Stakes	1948
Princess of Wales's Stakes	1948
Ormonde Stakes	1949

BAHRAM

IT IS A REASONABLE assertion that a horse's true merit can only be gauged by his first defeat, leaving aside super-champions like Nearco, Ribot, Ormonde and St Simon. Therefore any horse who retires unbeaten will always be liable to the accusation of 'he never beat a good horse'.

Foaled 1932
Trained in England

Such a horse was Bahram, the unbeaten winner of the Triple Crown in 1935. Bahram was bred and owned by the Aga Khan, at a time when the Imam had become by far the most substantial owner in the history of the British Turf. Between 1924-1937 he headed the Leading Owners' List seven times, while his breeding interests were served by five of the finest Studs in Ireland. It was scarcely surprising in the circumstances that several of Bahram's leading contemporaries were also owned by the Aga Khan. This factor has been used by Bahram's detractors to diminish his achievements.

Bahram, a good-looking and powerful son of Blandford, won all of his five races as a two-year-old. In the first of them, the National Breeders' Produce Stakes at Sandown, starting at 20-1, he beat his strongly-fancied stable companion Theft (gave 9lb) by a neck. In all of his remaining two-year-old races, including the Gimcrack and Middle Stakes, Bahram started at odds-on. He headed the Two-Year-Old Free Handicap with 9st 7lb ... just 1lb above Theft and another colt of the Aga Khan's in Hairan.

Bahram came to the 2000 Guineas without a preparatory race, having missed the Craven Stakes through being off-colour. The race resolved itself into a battle between Bahram and Theft, with Bahram running out ultimately an impressive winner by one-and-a-half lengths.

Bahram became a very warm favourite for the Derby, eventually starting at 5-4. His main ante-post rivals were Hairan and Theft. The only question mark about him was his stamina. Stable confidence was high, and as Bahram went to post, Bob Lyle, the distinguished correspondent for *The Times*, reported that he had never seen a horse move better. Prince Aly Khan confessed to a friend that he had struck the biggest bet of his life!

Early in the race Freddie Fox on Bahram found himself in a very tight spot and shouted to Harry Wragg on Theft to pull over. Wragg complied — and was later hauled before the stewards for his pains! Bahram took the lead over two furlongs out and won in majestic style. Theft was fourth and Hairan, ridden by Gordon Richards, unplaced.

Bahram was made 11-4 on to complete the Triple Crown and did so with the greatest of ease — by five lengths. The only drama

The Aga Khan is overwhelmed by congratulations as the unbeaten Bahram (Freddie Fox) returns to unsaddle after the Derby. Note the uninvited presence of tipster Ras Prince Monolulu in the background!

was an accident to Freddie Fox on the eve of the race. Charlie Smirke stepped in — as he did nineteen years later for the suspended Lester Piggott on Never Say Die.

The St Leger was Bahram's last race. The Aga Khan retired him to stud with eulogies of affection and a declaration that he would never sell the first Triple Crown winner since 1903.

He was a horse of magnificent presence. A favourite characteristic was for him to lean against the wall of a stable with his legs crossed, looking around him in a supercilious way. It was this studied indolence that occasionally made him less impressive than his critics demanded. But no horse beat him — nor did any extend him.

The tail-piece was sad. The Aga Khan sold him in 1940 to an American syndicate for $160,000. He never thrived in America and was eventually exported to Argentina where he died in 1956. At other times the Aga sold his Derby winners Blenheim and Mahmoud to America, and many British breeders never forgave him for the loss of three potentially great stallions. To cap this, at the start of the Second World War, the Aga sold almost all his horses in training and went to live in neutral Switzerland.

BIG RACES WON	
Derby	1935
2000 Guineas	1935
St Leger	1935
St. James's Palace Stakes	1935
Gimcrack Stakes	1934
Middle Park Stakes	1934

BALLYMOSS

Foaled 1954
Trained in Ireland

AMONGST THE REASONS that a great horse can fail to win the Derby are injury, inability to stay the trip and extreme bad luck in running. In the case of Ballymoss the prime reason was his ill fortune to be foaled in the same year as Crepello.

Of course there was another major factor. Ballymoss was a very backward horse who despite winning two Classics did not reach his pinnacle until a 4-year-old. Vincent O'Brien bought Ballymoss for 4500 guineas at the Doncaster Sales. It was early in Vincent's transition from top National Hunt trainer to Flat Racing 'wizard', and Vincent was hard on the look-out for owners. Through a mutual friend he met the American millionaire builder John McShain at Doncaster Races.

Ballymoss was a very average two-year-old, winning a minor race at Leopardstown from four starts. His reappearance in the Madrid Free Handicap was a disaster. He finished well back, and showed no enthusiasm. But the ground was heavy.

However, a month later, on good ground, he won the Trigo Stakes, beating his stable companion the great mare Gladness at 20-1. After a brilliant mixed gallop Vincent decided to send him to Epsom.

Crepello was a horse in 100,000 and he won the Derby with style by a length and a half. But Ballymoss at 33-1 beat the remainder comfortably and a month later, starting at 9-4 on, he won the Irish Derby with considerable ease.

Defeat in the Great Voltigeur Stakes was again blamed on soft going. I remember it well; it was a vile day and Lester Piggott, to the best of my recollection, was beaten on six fancied horses! So came the St Leger and another wet Yorkshire afternoon, spirits were in decline. But the light sandy soil at Town Moor inhibited Ballymoss far less than the bog of the Knavesmire, and Ballymoss ridden by T.P. Burns, won by a length from Court Harwell.

As a four-year-old, Ballymoss, like Busted ten years later, became an exceptional horse. He won the Coronation Cup, Eclipse Stakes, King George VI and Queen Elizabeth Stakes and finally a dramatic Prix de l'Arc de Triomphe.

Ballymoss galloped brilliantly before the 'Arc' and Vincent had a substantial ante-post bet. Everything had gone right. Then on the day of the race, the inevitable occurred... the skies opened and the rain poured down in torrents. Vincent tried desperately to cancel his bet, to no avail. Scobie Breasley, now Ballymoss's regular jockey, finished tailed off in the second race, and returned shaking his head in gloom. Viewing the recorded telecast of the race thirty years later, reveals the full extent of the impact of the rain: the horses seem

Ballymoss ('T.P.' Burns) overcomes soft ground to win the St Leger from Court Harwell (Scobie Breasley) and Brioche (Edward Hide).

to come home in slow motion! But Ballymoss, now at his peak of strength and maturity, and ridden by the artistic Breasley, somehow galloped through the mud.

During his career Ballymoss won £107,165 in stakes, establishing a new UK record. He was not a great stallion, but sired one Derby winner in Royal Palace. What he did do was launch Vincent O'Brien on his Classic path.

BIG RACES WON	
Prix de l'Arc de Triomphe	1958
St Leger	1957
Irish Derby	1957
King George VI & Queen Elizabeth Stakes	1958
Eclipse Stakes	1958
Coronation Cup	1958

BAYARDO

BAYARDO WAS, by common consent, one of the outstanding horses of the first half of the twentieth century. Yet he was beaten in both the 2000 Guineas and the Derby. Bayardo was trained by the 'Wizard of Manton' Alec Taylor for an awkward, irascible man named Mr A.W. Cox (whose *nom de course* was 'Mr Fairie').

Two weeks before his first appearance in the New Stakes at Royal Ascot, Otto Madden and some other jockeys travelled to Manton to ride in a trial, testing the stable's most promising two-year-olds against a three-year-old called Seedcake. Madden, riding Bayardo, won the trial easily by six lengths. One can imagine Alec Taylor's astonishment, therefore, when Madden told him on the eve of Ascot that he had accepted another ride in the New Stakes! 'I'm sorry,' stated Madden, 'but I'm afraid your two-year-olds can't be any good. That three-year-old I rode murdered them!' 'That wasn't the three-year-old you idiot,' exclaimed Taylor, 'That was Bayardo!'

It was the costliest mistake of Madden's life, as he lost the riding of Bayardo for good. Bernard Dillon rode Bayardo as a two-year-old and the legendary Danny Maher rode him for the remainder of his career. Bayardo was unbeaten in seven races as a two-year-old, but the following spring was cold and dry and the colt's feet, which were fleshy and shelly, gave Taylor considerable worry.

Taylor was loath to run his Champion in the 2000 Guineas, but the owner insisted. Bayardo, although odds-on, finished only fourth to The King's Minoru. Two weeks before Epsom Bayardo began to thrive, but on the day interference from the favourite Sir Martin, running down Tattenham Hill, cost him all of half a dozen lengths and Maher accepted defeat. Again, King Edward VII's Minoru was the hugely popular winner.

Thereafter Bayardo went from strength to strength. Over the next fifteen months he dominated the Turf in a way that few horses have done. He won the Prince of Wales's Stakes at Royal Ascot, the Eclipse, the St Leger (annihilating Minoru), three races at Newmarket in the autumn including the Champion Stakes, and the Liverpool St Leger.

As a four-year-old he won the Chester Vase narrowly, with Maher leaving it desperately late. Bayardo had gradually become quirky and would 'plant' for lengthy periods outside his box. Furthermore, at Newmarket he would refuse to canter down in front of the stands. Accordingly, Maher would weave his way through the coaches and carriages in the car-park, much to Bayardo's amusement.

It was this quirkiness that persuaded Maher to believe that Bayardo did not care to be in front for too long. Hence his riding at Chester. In the Ascot Gold Cup however, Bayardo pulled his way

Foaled 1906
Trained in England

Bayardo — brilliance tempered by quirks of character. Unbeaten as a two-year-old, he eventually won twenty-two out of twenty-five races.

to the front six furlongs from home to win as he pleased by four lengths, thus affording much delight to the critics of Maher's tactics.

Maher had his 'revenge', however, in Bayardo's final race, the Goodwood Cup. Starting at 20-1 on, Maher allowed the three-year-old Magic (receiving 36lb) almost a furlong's start, and failed by a neck to catch the younger horse.

Bayardo retired the winner of twenty-two of his twenty-five races. Sadly, he died at the age of eleven following a thrombosis, but his stud influence was considerable with his grandson Hyperion becoming one of the great prepotent stallions.

BIG RACES WON	
St Leger	1909
Gold Cup	1910
Eclipse Stakes	1909
Champion Stakes	1909
Prince of Wales's Stakes	1909
Liverpool St Leger	1909
Chester Vase	1910
Middle Park Plate	1908
Dewhurst Plate	1908

BRANTOME

ONCE UPON A TIME — indeed up to thirty years ago — the Ascot Gold Cup was considered the ultimate target of a four-year-old's career. Nowadays, sadly, the position is quite the reverse. To win a Gold Cup is a positive stigma for a potential stallion, and indeed no English Classic winner has won the Gold Cup for over forty years.

Foaled 1931
Trained in France

It was very different between the wars when the criterion of excellence in a thoroughbred was the ability to win over five furlongs as a two-year-old, and up to two-and-a-half miles as a four-year-old. Such a horse was Brantome, owned, bred and raced by Baron Edouard de Rothschild in France. A son of one of this century's greatest stallions, Blandford — sire of four Derby winners in seven years — Brantome was unbeaten in four races as a two-year-old, including the French Two-Year-Old 'Triple Crown', the Prix Robert Papin, Prix Morny and Grand Criterium. He was rated 7lb clear of his nearest rival, Admiral Drake, in the French Free Handicap.

His three-year-old season was interrupted severely by a persistent cough, which prevented him from running in both the French Derby and the Grand Prix de Paris. Nonetheless, he began the year by winning the French 2000 Guineas (at 10-1 on), and Prix Lupin — and ended it by winning the French St Leger and Prix de l'Arc de Triomphe, in brilliant style.

As a four-year-old, his target was duly made the Ascot Gold Cup. On the way he triumphed in the Prix du Cadran — the French equivalent — in record time for the race, and *turfistes* on both sides of the Channel looked forward to one of the great races for the Gold Cup, between Brantome and Windsor Lad.

Two things went wrong, however. Windsor Lad, the 1934 Derby winner, and also a son of Blandford, was withdrawn from the race by his owner, the bookmaker Mr Martin Benson, for fear of defeat. Then eleven days before the race, Brantome got loose and galloped down the main street at Chantilly. Although he skilfully avoided several cars, he lost three shoes and sustained an unpleasant cut before he was caught. His injury kept him off work for four days and his trip to Ascot was about to be abandoned. However, his sporting owner insisted upon running — and Brantome was beaten for the first time. When the news reached France no one was prepared to believe that he had finished out of the first three.

Brantome was never the same after Ascot, although he did win the Prix du Prince d'Orange at Longchamp in the autumn. But his record of twelve wins with over two million francs, from five furlongs — two-and-a-half miles — established him as one of the great French horses this century. But for his accident, he would probably never have been beaten.

Brantome returns after winning the Prix du Cadran (the French Gold Cup) in record time.

BIG RACES WON	
Poule d'Essai des Poulains	1934
Prix Royal Oak	1934
Prix de l'Arc de Triomphe	1934
Prix du Cadran	1935
Prix Lupin	1934
Prix Robert Papin	1933
Prix Morny	1933
Grand Criterium	1933

BRIGADIER GERARD

Foaled 1968
Trained in England

ASK A DOZEN 'experts' their formula for breeding a great horse and you will probably receive a dozen different answers. 'Breed the best to the best — and hope for the best!' is the traditional formula, but it is not a method approved by Brigadier Gerard's breeder and part-owner John Hislop.

To breed his champion, John sent a shy-breeding mare of medium-class pedigree to Queen's Hussar, a relatively unfashionable stallion whose nomination fee had dropped to 200 guineas. (I recall this fact vividly as I also sent a mare to Queen's Hussar in 1967, and bred a foal so moderate his name escapes me!) The result, nonetheless, to John's everlasting credit, was one of the greatest horses of the post-war era, who won his first sixteen races.

John Hislop, former champion amateur jockey, journalist, breeding expert and adviser, and company director, has excelled in many areas of horse racing. But he has never, on his own admission, been a rich man. It was fortunate therefore, that before 'The Brigadier' went into training as a yearling, his wife Jean had made him promise never to sell their cherished colt.

I recall having tea with Desmond and Molly Baring (The Brigadier's granddam Frisky Molly was allegedly named after my hostess) on the day that the powerful colt had won his third race, the Washington Singer Stakes. 'What did you think of him?' asked Molly, having heard me commentate on the race on BBC TV. 'I think he's good,' I replied. 'They've been offered £60,000 for him,' said Molly. 'I think they should take it!' I replied. To their credit they didn't, nor did they accept an offer of £250,000 before the 2000 Guineas, nor did they accept a genuine 'blank' cheque later in his career!

It was one of nature's ironic jokes that Brigadier Gerard was foaled in the same year as Mill Reef and My Swallow. The three of them composed the nucleus of possibly the finest field for the 2000 Guineas since the War. Mill Reef had won the Greenham Stakes in a common canter by four lengths; while My Swallow had beaten a useful horse owned by the author called Midnight Cowboy, with equal ease at Kempton.

The press and public considered the 2000 Guineas a two-horse race. Only the late Clive Graham in the *Daily Express* tipped The Brigadier. Brigadier Gerard did not just win, he went past his rivals as if they were standing still, to win by three lengths. At the time it was impossible to believe the result: I was convinced that Mill Reef had failed to 'run his race' — either because he was off-colour, or because the giant, coltish Minsky had frightened and intimidated him in the pre-parade ring. Mill Reef was never beaten again —

*Brigadier Gerard, winner
of his first 15 races,
including the 2000
Guineas, Eclipse and King
George VI & Queen
Elizabeth Stakes.*

which to a degree justified my beliefs — and sadly, the two great
horses never met again.

Brigadier Gerard did not run in the Derby because his owner
believed he would not stay. So the opportunity for a re-match did
not materialize until the following year on 15 August — in the
Benson & Hedges Gold Cup. Infuriatingly, six days before the race
Mill Reef pulled a muscie in his quarters and was withdrawn. Worse
was to follow: The Brigadier, after fifteen straight wins, was defeated
by the enigmatic Roberto. Ridden by the Panamanian Braulio Baeza
after Lester Piggott had declined the ride, the Derby winner made
every yard of the running in record time. It was The Brigadier's only
defeat.

He retired at the end of the season with a record comparable to the very best. Only two Classic winners this century (Pretty Polly and Bayardo) have won more races. He was a truly great champion.

BIG RACES WON	
2000 Guineas	1971
King George VI & Queen Elizabeth Stakes	1972
Eclipse Stakes	1972
Champion Stakes (twice)	1971-72
Sussex Stakes	1971
Queen Elizabeth II Stakes (twice)	1971-72
St James's Palace Stakes	1971
Prince of Wales Stakes	1972
Lockinge Stakes	1972
Middle Park Stakes	1970

BROWN JACK

Foaled 1924
Trained in England

IT IS A FACT of racing life that the public have a deeper affection for the jumping, year-to-year horses like Arkle, Sea Pigeon and Red Rum, than for the Flat Racing 'stars' who retire to stud after just two seasons' racing.

Brown Jack was probably the most popular flat-race horse this century. Yet ironically, in complete reversal of the normal trend, he began life as a hurdler — and then became a flat-race 'crack'! Brown Jack, by Jackdaw, was bred in Ireland by Mr George Webb, who sent him to Goff's Sales as a yearling in August 1925 — without his eliciting a single bid! After two private sales he was bought as a backward three-year-old in training for £750 by the Hon. Aubrey Hastings, with a long-term objective of winning the Champion Hurdle for his patron Sir Harold Wernher.

Despite starting his jumping career at Bournemouth and being viewed with a lack of interest verging on contempt by the lads in the yard, Brown Jack progressed throughout the season and went to Cheltenham for the Champion Hurdle a well-fancied 4-1 chance. It was only the second year of the Challenge Cup with a prize of just £680, but Brown Jack achieved the remarkable feat of winning the 'Hurdlers' Derby' within seven months of jumping his first hurdle. Watching the race was the ten times champion flat-race jockey Steve Donaghue, who declared to Hastings after the race: 'He'll win on the Flat — and I'll ride him'. Thus, remarkably, ended Brown Jack's hurdling career — and began a memorable chapter of Flat Racing history.

For the next seven seasons Brown Jack, ridden by Donoghue, never missed the Royal Ascot meeting. Within three months of winning the Champion Hurdle, he was handicapped with 7st 13lb in the Ascot Stakes — and won. In 1929 he was beaten a short head in the Ascot Stakes by Old Orkney — and three days later won the Queen Alexandra Stakes by four lengths.

In May 1929 Aubrey Hastings had died, but with the Wroughton stable taken over by his assistant Ivor Anthony, everything went on as before. In 1930 Brown Jack was unplaced in the Ascot Stakes — and once again won the Queen Alexandra Stakes three days later, beating his great rival Old Orkney. This pattern was repeated in 1931.

By now Brown Jack's popularity was immense, and his reception compared with that of a Derby winner. In 1932 he ran in the Gold Vase (unplaced) prior to his fourth success in the Queen Alexandra, while the following year the stable settled for just one foray — and won No. 5 in the 2 miles 6 furlong marathon.

In 1934, at the age of ten, he went to Ascot for the seventh and

Brown Jack and Steve Donoghue — the most popular and successful Royal Ascot combination this century.

final time — and for the first time since 1930, started odds against for 'his' race — indeed at one stage 3-1 was offered. The *Evening Standard* banners read simply: 'BROWN JACK TODAY'. Ivor Anthony was too nervous to watch the race and sat in the paddock under a tree. It was an epic race, Brown Jack and Solarium drew clear in the straight. Slowly, inch by inch, and then foot by foot, Brown Jack and Donoghue forged to the front to cheers the like of which had never been heard before. Afterwards there were scenes unprecedented at Ascot. Strong men wept unashamedly: reserved old ladies gathered their skirts and ran to the Unsaddling Enclosure; hats were thrown in the air. It was a fitting end to a remarkable career which also included a Doncaster Cup and a win and four seconds in the Goodwood Cup.

Gelded as a yearling, Brown Jack was kind, but idiosyncratic: lazy on the gallops, but like a lion on the racecourse. Steve Donaghue, the horseman supreme, loved him like no other horse — and he loved Donoghue. On their final photo-call, Brown Jack pushed his head forward and licked Steve's face from ear to ear.

BIG RACES WON	
Goodwood Cup	1930
Doncaster Cup	1930
Queen Alexandra Stakes (six times)	1929-34
Ascot Stakes	1928
Chester Cup	1931
Ebor Handicap	1931
Champion Hurdle	1928

CARBINE

Foaled 1885
Trained in Australia

IT TAKES A very special racehorse for his name to become part of the language. Such a horse was Carbine, who won the Melbourne Cup under a remarkable 10st 5lb. Ever since that famous day, Australian poker players have called two pairs of 'tens' and 'fives' a 'Carbine'!

Carbine was bred in New Zealand by two English expatriate parents, Musket and Mersey. Musket was lucky to be alive. His eccentric owner-breeder, Lord Glasgow, was so unimpressed by him as a foal that he ordered him to be shot. Happily for all concerned John Osborne, the stable jockey, pleaded for his life and Musket's salvation was clinched when Lord Glasgow died in March 1869. In 1878, after a successful racing career, but limited success at stud, Musket was exported to New Zealand where he was bred initially to half-bred mares. Eventually, he changed hands again and Carbine was foaled in 1886.

Carbine's career was extraordinary by any standards. Unbeaten as a two-year-old in New Zealand, he travelled to race for the superior prize money in Australia as a three-year-old. Unfortunately for his owner Dan O'Brien, Carbine was given an appalling ride by a jockey called Derrett in the V.R.C. Derby at Flemington, with the result that O'Brien offered him for sale — quite possibly to recoup gambling debts. He changed hands for 3000 guineas.

Thereafter Carbine scarcely looked back. At the Randwick Sydney Cup Meeting, he was beaten in the A.J.C. Autumn Plate (1½ miles) on the first day; won the Sydney Cup (2 miles) on the second day; and then won the All-Aged Stakes (1 mile), the Cumberland Stakes (1¾ miles) and the A.J.C. Plate (2¼ miles) at the same meeting!

As a four-year-old he was campaigned in a similar manner, culminating this time in winning all of his five races at the four-day Sydney Cup meeting! It was, however, as a five-year-old that he reached his zenith, notably with his remarkable Melbourne Cup triumph. Carrying 10st 5lb in a record-sized field of thirty-nine, he won Australia's greatest race in the then fastest-ever time of 3 minutes 28.25 seconds. The runner-up Highborn, receiving 53lb, later won the Sydney Cup under 9st 3lb. Not even Phar Lap's success in 1930 evoked greater scenes of enthusiasm.

In the autumn Carbine was retired with a career record of forty-three races, thirty-three wins, six 2nds and three 3rds. A bay horse, standing 15.3hh, he had a rather plain head with an unusual jagged white stripe. He made little impact at stud in Australia, but in 1895 the Duke of Portland acquired him to stand alongside St Simon at his Welbeck Abbey Stud in Nottinghamshire. Despite the worst slump in Australia's history, 2000 horse players stood at the docks to wave Carbine farewell.

Happily, Carbine justified his purchase by siring Spearmint, who went on to win the 1906 Derby. One hundred years on, Australia has only ever seen one comparable horse: Phar Lap.

Plain, stocky and short-backed he may have been, but Carbine became a legend in Australia and New Zealand.

BIG RACES WON	
Melbourne Cup	1890
Sydney Cup (twice)	1888-89
Champion Stakes, Randwick (twice)	1888, 1890
Flying Stakes, Flemington (twice)	1888-89
A.J.C. Plate (3m) (three times)	1888-90

CITATION

Foaled 1945
Trained in USA

ONE OF THE KEY assets in racing horses — as in gambling — is knowing when to stop. Nowadays owners are widely criticised for 'packing off' horses to stud too early in their careers. But only those closest to a horse can assess, with reasonable accuracy, when a horse's decline is imminent.

Citation was a horse who should almost certainly have retired at the end of his three-year-old career. Bred by the baking powder tycoon Warren Wright's Calumet Farm, Citation was a mature two-year-old, winning eight of his nine races, worth $115,690. His only defeat was at the hands of his stable companion, the brilliant filly Bewitch, in the Washington Park Futurity.

In his Classic season, Citation was almost unbeatable. He won nineteen of his twenty races, worth $709,470 — at the time a record sum for seasonal earnings. His only defeat came at the hands of a three-year-old called Saggy, over six furlongs, at Havre de Grace. Various reasons were put forward for this reverse, notably that he was carried wide on the final bend, and that Eddie Arcaro had not ridden him before. (His previous rider, Al Snider, had been drowned on a fishing trip off Florida Keys.) The truth is that his outstanding trainer, Ben Jones, had almost certainly left him a gallop 'short' — as was his habit — after a six-week absence from the track.

His Triple Crown was achieved in brilliant style. He won the Kentucky Derby by three-and-a-half lengths from his outstanding stable companion Coaltown; the Preakness by five-and-a-half lengths, and the Belmont by eight lengths. So little did the Classics tax him that in between he fitted in the Jersey Stakes at Garden State, New Jersey, which he won by eleven lengths in record time.

In the autumn, Citation was sent to California in a bid to surpass Stymie's record career earnings of $918,485, but after two wins which took him to within $50,000 of the target, he 'popped' an osselet, and was sent home to Kentucky to be bar-fired.

If Citation had been retired to stud at that point, he would now be regarded as one of the three great American colts this century, along with Man O'War and Secretariat. Sadly, however, his owners were obsessed with two racing landmarks. Firstly, Stymie's elusive record, and secondly, the alluring $1 million mark. So Citation returned to action thirteen months later, as a five year old, and immediately ran into a formidable opponent in Noor. For the next four months Noor inflicted defeat after defeat on Citation, initially in receipt of 22lb, and finally *giving* Citation 1lb. Citation finished second in seven out of eight races. After a further injury Citation returned to the track ten months later at the age of six, and eventually struck a winning run which took him past the 'magical million'.

Citation, a medium-sized horse by the Calumet stallion Bull Lea, out of a Hyperion mare bought from Lord Derby, rightly became a legend in American racing — and is commemorated by a life-size statue at Hialeah Park. But nowadays I wonder — should he have raced beyond the age of three...?

BIG RACES WON	
Kentucky Derby	1948
Preakness Stakes	1948
Belmont Stakes	1948
Gold Cup (Belmont)	1948
Jockey Club Gold Cup	1948
American Derby	1948
Jersey Stakes	1948
Flamingo Stakes	1948
Hollywood Gold Cup	1951

Citation (Eddie Arcaro), winner of 19 of his 20 races at two and three years, including the American Triple Crown.

COLOMBO

Foaled 1931
Trained in England

COLOMBO, UP UNTIL 1986, enjoyed the doubtful distinction of being regarded the unluckiest loser of the Derby this century. It is my view, however, that in the television age this myth would never have been perpetuated.

Colombo, a bay horse by Manna, was bought for a bargain 510 guineas, as a yearling, on behalf of the shipping magnate Lord Glanley. He won all of his seven two-year-old races including the New Stakes, Richmond Stakes and Imperial Breeders' Produce Stakes, and was clear top-weight in the Free Handicap with 9st 7lb. Some journalists were already calling him 'Horse of the Century'.

During the autumn his owner, a large, mercurial man with a thick walrus moustache, and dubbed by the racing public 'Old Guts and Gaiters', had negotiated to retain the Australian-born, French-based jockey Rae Johnstone for 1934.

Colombo won the Craven Stakes with ease, and in the 2000 Guineas started the shortest-priced favourite for forty years at 7-2 on. Colombo won by a length from Easton, but was far from spectacular. Nonetheless the racing world believed that only two factors could prevent Colombo from winning the Derby: either if he failed to stay, or if Rae Johnstone — who had served a two-year suspension in Australia for 'stopping' a horse for betting purposes — prevented him from winning. Johnstone, on his own subsequent admission, was offered £10,000 — a fortune in those days — to do just that.

Despite the doubts, Colombo went off favourite at 11-8. The dangers were considered to be Umidwar (H. Wragg), Windsor Lad (C. Smirke), Easton (G. Richards), and Brantome's No. 2 in France, Admiral Drake (E.C. Elliott). What happened in the race has been discussed ever since. Johnstone was tight on the rails running down Tattenham Hill, with Steve Donoghue in front of him and Smirke and Gordon Richards on his 'outer'. For some reason Johnstone didn't shout for room, which with his mount now beaten, Donoghue claims he would have given. So Colombo had to wait until well into the straight and then pull out to the wide outside. A furlong out Windsor Lad, Easton and Colombo were almost in line. The crowd roared themselves hoarse. But suddenly Colombo faltered, was beaten, and Windsor Lad forged away to win for Charlie Smirke.

In my view, had 'live' television existed, with expert analysts, as today, Johnstone would have been exonerated, and Colombo branded a non-stayer. Steve Donoghue, who had hoped to ride Colombo until Johnstone came on the scene, did not help to ease

the pain. 'Had I ridden him he would have won on the bit by lengths,' he stated.

On 29 June, after Colombo had been beaten at Royal Ascot at 5-1 on, Rae Johnstone was on his way back to France. For a generation of racegoers, the 1934 Derby was the race that Colombo and Rae Johnstone *lost*...

Colombo (Rae Johnstone) returns to scale after his 2000 Guineas success at 7-2 on.

BIG RACES WON	
2000 Guineas	1934
Craven Stakes	1934
New Stakes	1933
National Breeders' Produce Stakes	1933
Richmond Stakes	1933
Imperial Breeders' Produce Stakes	1933

CREPELLO

Foaled 1954
Trained in England

CREPELLO WAS ALMOST certainly one of the outstanding Derby winners this century. For many years Lester Piggott stated categorically that he was the best horse he had ever ridden. But sadly the strong, handsome 16.2½hh colt never had the opportunity to show the extent of his greatness.

Crepello was owned and bred by the late Sir Victor Sassoon, who was seventy-five years old when Crepello began to race. With much of his year spent abroad, Sir Victor always liked to have runners at Royal Ascot. The trainer, Murless, with little else available and against his judgment, ran the backward Crepello in the Windsor Castle Stakes. The ground was firm and Crepello, always straight in front, was far from ready for a hard race. Tenderly ridden by Lester Piggott, he was beaten a short head by Fulfer.

A week later Murless felt a tiny notch on Crepello's suspensory ligament. The great trainer hated anyone other than himself to touch his horses' legs so he ordered a cloth bandage, known as a 'Newmarket cloth', to be sewn on each of Crepello's forelegs. He wore them throughout his career — and all that time the leg, on such a fine horse, was a worry to Murless. Crepello did not run again until the autumn, when he finished fourth to Pipe of Peace in the Middle Park Stakes and then won the Dewhurst Stakes comfortably.

In the spring of 1957, Murless took a rare step. Never much of a bettor, he took odds of 66-1 to £100 that Crepello would win the 2000 Guineas and Derby. After a dry spring and firm ground, Crepello went to the 2000 Guineas without a preliminary race. Held together beautifully by Lester Piggott, he struck the front 200 yards out and won comfortably by half a length.

Crepello was now firm favourite for the Derby and galloped brilliantly, but the combination of firm ground and the threat of 'nobblers' caused him to ease in the market to 11-4. On the day, however, he hardened to 6-4 and again, superbly ridden by Piggott, he swept past Ballymoss to win by a length and a half.

Sadly, it was to be his last race. He was withdrawn on the morning of the King George VI & Queen Elizabeth Stakes after a downpour had made the ground soft and false; and then, whilst in training for the St Leger, his tendons finally showed signs of strain and he was retired to stud. Only Piggott and Murless have an inkling as to how good Crepello was. With his legs in mind, Piggott never really let him down, so he was never fully extended.

Busted apart, Crepello proved a better sire of fillies and brood mares than of colts. He was certainly a great racehorse — and trained by an equally great trainer.

BIG RACES WON	
Derby	1957
2000 Guineas	1957
Dewhurst Stakes	1956

Crepello, the tall but striking winner of the 1957 2000 Guineas and Derby. Note the 'Newmarket cloths' that he always wore after his first race.

DAHLIA

Foaled 1970
Trained in France

JUST AS 1968 had seen the birth of two great colts in Mill Reef and Brigadier Gerard, 1970 produced two of the great post-war fillies in Allez France and Dahlia.

They were formidable rivals, and bear fascinating comparision:
— Dahlia never beat Allez France in six encounters — but won
£497,741, a record for a European horse.
— Allez France never won outside of France. Dahlia won in France,
England, Ireland, Canada and the USA.
— Allez France was consistent and won thirteen of her twenty-one
races. Dahlia never bloomed until June or July and ran many
indifferent races.

Dahlia was tough, and at her best was spectacularly brilliant. Her
success in the 1973 King George VI & Queen Elizabeth Stakes was
one of the staggering big-race victories I have ever seen. Last with
half a mile to race, she swept past a field that included Rheingold
and Roberto to win by six lengths going away. A week earlier Dahlia
had beaten the four-lengths Oaks winner Mysterious by three lengths
in the Irish Oaks — a result which, at the time, nobody believed!

After an injury-affected autumn, Dahlia went to America for the
Washington International and showed her love of travel by winning
easily from Big Spruce. She failed to win until July as a four-year-
old, and along the way jockey Bill Pyers was sacked.

Lester Piggott teamed up with the mare in the 'King George' and
the Benson & Hedges Gold Cup, and won both comfortably. Once
again an American autumn campaign was planned and she duly
won the Man O'War Stakes and Canadian International
Championship before meeting with defeat in the Washington
International.

Dahlia was again 'cold' in the spring of 1975 and Piggott was
temporarily given the 'sack'. But she came good to win a second
Benson & Hedges before tailing right off in the autumn and retiring
to stud.

Dahlia was trained with a mixture of volatility, genius and
inspiration by Maurice Zilber for the Texan oil and metals magnate
Nelson Bunker Hunt. Unlike Allez France, she has proved a success
at stud, foaling a dual Group 1 winner in Dahar (by Lyphard), and
a Group 3 winner in Rivlia (by Riverman).

BIG RACES WON	
Irish Guinness Oaks	1973
King George & Queen Elizabeth Diamond Stakes (twice)	1973-74
Benson & Hedges Gold Cup (twice)	1974-75
Grand Prix de Saint Cloud	1974
Prix Saint-Alary	1973
Man O'War Stakes	1974
Canadian International Championship	1974
Washington D.C. International	1973

OPPOSITE: *Dahlia, the twentieth century Marco Polo (female variety!) — winner of $497,741 in France, England, Ireland, Canada and the USA.*

DANCING BRAVE

Foaled 1983
Trained in England

IN APRIL 1985, after Walter Swinburn had been suspended for a riding offence at Epsom, I observed on TV: 'It has always been a mystery to me why the world's greatest Flat Race should be run on one of the worst racecourses'. Considerable comment was engendered by the remark, with the popular riposte: 'Well the best horse nearly always wins; you've never seen a *great* horse beaten in the Derby...'

It was ironic therefore, that a year later just such a situation came about. Dancing Brave could certainly be compared with any of the great horses of the past thirty years — but he lost the Derby.

A medium-sized bay horse by Lyphard, Dancing Brave ran just twice as a two-year-old, winning minor races over a mile at Sandown and Newmarket. After overcoming soft ground in the Craven Stakes and winning comfortably by a length, he started 15-8 favourite for the 2000 Guineas, despite never having beaten an opponent of quality. His performance, however, was spectacular, brilliant acceleration enabling him to win by three lengths from the Free Handicap winner Green Desert.

His trainer, Guy Harwood, now had to decide whether to restrict him to one mile — or take a chance on his stamina in the Derby. Encouraged by his jockey. Greville Starkey, who made a public statement shortly before the race that 'The Brave' was 'bomb-proof', and was 'sure to win', Harwood grasped the nettle and sent his star colt to Epsom.

As with Colombo's Derby, the race will be argued about for many years, and, as with Colombo, the jockey received the blame! Starkey was accused of setting The Brave an impossible task. It was my view at the time, and remains so, that Dancing Brave was beaten because he hung inwards when his rider wanted to improve his position. He continued to 'lean in' well into the straight; and by the time that Starkey had pulled him out, balanced him, and launched him, it was just too late. Shahrastani held on by a rapidly diminishing half length.

It was Dancing Brave's only defeat in Europe. He won the Eclipse Stakes by four lengths and the King George (ridden by Eddery), by a diminishing three parts of a length confirming that he barely stayed a mile and a half.

His autumn campaign was directed towards the Prix de l'Arc de Triomphe where, ridden again by Eddery, he came alarmingly late to win in brilliant style, and record time, from one of the strongest fields since the War.

Dancing Brave was almost the complete racehorse. He had speed, acceleration and he stayed (just) a mile and a half. He was blessed too, with a perfect temperament. He retired to stud at Newmarket

with a valuation of £14 million, where his progeny will be greeted with rare interest.

Dancing Brave (Pat Eddery) shows brilliant acceleration to win one of the finest 'Arc de Triomphes' in the history of the race from Bering (Gary Moore) and Triptych (Angel Cordero).

BIG RACES WON	
2000 Guineas	1986
King George VI & Queen Elizabeth Diamond Stakes	1986
Eclipse Stakes	1986
Prix de l'Arc de Triomphe	1986
Craven Stakes	1986

DANTE

Foaled 1942
Trained in England

DANTE, WHO WAS bred and raced by Sir Eric Ohlson of Belvedere, Scarborough, was the only Northern-trained horse to win the Derby in the past 100 years.

He was also a classic example of the role of fate in racing. In 1941, Sir Eric bought his dam, Rosy Legend, from the sale of the late Lord Furness's bloodstock for 3500 guineas. The foal, a brown colt by Nearco, was sent by Sir Eric to the Yearling Sales, but failed to reach a reserve of 3500 guineas. Sent into training with Matt Peacock at Middleham, Yorkshire, the Nearco colt remained 'on offer' throughout the autumn, but failed to find a buyer. So the reluctant Sir Eric was compelled to race Dante — and soon realised his good fortune.

Dante won all his six two-year-old races, ending up with the Middle Park Stakes. He headed the Free Handicap with 9st 7lb, 1lb ahead of the Manton-trained Court Martial. Already an idol in the North of England, he reappeared at wartime Stockton, and was so impressive in appearance and performance that he started even money favourite for the 2000 Guineas. To the dismay of the whole of Yorkshire, however, he was beaten a neck by Court Martial. Two days before the race, Dante had appeared to be suffering from impaired vision and it was thought that he had been struck in the eye by a flint. Court Martial challenged on his 'blind' side, and Dante's rally came all too late.

The 1945 Derby was run for a final time at Newmarket, as Epsom was not yet in a state of repair — although the war had been over for a month. With Court Martial unlikely to stay, Dante, ridden by Willie Nevett, was made favourite at 100-30 and duly won by two lengths from Midas, with Court Martial a further neck away third. The north of England treated the result like a second V.E. Day: the famous Middleham bell tolled, and at the Dante Ball, 'Cock of the North' Nevett was carried shoulder-high.

Dante was now an odds-on favourite to complete the Triple Crown on Yorkshire soil, and the bookmakers had collossal liabilities. However, in August disturbing rumours began to circulate as to Dante's well-being. As late as 22 August there were firm denials from the stable that anything was amiss, but on 25 August Dante was scratched — and was never to race again. It transpired that, far from suffering a physical injury, Dante was the victim of a far more serious eye disease which eventually left him entirely blind.

Whatever the rights and wrongs of the affair, the deception created a scandal which left deep scars for years to come. Happily, Dante's ocular disability was not hereditary, and he sired two Classic winners in Darius and The Queen's Carrozza.

BIG RACES WON	
Derby (wartime)	1945
Middle Park Stakes	1944
Coventry Stakes	1944

A.G. Haigh's portrait of Dante, painted in the year of his Derby triumph.

ECLIPSE

Foaled 1764
Trained in England

ECLIPSE, WHOSE NAME is borne by the oldest Group 1 mile-and-a-quarter flat race, was the first truly great racehorse.

A grandson of the Darley Arabian, he was bred by William Duke of Cumberland, at Windsor Forest. On the Duke's death in 1765, he was bought by a Smithfield meat salesman called William Wildman for seventy-five guineas. A massively-built lengthy chestnut colt with a white stocking on his off-hind leg, Eclipse was so temperamental as a young horse that his owner considered gelding him. To have done so would have undermined the entire future of the Stud Book over the next 200 years!

Eclipse did not race until he was five, when Wildman took him

Eclipse, in full stride — the famous Sartorius oil painting.

to Epsom for a £50 Plate to be run in three four-mile heats. The course began in the region of Lord Derby's house, The Oaks, and would finish on the Downs. He won the first heat easily, whereupon the legendary Irish gambler Colonel Dennis O'Kelly bet that he could place all five runners in the second heat in the correct order. The bet was accepted, and O'Kelly stated that his forecast was: 'Eclipse first, and the rest nowhere!' — meaning that Eclipse would finish a distance (240 yards) in front of his rivals. Eclipse did so and O'Kelly collected. . . . A month later, O'Kelly bought a half-share in Eclipse for 650 guineas, and eventually the other half for 1000 guineas, after a game of chance over the price.

Under O'Kelly's guidance, Eclipse became a legend. He was never beaten, and never extended, in eighteen races. Indeed he was so vastly superior to any possible rival it was almost impossible to make a match for him. It was said that Eclipse could run a mile in a minute — a claim that casts serious doubts upon the accuracy of reporting at the time!

Eclipse was the sire of three of the first five winners of the Derby, and almost all the great horses of the twentieth century trace back to him. On his death his anatomy was examined in detail by an eminent young French veterinarian whose paper on the subject was largely responsible for the foundation of the Royal Veterinary College of London. His purpose had been to determine the reasons for Eclipse's amazing speed, generally attributed to his exceptional heart-room. Eclipse's skeleton was eventually re-assembled, and now stands in the National Horse Racing Museum in Newmarket.

EPINARD

Foaled 1920
Trained in France

WHEN THE FRENCH produce a good horse he is often very good indeed, and Epinard most definitely comes into that category. Jack Leach, ex-jockey, author and journalist, described him as the most fascinating horse he had seen. 'He was fantastic,' he wrote.

Epinard was owned and bred by M. Pierre Wertheimer, whose family still race in Paris. Recent 'Arc' winners in Ivanjica and Gold River have carried the Wertheimer colours.

As a yearling, Epinard did not impress his breeder and he was almost sold. Eventually, however, he was sent into training with Eugene Leigh, a French-based American.

He began his two-year-old career at Deauville in the Prix Yacowlef which he won by five lengths, in a canter from what Willie Pratt — one of the leading French trainers of the time — considered his best two-year-old. In the Prix Morny, however, he was hopelessly left, and met with his only defeat over the next fourteen months. His remaining two-year-old races included the Grand Criterium, Criterium de Maisons-Laffitte and the Prix de la Forêt, all of which he won in magnificent style.

Epinard (Everett Haynes) — his name means 'spinach' ... but he was no 'Popeye'.

By now he was considered one of the best two-year-olds ever seen in France. Because his owner-breeder had thought so little of him as a foal, he had not been entered in the Prix du Jockey Club (the French Derby). Nonetheless, he began his three-year-old career with four impressive wins. It was now that the plan took shape to send him to England. At first the Royal Hunt Cup was chosen, but after consideration the stable decided to send a 'sighter' in the five-year-old Select. The Stewards Cup — in those days a race of collossal prestige, and a major gambling medium — was chosen for Epinard. He was given 8st 6lb by the handicapper — more than any three-year-old had ever carried to victory. Nonetheless, Epinard was backed from 33-1 to 7-2 and, ridden by the American Everett Haynes, he staggered his rivals by winning in a canter by two lengths.

Epinard travelled back to France a national hero, but returned to England in the autumn facing another 'impossible' task. This time he was set 9st 2lb in the Cambridgeshire. Only Foxhall, forty-two years earlier, had won the great race with nine stone as a three-year-old. The going was firm in France, and Epinard was prepared at Singleton, near Goodwood. In the last week he was stabled at Newmarket. This is where Jack Leach comes into the story. According to Leach, he rode in a gallop in the week of the race,

Epinard ... 'a horse and a half, and the greatest runner I ever saw,' according to Jack Leach.

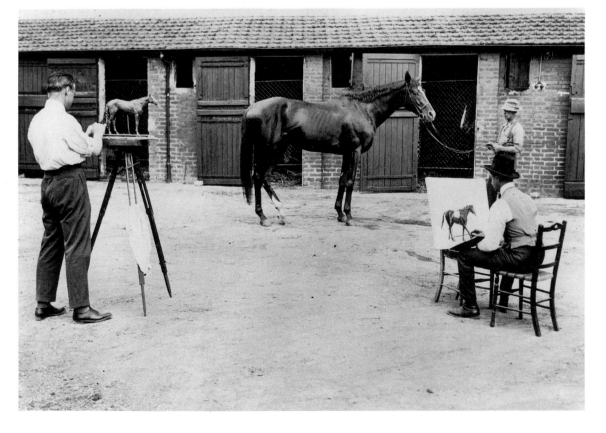

over seven furlongs on racecourse side — and noticed that Epinard was working over a mile on a parallel gallop. It seemed to Leach that the two groups of horses jumped off at the almost identical moment — with Epinard a furlong behind Leach's group. Leach writes in his book *Sods I Have.Cut On The Turf*: 'We jumped off and came a good gallop. As we passed Felix [his brother], Epinard was with us. In fact he pulled up in the bunch as if he had been with us all the way. I have never been so astonished in my life...!'

Epinard started favourite at 3-1 for the Cambridgeshire, but his rider had been persuaded to tack over to the stands rails from his high draw. He did so violently, seemingly six lengths clear, and never gave his mount a breather throughout. He was caught and beaten in the last strides by Michael Beary riding the Earl of Coventry's filly Verdict, carrying 7st 12lb. The following season Verdict won the Coronation Cup! Epinard received an astonishing reception. Leach concludes: 'Epinard was a horse and a half, and the gamest runner I ever saw!'

BIG RACES WON	
Prix d'Ispahan	1923
Grand Criterium	1922
Prix de la Forêt	1922
Criterium de Maisons-Laffitte	1922
Stewards Cup	1923

GAY CRUSADER

GAY CRUSADER was described by the great Steve Donoghue as the best horse he ever rode. As such he earns a place in any list of great horses. He was bred by his owner Mr A.W. Cox, by Bayardo, out of a daughter of Galeothia, both of whom had won Classic races for Mr Cox. It cannot be held against Gay Crusader that he gained his 'Triple Crown' in 1917, but this austere year imposed the most extreme restrictions on racing. Only forty-five meetings took place, all at Newmarket, and the September Stakes — the wartime substitute for the St Leger — attracted only three runners.

Gay Crusader, like Bayardo, was trained by the brilliant Alec Taylor at Manton. In the spring of 1917, Taylor had two leading 2000 Guineas contenders in Gay Crusader and Magpie. There was little between them on the form book, and Taylor was anxious to 'try' them before the Classic to determine which was the better. Donoghue, who was retained by Mr Cox, drove his patron to Manton to watch the gallop, but on arrival Mr Cox, true to character, became awkward and insisted that Gay Crusader should only be galloped with his own horses. So Gay Crusader worked with Mr Cox's Kwang-Su, a four-year-old that had been beaten by a head in the Derby the previous year; and Magpie's gallop was postponed to the following day. Although Donoghue rode in both gallops, it was the veteran Otto Madden who rode both Gay Crusader and Magpie. Both horses worked exceptionally well. Neither Donoghue nor Madden, who was to ride Magpie in the '2000', could decide which colt had the better chance. Nowadays the matter would be academic, but in those days betting was still all-important and the stable's owners would all wish to be on the 'right one' — not to mention Steve's 'punters'!

The race was an epic. Magpie and Gay Crusader, the favourite at 9-4, drew right away from the others and ran neck and neck. Donoghue felt that Magpie was going every bit as well as Gay Crusader and, as a lazy horse, would respond better than Gay Crusader to a crack with the whip. Accordingly he rode so tight to Magpie, who was on his left, that Madden, a little rusty after temporary retirement, could not bring down his whip. Nor did Madden have time to pull it through to his left hand. The two horses flashed past the post locked together, with Gay Crusader the winner by a neck. Sadly the two horses never met again, as soon afterwards Magpie was sold to go abroad.

Gay Crusader thrived in the weeks leading up to the Derby — run on 3 July — and won easily by four lengths. As well as the September Stakes, he won the Newmarket Gold Cup (2½ miles), the Champion Stakes (1¼ miles), the Lowther States (1¾ miles)

Foaled 1914
Trained in England

51

Gay Crusader, a handsome, kind and genuine horse.

and the Limekiln Stakes (1¼ miles). Unfortunately, he broke down the following season with a clean sweep in the Cup races at his mercy.

The reason that Donoghue rated him so highly was his ability to quicken like a sprinter at the end of a two mile gallop. A handsome, kind and genuine horse, his picture always had pride of place over Steve's fireside.

BIG RACES WON	
Derby	1917
2000 Guineas	1917
September Stakes (wartime St Leger)	1917
Newmarket Gold Cup	1917
Champion Stakes	1917

GLADIATEUR

FEW HORSES MERIT a full-sized statue in their memory. Gladiateur — 'The Avenger of Waterloo' — is one, and it can be seen on entry to the 'Tribunes' at Longchamp racecourse.

Foaled 1862
Trained in France

Gladiateur was the first French-owned and bred horse to win the Derby; indeed he won the English Triple Crown. Owned and bred by Count Frédéric de Lagrange, Gladiateur was sent to Newmarket to be trained by Tom Jennings. Born in Cambridgeshire, Jennings had been apprenticed and had ridden in France and was appointed the Count's private trainer in 1851. Six years later he took some horses to Phantom House, Newmarket, to compete in the more prestigious English racing scene and remained a resident at headquarters until his death in 1900. His brother Henry took over the Count's other horses at Compiègne.

Gladiateur was a large, plain, angular horse who was trodden on as a foal leaving him with an ugly enlargement on his off-fore fetlock joint for the rest of his life. Nonetheless, Jennings backed him for the Derby to win over £10,000 when he was a yearling. As a two-year-old he was backward and did not run until the autumn, when he won two of his four races (one a dead heat). He was still backward the following spring, having been 'blistered' in the autumn and confined to his box for much of January and February. Nonetheless, he won the 2000 Guineas in a field of twenty-nine — and suddenly the insular English racing public began to question the invincibility of the British Thoroughbred.

Before the Derby, Gladiateur was subjected to a trial of amazing severity, giving 8lb to Fille de l'Air, who had won the Oaks the previous year, and 35lb to two other four-year-olds. He came through it with ease, persuading Jennings that he was a 'certainty' for the Derby. In a field of twenty-eight, and after half-an-hour of false starts, there was only a brief moment of doubt when his jockey Harry Grimshaw, short-sighted at the best of times, appeared to have allowed two rivals to slip him. On a shout from a fellow jockey, Grimshaw let his horse go — and the race was over.

Three weeks later he travelled to France for the Grand Prix de Paris where he was cheered to the echo by 150,000 wildly excited Frenchmen. He won the St Leger virtually on three legs, but such was the bigotry against the French at the time that the owner of the runner-up, a Mr William Graham, lodged an objection on the grounds that he was a four-year-old!

Perhaps his greatest performance came as a four-year-old in the Gold Cup. His leg was worse than ever, and Grimshaw was instructed to nurse the great horse down the hill of the far side. Such was Grimshaw's shortsightedness that, according to

contemporary accounts, he allowed the leader, Breadalbane, to be 300 yards ahead at Swinley Bottom. At last Gladiateur was allowed to stride along and incredibly won the race by forty lengths! He ended the season unbeaten in six races, an undying testimony of the skill of his trainer. Sadly, neither in France nor England was he a great success at stud, and he died of navicular disease in 1876.

BIG RACES WON	
Derby	1865
2000 Guineas	1865
St Leger	1865
Grand Prix de Paris	1865
Prix Royal Oak	1865
Newmarket Derby	1865
Gold Cup	1866
La Coupe	1866
Grand Prix de l'Impératrice	1866
Grand Prix de l'Empereur	1866

GRUNDY

Foaled 1972
Trained in England

EVERY FEW YEARS some enterprising entrepreneur — usually American — creates the 'Race of the Century'. There has only been one 'Race of the Century' — at least on the Flat — in my lifetime, and that was Grundy v Bustino at Ascot in July 1975. Grundy won.

Grundy was bought for 11,000 guineas by Keith Freeman on behalf of Dr Carlo Vittadini in October 1973. The agent's limit was 10,000 guineas, but luckily he exceeded it. He was not the type of horse to appeal to every eye: a pale, rather washy chestnut, with flaxen mane, three white feet and a jagged blaze. He reminded the author greatly of a horse he was lucky enough to own called Midnight Cowboy. Indeed Grundy's owner was once quoted as saying of his horse: 'He looks more like a horse for a cowboy than for the racecourse ... I must admit I am not altogether happy with his colour.'

Grundy (Pat Eddery) beats Bustino (Joe Mercer) in 'The Race of the Century' in a new Ascot course-record time.

But could he gallop! As a two-year-old Grundy was unbeaten in four races, and topped the Free Handicap. He won the Dewhurst Stakes by six lengths from Steel Heart who had won the Gimcrack and Middle Park Stakes. His three-year-old career began badly when a kick in the face interrupted his preparation and he was beaten for the first time in the Greenham Stakes by Mark Anthony. Nonetheless, he appeared to come on for the race at home and remained favourite at 7-2 for the 2000 Guineas.

May 3rd, 1975, was one of the unhappiest days in the history of the Turf. For several weeks there had been simmering in Newmarket a stable lads' dispute over conditions and wages. At dawn it transpired that evil hands had dug up a section of the Rowley Mile course near the 2000 Guineas start. Shortly before the race, a rabble of stable lads, flying pickets, and other individuals who had infiltrated the racing industry in the previous months, staged a disgraceful demonstration on the course itself. A few outraged individuals tried bravely to remonstrate with them, but were merely laughed at. Because of the uncertainty of the situation the starter decided to start the race by flag, several yards in front of the stalls. Eventually, fifteen minutes late, the race was 'off'. Grundy hit the front, looked likely to win, but was then beaten for speed by the Italian colt Bolkonski. In the last fifty yards he was coming back at the winner. Gianfranco Dettori, Bolkonski's jockey, was one of the few unaffected by the affair. 'Call this a riot? We have worse than this every Sunday in Italy!', he joked.

That was Grundy's last defeat until August. He won the Irish 2000 Guineas by one-and-a-half lengths, in the manner of a horse who would stay. He won the Derby by three lengths from the filly Nobiliary, and the Irish Sweeps Derby even more impressively by two lengths from Vincent O'Brien's runner King Pellinore.

And so to the 'King George', and the most enervating horse race I have ever seen. The four-year-old Bustino, trained by Dick Hern, was assisted by not one but two pacemakers, Kinglet and Highest, who went off at a six-furlong pace. There was no pause for breath. Bustino took it up four furlongs from home, and Grundy went in pursuit. In the straight, battle was joined. Hard driven by Eddery, but answering his call, Grundy took the lead a furlong from home, but still Bustino would not give in. The roof of the Grandstand felt it would lift. Each horse was now racing from instinct and memory. For a split second it seemed that Bustino would rally ... that Grundy would crack ... then 'Grundy wins!' The distance was half a length, the time an incredible 2 minutes 26.98 seconds, beating the previous record by a staggering 2.36 seconds.

Grundy raced only once more — in the Benson & Hedges Gold Cup three weeks later — but his Herculean achievement had taken its toll mentally, if not physically, and he ran the one disappointing race of his life and was retired to stud. The generosity of Dr Vittadini enabled him to stand at the National Stud at a valuation of £1 million (less than half his international value), but sadly he was not a success and was exported to Japan in 1984.

BIG RACES WON	
Derby	1975
Irish Sweeps Derby	1975
Irish 2000 Guineas	1975
King George VI & Queen Elizabeth Diamond Stakes	1975
Dewhurst Stakes	1974
Champagne Stakes	1974

HABITAT

HABITAT WAS A very good, but not *great* racehorse, but, as by far the most successful commercial stallion of the 'seventies and early 'eighties in England and Ireland, he earns a place amongst the élite.

A son of Sir Ivor's sire Sir Gaylord, out of a mare called Little Hut, who was later to breed Northfields, Habitat was bought for $105,000 by Mr Charles Engelhard at the Keeneland Sales, and sent to Fulke Johnson Houghton at Blewbury.

It was soon clear that Habitat would be difficult to train. He was a rather shouldery heavy-topped colt, with an extremely suspect off-fore leg. Accordingly, in the dry summer of 1968, when so many horses — including Sir Ivor — were jarred up, the Johnson Houghtons did not do a great deal with him, and he did not race.

After defeat in his first two races as a three-year-old at Sandown and Windsor, he broke his duck in a one-mile maiden race at Haydock. To the astonishment of students of form, he went straight on to the prestigious Lockinge Stakes at Newbury, to take on, as

Foaled 1966
Trained in England

Habitat, the greatest commercial stallion of the modern-day era, who still commanded a stallion fee of IR£80,000 at the age of twenty-one.

an inexperienced three-year-old, top milers like Tower Walk, Jimmy Reppin, Wolver Hollow and Lorenzaccio. Backed from 20-1 to 10-1 he won — and never looked back.

After a narrow defeat at Royal Ascot in a rough race with the 2000 Guineas' winner Right Tack, he won the Prix Quincey at Deauville, the Wills Mile at Goodwood, and the Prix du Moulin at Longchamp, beating Right Tack and Welsh Pageant. Meanwhile, he was acquired, shrewdly, by the late Capt. Tim Rogers for his Airlie Stud, for £400,000. By the mid 'eighties, his nomination fee alone had reached £100,000!

Habitat was soon awarded a private paddock at the Grangewilliam Stud — part of the Airlie complex — where he would stalk about happily each afternoon, after stallion duties, in the long grass. Cynics claimed that the length of the grass was designed to conceal his almost deformed off-fore leg. Yet within a matter of years he had become the most prolific sire of Patten Race winners to stand in the British Isles since the last war. With rare exceptions, his weaknesses were never transmitted to his stock. Ironically, however, none of his brilliant male progeny has ever become a top stallion himself. Habitat was put down aged twenty-one, on June 23rd 1987.

BIG RACES WON	
Prix du Moulin de Longchamp	1969
Lockinge Stakes	1969
Prix Quincey	1969
Wills Mile	1969

HAMBLETONIAN

HAMBLETONIAN WAS ONE of the most famous and successful horses ever to be bred and raced in the north of England. A grandson of Eclipse, he was bred by John Hutchinson, a former stable lad who, through hard work, ambition and shrewd betting, became one of the most successful owners and bloodstock breeders in the north.

Hambletonian was bought privately from his breeder by Sir Charles Turner as a three-year-old in August 1795. Within the week he had won a 100 guineas two-mile sweepstake, and a fifty guineas sweepstake at York. A month later, Hambletonian was 6-4 on in a field of five for the St Leger, which he duly won, going on to win the Doncaster Cup (four miles) the next day. The following year Sir Charles Turner was married and, at the stipulation of his father-in-law-to-be, was compelled to give up racing. Hambletonian was bought by his neighbour in North Yorkshire, Sir Henry Vane-Tempest, and having met with the only defeat of his life at York, when he ran off the course, he again won the Doncaster Cup.

It was as a six-year-old that he took part in his most famous race, the match for 3000 guineas over four miles on the Beacon course

Foaled 1792
Trained in England

The famous Sartorius painting of Hambletonian's match with Diamond at Newmarket, 1798.

at Newmarket, with Mr Cookson's Diamond. Hambletonian was ridden by Frank Buckle, the man who held the record for Classic wins until Piggott surpassed it, and Diamond by Denis Fitzpatrick.

The match attracted collossal interest. Every bed and stable within twenty miles of Newmarket was occupied, and many thousands of Yorkshiremen travelled south to back their champion. The race itself was a dour battle. At the distance, the two horses were head to head, and at the Judge, Hambletonian had it by 'half-a-neck'. According to the *Sporting Magazine* correspondent: 'The little horse, [Diamond] who ran remarkably well, was both whipped and spurred forty times more than was necessary or advantageous'. Wagering had been exceptionally heavy, and Sir Harry was back in London by ten o'clock that evening to tell his friends the result. The following day he rode his great horse in Hyde Park.

Hambletonian's influence, through a dozen generations, emerged in the pedigree of Fighting Charlie, the Gold Cup winner of 1965 and 1966. Fighting Charlie was owned by Lady Mairi Bury, daughter of the seventh Marquess of Londonderry, and a direct descendant of Sir Harry Vane-Tempest. Lady Mairi still possesses the famous life-size painting of Hambletonian by Stubbs.

BIG RACES WON	
St Leger	1795
Doncaster Cup (twice)	1795-96

HUMORIST

THE STORY OF HUMORIST is one of the saddest in the history of the Turf. Owned and bred by Mr Jack Bernato Joel — father of Mr Jim Joel — and trained at Wantage by Charlie Morton, Humorist was always a horse of delicate health, and was never a good 'doer'.

After a first season highlighted by a close second in the Middle Park Stakes, Humorist made exceptional progress in the winter, and started favourite at 3-1 for the 2000 Guineas. Three furlongs out Humorist was in the lead going easily, and running down the hill into the Dip he looked sure to win. However, his stride began to shorten on the rising ground, and he was caught and beaten by the Manton horses Craig an Eran and Lemonara.

His jockey Steve Donoghue was blamed for taking matters too easily, and being 'caught napping', but from the first time he had

Foaled 1918
Trained in England

Humorist — the bravest of the brave. Within three weeks of his dramatic Derby win from Craig an Eran, he was dead from a massive haemorrhage.

ridden Humorist (in the Woodcote Stakes at Epsom the previous June), he had experienced the same sensation: from pulling 'double', Humorist would die in his hands at the end of his race. Nonetheless, the way in which he had handled the gradients of Epsom that day encouraged Donoghue to believe that he was a Derby horse — providing he stayed.

After the Guineas, Humorist was 16-1 for the Derby, but when Donoghue was released by Lord Derby to ride Humorist, he became a well-backed third favourite at 6-1. After several false starts, Humorist was well away and perfectly placed on the rails at the top of the Hill. Donoghue let him go two furlongs out, and after a fierce struggle with Craig an Eran, Humorist answered his rider's calls with superb courage and resolution to win by a neck. It was Steve's first Derby. Afterwards, amidst the euphoria, few noticed Humorist standing in the Winners' Enclosure, sweating, trembling and with his head on the ground. Morton was so concerned that he kept him at Epsom overnight.

With his weak and delicate constitution, Humorist would run up light at the slightest pretext.

Humorist was intended to run in the Hardwicke Stakes, but broke a blood vessel on the eve of the meeting and was withdrawn. The following Saturday, Sir Alfred Munnings visited Letcombe Regis to make some sketches of Humorist for a painting. After lunch on the Sunday, before which Munnings and Morton had shared two bottles of champagne, Munnings dozed off pleasantly in the shade of a yew tree. He was awoken rudely by a fearsome commotion. 'Wake up Mr Munnings — Humorist is dead!' A horrifying sight greeted Morton and Munnings ... a dark, dried-up trickle of blood on the white chalk outside the end box of the yard. Inside, the scene was gruesome. Humorist lay dead on the straw, his head close to the door — the upper ear pricked, an eye still open. There was blood in great splashes all over the box where he had spun round in his terror, and plunged and reared. It was a vision that remained with Munnings for the rest of his life.

Now it was clear to Donoghue and Morton why Humorist had seemed to 'die' at the end of his races. A post-mortem showed that he was suffering from an advanced and long-standing tubercular lung condition, and that he almost certainly had had only one lung functioning when he won at Epsom. He died from a massive haemorrhage.

Humorist was buried with a headstone at Mr Joel's Childwick Bury Stud — a tribute to one of the bravest horses that ever lived.

BIG RACES WON	
Derby	1921
Woodcote Stakes	1920
Buckenham Stakes	1920
Clearwell Stakes	1920

HYPERION

Foaled 1930
Trained in England

HYPERION WAS NOT only an outstanding racehorse, but also one of the most successful and influential sires this century. I was lucky enough to 'interview' him at the Woodland Stud, Newmarket, a few months before his death in 1960. The headline on my article was 'The Daddy of Them All'!

Hyperion was bred by the 17th Earl of Derby, by Gainsborough, out of the small, but superbly symmetrical mare Selene. It was obviously from his mother that Hyperion inherited his lack of inches — he stood just 15.1½hh — and much of his huge popularity stemmed from his lack of size.

Hyperion was not only small, but lazy, and his gallops gave no indication that he would win the New Stakes at Royal Ascot — which he did by three lengths. In the autumn he was easily beaten by the very fast Manitoba in the Boscawen Stakes over five furlongs, although the performance was excused as he had been badly plated. Two weeks later he won the Dewhurst Stakes (7 furlongs) in good style.

Hyperion was trained by the Hon. George Lambton and ridden by Tommy Weston. At one stage neither looked likely to continue their association with Lord Derby in 1933. Lambton had for some years been suffering from ill-health, while Lord Derby was convinced that Weston had either lost his nerve, or was pulling his horses. Nonetheless, the team remained intact and Hyperion began his season by winning the Chester Vase in lazy but impressive fashion. This was Hyperion's only race before the Derby, but Lambton subjected the lazy little colt to some searching gallops, and he was made 6-1 favourite.

On Derby Day, Lambton was too ill to travel to Epsom, but Hyperion, led by his pacemaker Thrapston (ridden by Steve Donoghue), took command of the race in the straight to win by four lengths. It was an immensely popular result. He was judged to be the smallest Derby winner since Little Wonder in 1840, who stood less than 15hh yet was said to be a four-year-old. Hyperion won the Prince of Wales's Stakes at Royal Ascot, but training problems, notably a stifle injury, looked like ruling him out of the St Leger. However, after several 'scares', Lambton was able to get him to post and, starting 6-4 favourite, he made all the running to win by three lengths from Felicitation.

At the end of the season Lord Derby pursued his resolve to 'retire' Lambton, much against the great man's wishes. Lambton continued training for other patrons and was bitterly resentful towards his former employer. Colledge Leader took over Hyperion, but completely underrated his need for — and capacity for — work,

with the result that he went to Ascot for the Gold Cup only half fit. Felicitation won easily by eight lengths with Hyperion on third. Hyperion ran only once more and was beaten a short head in a two-horse race.

Hyperion was champion sire six times, siring seven Classic winners amongst the winners of 752 races worth £633,000 in the British Isles. But his greatest influence was as a sire of broodmares. His daughters included the dams of Alycidon, Carrozza, Citation, Parthia, Ribocco and Ribero. Above all he was a delightful and lovable character who left an enduring impression upon anyone who came into contact with him. I was proud to have met him.

'The Daddy of Them All.' Despite his lack of inches, Hyperion became one of the most influential sires of the twentieth century.

BIG RACES WON	
Derby	1933
St Leger	1933
Chester Vase	1933
Prince of Wales's Stakes	1933
Dewhurst Stakes	1932
New Stakes	1932

ISINGLASS

Foaled 1890
Trained in England

ISINGLASS WAS A big, tall, rather leggy horse with far from the best of forelegs. But, in his time, he had the reputation of being one of the finest horses ever to race. The claims must be taken seriously, for he was foaled during a 'Golden Age' of the Turf — the era of Ormonde, St Simon, Galtee More and Flying Fox.

Although he won the Triple Crown, his record does not do justice to his reputation. He ran just three times as a two-year-old, winning all three, notably the Middle Park Stakes from Ravensbury, Le Nicham and Raeburn. These four horses were to see a great deal of each other during their careers.

The spring of 1893 was exceptionally dry, and Isinglass's trainer, James Jewitt, and Captain Machell, the owner's racing manager, had a series of furious rows as to whether he should be trained for the 2000 Guineas. Machell insisted in having his way and as the Newmarket training grounds were already hard as concrete, Isinglass was taken out twice a day to do strong canters on the tan gallop on Bury Hill. Despite Jewitt's forebodings, Isinglass went to post a firm favourite at 5-4 on for the 2000 Guineas — and duly won, but only by three parts of a length from Ravensbury. Two weeks later he gained an easier win in the Newmarket Stakes, beating Ravensbury into third place. Now Isinglass was made 9-4 on for the Derby, but Epsom was at its awful, bare, unyielding worst, and Isinglass galloped like a cat on hot bricks. Nonetheless, when Tom Loates set about him he quickened to beat the luckless Ravensbury by a length and a half.

In the St Leger, Isinglass won again from Ravensbury, but ten days later he met with the only defeat of his career, over a mile at Manchester, where he narrowly failed to concede 10lb to another old rival in Raeburn. Apart from the distance of the race, Isinglass had been compelled to make his own running.

In his four-year-old season, the dry weather persisted and Isinglass did not run until July. Finally the weather broke, and it rained incessantly for ten days before the Eclipse Stakes — in those days a race double the value of the Derby. At last Isinglass had the conditions he wanted and won in a canter from Ladas, the 9-2 on winner of the Derby, and poor Ravensbury. It was this race above all which established his reputation.

Isinglass ran only once as a five-year-old, winning the Gold Cup with ease. His eleven victories earned him £57,455, a record sum which, remarkably, was not surpassed until 1952. A photograph in the 1895 *Racing Illustrated* shows him to be exceptionally upright on his fetlock joints, and at some stage to have been bar-fired. His achievements do great credit to Jewitt and Captain Machell.

BIG RACES WON	
Derby	1893
2000 Guineas	1893
St Leger	1893
Eclipse Stakes	1984
Gold Cup	1895
Princess of Wales's Stakes	1894
Jockey Club Stakes	1894
Newmarket Stakes	1893
Middle Park Stakes	1892

Triple Crown winner Isinglass. His stake earnings of £57,455 remained a record — despite inflation — for almost 60 years.

KELSO

Foaled 1957
Trained in USA

WE LIVE IN an age of reform. Starting stalls, camera patrol, overnight declarations, ownership syndicates, trade unions, lady trainers and female jockeys are all recent horseracing phenomena. In 1986, almost the last bastion fell. After 200 years, geldings were allowed to run in Group 1 races (i.e. the 'King George' and Ascot Gold Cup).

Why are we prejudiced against geldings? They are easier to train, more durable and more reliable. Their only shortcoming is that their appearance is less spectacular — they rarely have that magnificent thoroughbred 'bloom' in summer — and, of course, they cannot breed.

Kelso was a gelding, and for half a decade he dominated American racing. He was the great crowd-puller of the 'sixties and had over 70,000 race fans cheering for him whether they had backed him or not. He was Horse of the Year an incredible five times, and he

took part in some of the most memorable races on the American Turf.

Kelso, bred by his owner Mrs Allaire du Point, was found to be a 'rig' as a two-year-old — that is to say his reproduction organs had not developed properly — and he was gelded to alleviate the discomfort they caused him. He won one small race at Atlantic City and looked nothing special. As a three-year-old, now trained by Carl Hanford, a former jockey, he didn't race until June 28th. But in the next four months he won eight of his nine starts, usually in spectacular times — notably an American record for two miles (3 minutes 19.4 seconds) in the Jockey Club Gold Cup. He was Champion Three-Year-Old despite his late start, and Horse of the Year.

Kelso's return to action at four was delayed by stifle trouble, but he enjoyed another collossal season. A major highlight was his sweep of New York's 'Handicap Triple' — the Metropolitan, Suburban

Kelso (Milo Valenzuela) wins his second 'Suburban', the second leg of New York's 'Handicap Triple'.

and Brooklyn Handicaps — only twice previously achieved. In all he won seven of his eight starts on dirt, including a second Jockey Club Gold Cup. He was again Horse of the Year. Eddie Arcaro was now his regular jockey.

In twelve races the following year, Kelso started odds against only twice! He had minor problems all year and didn't peak until autumn. In all he won six races, notably the Woodward Stakes, and Jockey Club Gold Cup by ten lengths in a track record time. By now he had earned $1 million — and was Horse of the Year for an unprecedented third time.

In 1963 Kelso had his biggest money year. He won nine of his twelve races and earned $569,762. His jockey was now Milo Valenzuela. A record 71,876 people came to see him at Aqueduct on Labour Day and cheered him to a five-and-a-half lengths victory.

The following season — with Kelso now seven — was perhaps the most sensational. A clash with Gun Bow in the 'Aqueduct' at nine furlongs, saw a thrilling three-quarter-length win for 'The Champ'. A crowd of over 64,000 gave him the biggest welcome since Native Dancer. A month later the two principals re-met over ten furlongs of sheer excitement in the Woodward. This time, the blinkered Gun Bow had it by a short head. There followed Kelso's fifth successive victory in the Jockey Club Gold Cup — by five-and-a-half lengths, in record time. The purse pushed him past Round Table's record earnings with $1,803,362.

Now just one challenge remained — to win the Washington D.C. International on grass. It was his fourth try, after three seconds. He did it — in a track record of 2 minutes 23.8 seconds. He was now Horse of the Year for the fifth time. Kelso was a legend.

The end came when he fractured an off-fore sesamoid bone in March 1966. He had earned $1,977,896 — a record that lasted for over a decade. The lanky, brown gelding with the yellow ribbon on his bridle, left the track for ever — never to be forgotten. Like Brown Jack, he was a horse who gave geldings a good name.

BIG RACES WON	
Washington D.C. International	1964
Jockey Club Gold Cup (5 times)	1960-64
Woodward (3 times)	1961-63
Aqueduct (twice)	1963-64
Suburban Handicap	1961
Brooklyn Handicap	1961
Metropolitan Handicap	1961
Seminole Handicap	1962
Gulfstream Park Handicap	1963

KINCSEM

KINCSEM WAS CERTAINLY the best thoroughbred to come out of Hungary, and probably one of the best mares ever to race in Europe. Bred at the Hungarian Imperial Stud at Kisber, and owned by one M. de Blascovitz, Kincsem was by Cambuscan out of a mare called Water Nymph. Her paternal grandsire was the St Leger winner Newminster, a son of Touchstone.

Kincsem began her career in Hungary and won twenty-seven races in her first two seasons, including the Hungarian 2000 Guineas and Oaks, and the Austrian 2000 Guineas and Derby. How competitive was the standard of racing in Hungary is hard to evaluate. The Hungarian Jockey Club was founded in 1869 under the title of the Pester Jockey Club, so institutionalised racing was fairly young. Kisber, winner of the 1876 Derby, was, like Kincsem, bred at the Imperial Stud, but from English parents. There were a few private studs, whose owners included Count Esterhazy and Count Batthyany — names that have survived Hungary's social and military upheavals.

Foaled 1874
Trained in Hungary

Emil Adam's painting of the remarkable Hungarian mare Kincsem, unbeaten in 54 races.

In 1878, M. de Blascovitz decided to broaden his filly's horizons and brought her to England to run in the Goodwood Cup. A big, lengthy filly, standing 16.1hh — and rather unkindly described as 'long as a boat' — she galloped her two rivals into the ground and won easily. From Goodwood she was shipped to the Normandy coast, and over a very different course and a shorter distance she routed the French in the Grand Prix de Deauville. From there she travelled north-east to Germany and completed a remarkable International treble in the Grosser Preis von Baden at Baden-Baden on the edge of the Black Forest — a race she had also won twelve months earlier. This was the only close finish in her career, and she won only after a deciding heat.

Kincsem remained in training as a five-year-old winning a further twelve races, including a third Grosser Preis von Baden. She was finally retired the unbeaten winner of fifty-four races, from five furlongs to two-and-a-half miles, and carrying weights up to 12st 1lb. A bronze statue of Kincsem can be seen in the Newmarket Horseracing Museum.

BIG RACES WON	
Goodwood Cup	1878
Grand Prix de Deauville	1878
Grosser Preis von Baden (three times)	1877-79
Austrian 2000 Guineas	1877
Austrian Derby	1877
Hungarian 2000 Guineas	1877
Hungarian Oaks	1877

LA FLECHE

LA FLÈCHE WAS one of the outstanding fillies of the nineteenth century, and was most unlucky not to have won the Derby. Bred by Queen Victoria at the Royal Stud at Hampton Court, La Flèche was a bay filly by St Simon out of Quiver, and thus an own sister to the Oaks and St Leger winner Memoir. As a yearling she was bought for the then staggering record price of 5500 guineas by Baron Maurice de Hirsch, a German Jew who had amassed a fortune in business. Presumably the Baron was advised from the outset by his close friend the Prince of Wales, and by the Prince's manager Lord Marcus Beresford, for La Flèche was sent to the Royal trainer John Porter at Kingsclere.

La Flèche was unbeaten in four races as a two-year-old, including two within two days at Goodwood. She was winter favourite for the 1000 Guineas and won in a canter. Before the 2000 Guineas, the stable's outstanding colt Orme fell ill — probably poisoned — and was therefore unable to run in the Derby. La Flèche was therefore made favourite for the Derby at 11-10. She was ridden by George Barrett who had won the Triple Crown the previous season on Common, but whose behaviour was becoming increasingly erratic. In the Derby, Barrett lay far out of his ground in the early stages, shouting and gesticulating at the other jockeys as if drunk. La Flèche had an impossible task at Tattenham Corner, lying a full ten lengths from the leader, but she ran on with terrific courage to finish second, beaten three-quarters of a length to the 40-1 outsider Sir Hugo. Two days later, despite her hard race, she won the Oaks.

Orme and La Flèche both ran in the St Leger, with Barrett on Orme, and Jack Watts on La Flèche. Rumours had reached Orme's owner, The Duke of Westminster, that Barrett had been bribed by bookmakers to 'stop' Orme, and the owner made the mistake of informing Barrett in the paddock that his riding would be watched closely. Barrett, in a rage, rode Orme into the ground and La Flèche won comfortably by two lengths from Sir Hugo. Orme was unplaced. La Flèche went on to win the valuable Lancashire Plate at Manchester, the Grand Duke Michael Stakes, the Newmarket Oaks and finally, remarkably, the Cambridgeshire, under 8st 10lb where she beat a fair horse called Pensioner, who carried 6st 4lb.

At the end of the season, the Prince of Wales's horses were moved from John Porter's stable to that of Richard Marsh, and La Flèche — who had been considerably more successful than the Royal string — went with them, together with nineteen others belonging to Baron de Hirsch. This shattering blow to John Porter has never been adequately explained, although the official reason was that the Prince

Foaled 1889
Trained in England

La Flèche, one of the great fillies of the nineteenth century, at stud in Yorkshire.

would have more opportunity to see his horses at Newmarket than Kingsclere. The suspicion exists, however, that there may have been friction between the likeable, quick-witted, Lord Marcus Beresford and the serious, humourless, John Porter. In any case, the Royal horses were moderate and had achieved no success.

La Flèche, who stood 15.3hh, was a wiry, greyhound type of filly in training and was always at her most effective when she looked at her worst. In the spring of 1893 she was covered by Morion and did not run until the 'Eclipse', where it was patently clear that she was not in foal as she was 'squealing' in season — so much so that the blacksmith could not plate her. To the chagrin of her connections, and to the delight of John Porter, she was only third behind Orme, now ridden by Mornington Cannon. La Flèche was again out-of-sorts when Orme beat her in the Gordon Stakes at Goodwood but, looking terrible, she came back in the autumn and won the Liverpool Cup under 9st 6lb. As a five-year-old, she landed odds of 5-2 in the Gold cup, but was beaten by the luckless Ravensbury in the Hardwicke Stakes the following day.

On Baron de Hirsch's death in 1896, she was sold by auction

for 12,600 guineas to the Sledmere Stud of Sir Tatton Sykes. There she bred six foals, the best of which was John O'Gaunt, who finished second in the 2000 Guineas and Derby. Latterly, she proved impossible to get in foal.

BIG RACES WON	
Oaks	1892
1000 Guineas	1892
St Leger	1892
Gold Cup	1894
Cambridgeshire	1892
Lancashire Plate	1892
Liverpool Cup	1893
Newmarket Oaks	1892
Molecomb Stakes	1891
Champagne Stakes	1891

MAN O'WAR

Foaled 1917
Trained in USA

MAN O'WAR was one of those horses that those who saw him race have always asserted was the best ever. He possibly was. Winner of twenty of his twenty-one starts, in two seasons, his record and reputation were unmatched until the arrival of Kelso.

Man O'War was a big, strong, chestnut colt, standing, eventually, 16.2hh. He was bred by Major August Belmont II who was chairman of the American Jockey Club, and one of the most powerful men in US racing. Although sixty-four years old, the Major's concern over the war in Europe was such that he offered his services as a commissioned officer. His acceptance led to the sale at Saratoga of all his yearlings in 1918 — amongst them Man O'War. He was bought for $5000 by the Pennsylvanian textile magnate, Samuel D. Riddle, and sent to Louis Feustel to train.

His first start was at Belmont Park, which he won by six lengths. There followed five more victories before the one and only defeat of his career. This happened in the Sanford Memorial Stakes at Saratoga on August 13th, 1919. Man O'War was side on at the tapes: he whipped round, and lost several lengths. In the straight he ran into a wall of horses, switched to the outside, and just failed to get up by half a length. The winner's name, appropriately, was Upset. Thereafter, he won fourteen stakes races in succession. For some reason he was not entered for the Kentucky Derby, but he won the Preakness and the Belmont with ease.

Now, in his second season, he had a new jockey in Clarence Kummer, his original rider, Johnny Loftus, having been refused a licence in 1920 — according to some sources because of rumours following Man O'War's defeat at Saratoga. His eleven races yielded wins by margins between a length and a half, and 100 lengths! He was odds-on every time that he raced (three times 100-1 on), and he established five separate time records between one mile and 1 mile 5 furlongs. His records for 1 mile 3 furlongs, set up in the Belmont (2 minutes 14.2 seconds) and 1 mile 5 furlongs (2 minutes 40.8 seconds) lasted almost fifty years.

In the Potomac Handicap at Havre de Grace, under 9st 12lb, he conceded 30lb to the runner-up Wildair, a good Stakes winner, with the Kentucky Derby winner Paul Jones, also receiving lumps of weight, last of the four runners. His final appearance was in the Kenilworth Park Gold Cup in Canada, worth $80,000 (the biggest stake he ever won) where, starting at 6-1 on, he annihilated a top handicapper called Sir Barton, by seven lengths.

Man O'War was retired to stud at the end of his three-year-old season at Faraway Farm, Lexington, Kentucky — a complex built especially for the great horse. At his owner's whim he was restricted

to twenty-five mares a year, most of them the property of either his owner, or his friends. For this reason he achieved less success at stud than he might have done otherwise. Nonetheless, he became leading sire in 1926, and four of his sons and one daughter won over $100,000. His best son was War Admiral.

Man O'War died on 1st November, 1947, in his thirty-first year. His direct line of offspring include Never Say Die, Sir Ivor, Damascus and Buckpasser. Man O'War is commemorated by a statue, a memorial park, and one of America's great races. He is certainly a contender for the title 'The Greatest'.

A candidate for 'The Greatest'. Man O'War, winner of twenty of his twenty-one races.

BIG RACES WON	
Preakness Stakes	1920
Belmont Stakes (record)	1920
Lawrence Realization Stakes (record)	1920
Kenilworth Park Gold Cup	1920
Travers Stakes	1920
Jockey Club Stakes (record)	1920
Potomac Handicap	1920
Belmont Futurity	1919
Hopeful Stakes	1919

MELD

Foaled 1952
Trained in England

MELD WAS ALMOST certainly the greatest filly of my lifetime, although sadly I was too young to see her race. Bred 'in the purple' by Alycidon out of Daily Double, from the famous Double Life family, she was treated like a queen from the moment she arrived at Freemason Lodge from Sir Harold and Lady Zia Wernher's stud.

A strong, well-made, attractive filly, Meld was just starting to catch the eye in the spring when she split a pastern and spent two months in her box. Accordingly, she did not run until the autumn, when, as second string to the Queen's colt Corporal and ridden by Stan Smith, she was beaten a length by her stable-companion over five furlongs at Newmarket. The following months she won comfortably over six furlongs at Newmarket, and impressed many — including her jockey Harry Carr — as a likely winner of the Oaks.

Now in his ninth season as stable jockey to Captain (later Sir) Cecil Boyd-Rochfort and still awaiting his first Classic winner, Carr decided to take Meld under his wing. He rode her from the yard every morning and came to understand her every quirk. Prepared for the 1000 Guineas without a preliminary race, and still lacking experience, Meld won her first Classic comfortably by two lengths from Aberlady.

Regarding the Oaks, there were only two worries: first, whether a filly with such a brilliant speed would stay — although her pedigree suggested she would; and second that the Oaks would be her first race away from Newmarket. Neither factor created a problem. In front before Tattenham Corner, she was briefly headed by Ark Royal

Meld (Harry Carr) despite having coughed overnight, wins the St Leger from Nucleus (Lester Piggott).

and then stormed away to beat that good filly by six lengths.

Because of the 1955 rail strike, Royal Ascot was postponed until July, and Boyd-Rochfort decided to bring Meld back to a mile in the Coronation Stakes rather than aim for the King George VI & Queen Elizabeth Stakes over a mile and a half. Meld beat the outstanding Gloria Nicky by five lengths, and Scobie Breasley, who rode the runner-up, told Harry Carr that he had rarely, if ever, seen such acceleration in a filly.

The next two months leading up to the St Leger were nerve-wracking for Boyd-Rochfort, Carr and the stable's new assistant trainer, the outstanding horseman Bruce Hobbs. In a hot, dry autumn, Newmarket was beset with the worst coughing epidemic in living memory. The proud, 1500-horse training centre became a ghost town as stable after stable fell victim. Meld was isolated and would walk and exercise on her own. Many was the brush between Carr and the autocratic heathmen, when Meld was taken on 'forbidden territory', to avoid other horses.

As the St Leger drew closer, the tension became intolerable. All but three of Boyd-Rochfort's fifty-five horses had gone down with the cough. On the morning of the race, rumours spread like wildfire, that Meld had coughed in the racecourse stables overnight. Harry Carr was assured by the travelling head lad George Archibald, that all was well. Cantering to post, Carr knew that it was not, and resolved not to give her a hard race. It was because of Carr's affection for the filly that the stable had tried to keep the truth from him — that Meld had coughed. Luckily, Meld was in a different class to her rivals and her quality and courage carried her through, although by only three parts of a length from Lester Piggott's mount Nucleus. Piggott threw down a frivolous objection for crossing, which was quickly thrown out. The following morning Meld had a temperature of 103° and she lay on the floor of her box for forty-eight hours.

Meld thus became one of only four fillies this century to win three or more Classics. Sceptre, Pretty Polly and Sun Chariot were the others. Oh So Sharp completed the 'Fillies' Triple Crown' in 1985. Although her stud career was not a consistent success, she nonetheless achieved the rare feat nowadays for a Classic filly, of breeding a Derby winner in Charlottown.

BIG RACES WON	
Oaks	1955
1000 Guineas	1955
St Leger	1955
Coronation Stakes	1955

MILL REEF

Foaled 1968
Trained in England

IT WAS ON June 9th, 1970, that I first set eyes on Mill Reef. The purpose of my visit to Ian Balding's Kingsclere stables was to film a preview for Royal Ascot. The subject was a possible Royal winner in Magna Carta. After Magna Carta had galloped, two other horses came towards us down the gallop. One horse was cruising, doing nothing, about twenty lengths in front of the other. 'What's that?' I asked, assuming indifference. 'That's Mill Reef,' replied Balding quietly. A week later Mill Reef won the Coventry Stakes by eight lengths and became 16-1 favourite for the 1971 2000 Guineas. It was the beginning of a long love affair. But my admiration had as much exclusivity as a man besotted by Princess Stephanie of Monaco. In short, to know him was to love him.

Mill Reef was bred in Virginia by his owner, the multi-millionaire American philanthropist, Mr Paul Mellon. A perfectly-moulded, but quite small colt by Never Bend, never standing more than 15.2hh, he was always the supreme athlete ... handy and perfectly balanced with a superlative temperament. As a yearling he was judged by Paul Mellon's American trainer to be a shade long in the pastern for American racing, so, to the infinite good fortune of Ian Balding — and British racing — he was sent to England.

Predictably, he came to hand early, and won his first race at Salisbury in May, beating a 9-2 on shot, Fireside Chat, by four lengths. It was four weeks later that I saw him at Kingsclere. His two-year-old programme was dramatic. After Ascot he went to France for the Prix Robert Papin to clash with the precocious, well-grown, My Swallow. After a terrible journey, and a gruelling race, he succumbed by a short head. At York, the going became a quagmire on the morning of the Gimcrack Stakes. Anxious lest his small feet would make him ill-suited to soft ground, and determined that he should not undergo another hard race, Balding was on the point of withdrawing him. Mr Mellon said: 'Let's run,' Mill Reef floated through the mire, his tiny feet barely making a mark, and won by ten lengths. He struggled to win the Imperial Stakes, but wound up the year with a four-length win in the Dewhurst Stakes.

The events leading up to the 2000 Guineas are described in the passage devoted to Brigadier Gerard. Suffice to say that I shall always believe that Mill Reef failed to give his true running. His defeat in the '2000', combined with an American theory that 'sons of Never Bend never train on', made him an easy-to-back favourite for the Derby at 100-30. He won easily by two lengths, from Linden Tree and Irish Ball.

His next race was one of his great ones. In the Eclipse Stake, he was opposed by the top French middle-distance horse Caro, who

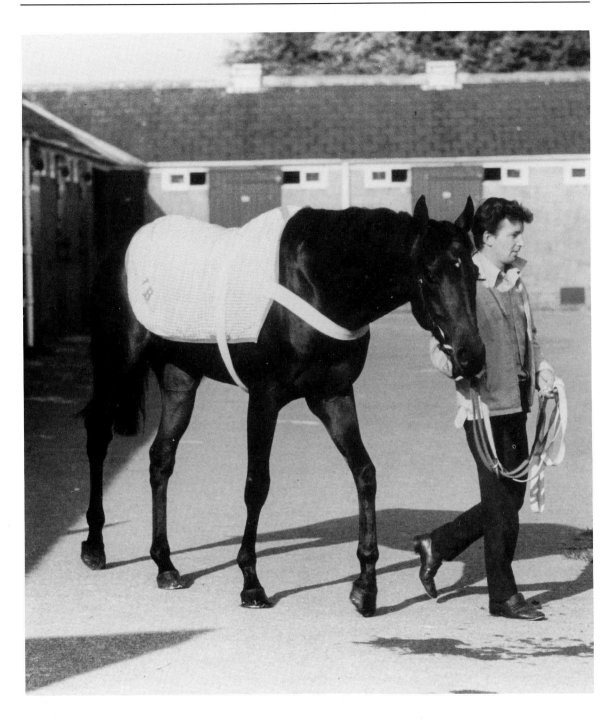

had won the Prix Ganay in record time from an exceptionally strong field. Mill Reef annihilated him by four lengths. Later in the month he ran away with the 'King George' by six lengths. His autumn target was the Prix de l'Arc de Triomphe, which he won easily by three lengths, from an outstanding filly in Pistol Packer.

His first race as a four-year-old was one I shall always remember.

Mill Reef and his devoted lad John Hallum, who nursed him through months of convalescence after the accident that left his fetlock like a 'bag of marbles'.

He won the Prix Ganay by ten lengths ... which looked closer to twenty. He simply galloped away from his rivals. After that came a catalogue of disasters. After struggling to beat Homeric in the Coronation Cup, he went down, predictably, with a virus. In early August he knocked a tendon and pulled a muscle in his quarters. Finally, on the gallops, on a fateful August 30th, Mill Reef's near-fore was shattered into smithereens. By a series of miracles of modern veterinary science — aided by his indomitable courage — he was rescued for a spectacularly successful stud career at the National Stud. His death in 1986 left a void which will take many years to fill.

BIG RACES WON	
Derby	1971
King George VI & Queen Elizabeth Stakes	1971
Eclipse Stakes	1971
Prix de l'Arc de Triomphe	1971
Coronation Cup	1972
Prix Ganay	1972
Gimcrack Stakes	1970
Dewhurst Stakes	1970
Imperial Stakes	1970
Coventry Stakes	1970

MUMTAZ MAHAL

A POPULAR JOURNALISTIC cliché, which the author is occasionally prone to use, is the expression 'flying filly'. Mumtaz Mahal was the original 'Flying Filly'. Bought as a yearling by the Hon. George Lambton on behalf of the Aga Khan, the daughter of The Tetrach cost 9100 guineas — the top price of the year — at the Doncaster Yearling Sales. The price came as no surprise. The strapping grey filly was well-grown and exceptionally well developed, with power allied to quality. She was a superb athlete, with an eye-catching rangy action.

Trained by Dick Dawson at Whatcombe, she made her first appearance at Newmarket in May and won by three lengths from Straitlace — who was to win the following year's Oaks! The official hand time was 57.8 seconds which has never been surpassed. Odds of 4-1 were laid on Mumtaz Mahal in the Queen Mary Stakes at Royal Ascot which she won by ten lengths, in another exceptionally fast time. There followed successes in the National Breeders' Produce Stakes (100-6 on), the Molecomb Stakes (40-1 on — against a single opponent), and the Champagne Stakes (100-8 on) — her first race over six furlongs.

Foaled 1921
Trained in England

The 'Flying Filly' and George Hulme, who partnered her throughout her brilliant two-year-old career.

Her final two-year-old race was the Imperial Produce Plate over six furlongs at Kempton. The rain poured down all morning, making the ground heavy, and Dick Dawson seriously considered withdrawing the filly. However, the Aga Khan was not present to sanction such a decision and the opposition appeared moderate, so Dawson decided to take a chance. Paddock critics took the view that the Flying Filly had run up light, and 3-1 could be laid on. Mumtaz Mahal never dominated the race in her usual fashion and was caught in the last half furlong by the colt Arcade. Nonetheless, she headed the Free Handicap.

No one expected Mumtaz Mahal to stay a mile as a three-year-old, but she was nonetheless trained for the 1000 Guineas. Six lengths clear at The Bushes, she weakened rapidly on the rising ground, and was caught and beaten half a length by Plack. After finishing unplaced in the Coronation Stakes, she reverted to sprinting, and won the King George Stakes (6 furlongs) at Goodwood, and the Nunthorpe Stakes (5 furlongs) at York — the latter by six lengths.

Mumtaz Mahal was relatively successful at stud, breeding six winners, but notably as a dam of broodmares. Her grandsons included Nasrullah, Mahmoud, Abernant and Migoli, while a notable granddaughter was Petite Etoile. Above all she was another remarkable testimony to the judgement of the Hon. George Lambton.

BIG RACES WON	
National Breeders' Produce Stakes	1924
Champagne Stakes	1924
Queen Mary Stakes	1924
Nunthorpe Stakes	1925
Molecomb Stakes	1924
King George Stakes	1925

NASRULLAH

NASRULLAH WAS NOT a great racehorse, but he became one of the most successful and influential sires of the twentieth century. He was owned and bred by the Aga Khan, who maintained a greatly reduced string of horses with Frank Butters at Newmarket during the war, while he himself was in self-imposed exile in neutral Switzerland.

Nasrullah was a big, fine, bay horse by Nearco out of Mumtaz Begum, who was a daughter of Mumtaz Mahal. It would be hard to conceive a better pedigree. He was a victim of having to race during the war years: every race that he ever ran in was at Newmarket where, in addition, he spent every morning of his racing life. Understandably, he came to hate the place.

As a two-year-old he ran four times, winning the Coventry Stakes and a minor two-horse race. In the Middle Park Stakes he had a desperately hard race against Ribbon, going down by a neck. Probably he always remembered that afternoon. The following season Gordon Richards accepted a second retainer to ride for the Aga Khan and Frank Butters, as Fred Darling now had only sixteen horses, most of them moderate. Gordon was immediately impressed with Nasrullah's ability and stated that he had never ridden a better mover. But already, his temperament was a major problem. His antics would bring the entire Butters string to a halt, and Gordon

Foaled 1940
Trained in England

The magnificent but high-mettled Nasrullah, who became one of the most influential stallions of the post-war era.

would duck and weave through gaps in the Devil's Ditch to try to make him work at all.

Nonetheless, he behaved reasonably well, winning comfortably on his reappearance in the Chatteris Stakes, and was made favourite for the 2000 Guineas. In the Classic, however, he infuriated Gordon by running in snatches, and refusing to let himself go. Gordon reckoned he could have won by lengths; instead he was fourth, beaten in a finish of heads and short heads. In the Derby he ran a better race despite hanging to the right at a crucial stage. For a moment he looked like winning, but was finally beaten by a head and half a length by Straight Deal and Umiddad. In the St Leger he failed to stay, but he ended his career by winning the Champion Stakes in good style.

On retirement, Nasrullah was bought by Joseph McGrath for 19,000 guineas and stood at stud in Ireland until he was sold to America for £130,000 in 1950. He was four times Champion Sire in America where his notable winners included Nashua, Bold Ruler and Bold Eagle. In Europe he had left behind Never Say Die (Derby), Nearula (2000 Guineas), Musidora (1000 Guineas and Oaks), and Belle of All (1000 Guineas). Amongst his offspring who became successful stallions were Grey Sovereign, Princely Gift and Red God. All three possessed and passed on their sire's 'gunpowder'.

BIG RACES WON	
Champion Stakes	1943
Coventry Stakes	1942

NATIVE DANCER

MOST OF THE HEROES of this book are kind, courageous, thoroughly likeable individuals, who commanded affection and respect. Native Dancer was none of these things, with the possible exception of courageous. He was, however, a sensational racehorse.

Foaled 1950
Trained in USA

Native Dancer was a big, grey, calculating bully and nasty with it. No one could relax in his presence. An unwary groom would be lifted off the ground with Native Dancer's teeth, while more than one exercise rider was pulled off by a grab at his foot. When he was turned out he would come to the gate when he was ready, and woe betide anyone who ventured into his field. His one Achilles' heel was threat of the whip, which he resented, but feared. In between all this nonsense, he was generally judged the greatest American racehorse since Man O'War thirty years earlier.

Bred by Alfred G. Vanderbilt at his Sagamore Farm in Maryland's Worthington Valley, he was trained for the owner-breeder by Bill Winfrey. As a two-year-old, he won all nine starts, worth $230,495. He was odds-on in every race after his first, and in the Futurity at Belmont Park, he equalled the world record for six-and-a-half furlongs in 1 minute 14.4 seconds. He was never again to start odds against.

Between seasons he developed into a powerhouse of a horse, standing 16.3hh. After landing odds of 10-1 in the Wood Memorial at Jamaica, he was shipped to Louisville for the Kentucky Derby at Churchill Downs. No one could envisage defeat — but for the first and only time in his career, the race went wrong. After half a mile 'The Dancer' collected a hefty bump from another runner and lost his place. At the top of the straight, two furlongs out, The Dancer had moved into fourth on the inside. Eric Guerin, his jockey, kept to the fence — and was stopped. Late — too late — Guerin switched to the 'outer'. Native Dancer closed … and closed … but the post came three strides too soon. Dark Star had become the only horse ever to beat The Dancer. Guerin was accused of taking the colt 'just about every place on the track except the Ladies Room'!

The Dancer had swift consolation in the Withers Stakes before landing odds of 5-1 in the 'Belmont' and 5-2 in the 'Preakness'. In the Belmont, Dark Star broke down and Native Dancer won by only a neck doing no more than he had to. In the Preakness, he worked harder and won in 2 minutes 28.6 seconds, the third fastest time in the history of the race. There followed the Dwyer Stakes (20-1 on), the Arlington Classic (by nine lengths), the Travers (by five-and-a-half lengths) and finally the American Derby. That was one of his most remarkable wins. Native Dancer was lame at the gate, and Eddie Arcaro, standing in for Guerin, wanted to withdraw.

A great big, grey bully, but a sensational racehorse. Native Dancer feared only one thing — the whip.

Three furlongs out Native Dancer was almost last, and going nowhere. Arcaro picked up his whip, gave his mount a sharp smack, whereupon The Dancer took off and flew past his field. Was it courage? — or fear of the whip? Arcaro called him 'all heart — and then some'. Maybe so — but he was smart. Bud Troyer, his exercise rider as a stallion, relates in *Classic Lines* (by Patrick Robinson and Richard Stone Reeves): 'He hated the whip, and as long as I walked out holding one, he was well behaved. Any day he saw me without a whip, he would immediately try to throw me off, or refuse to move.'

The Dancer ran three times as a four-year-old, a campaign highlighted by a dramatic win in the Metropolitan Handicap, making up seven lengths in the straight, and getting up to win by a neck. In August he was retired as his foot problem became worse. In twenty-one wins from twenty-two starts, he had won $785,240.

Native Dancer made an immediate impact at stud. His sons Kauai King (1966) and Dancer's Image (1968) won the Kentucky Derby, while his daughter Natalma was the dam of the great Northern Dancer. In Europe he was the sire of Hula Dancer and the grandsire of Sea Bird II. But in all these great offspring, his moodiness and cussedness was never far away. He was great — but too clever by half!

BIG RACES WON	
Belmont Stakes	1953
Preakness Stakes	1953
Arlington Classic	1953
American Derby	1953
Wood Memorial	1953
Dwyer Stakes	1953
Metropolitan Handicap	1954
The Futurity	1952
The Hopeful	1952
The East View Stakes	1952

NEARCO

Foaled 1935
Trained in Italy

THE STORY OF Nearco is a story of the fulfilment of one man's work of a lifetime. Nearco was bred and trained by Signor Federico Tesio, a chauvinistic, but gifted, Italian ex-Cavalry Officer, who was almost solely responsible for putting the Italian-bred racehorse on the international map.

Tesio was a small, fussy, fastidious and egocentric man, with a brilliant mind and ill-concealed contempt for intellectual inferiors. In wartime 1915, he travelled to Newmarket Sales and bought a mare called Catnip for 75 guineas. Although Catnip was an unprepossessing individual and had gained her only success in a £100 nursery at Newcastle, she was nonetheless beautifully bred by Spearmint, winner of the 1906 Derby, out of Sibola, who won the 1899 1000 Guineas. In 1987 such a filly's value would be nearer £250,000!

Catnip proceeded to breed a sequence of important winners, amongst them a filly called Nogara who won the Italian 2000 and 1000 Guineas. More important, Nogara became the dam of Nearco. As so often happens, there was an element of luck in Nearco's breeding. After deep thought, Tesio decided to send Nogara to Lord Derby's outstanding stallion, Fairway, but the little Italian was late in applying for a nomination and the Stud were rigidly strict in restricting Fairway to forty-two mares. In a state of outrage, Tesio reluctantly decided to visit Fairway's own brother Pharos who was standing in France. The resultant foal was small, but strong, stocky and robust. He was a 'leader' and a bully in the lush paddocks at Olgiata near Rome, the property of Mario Incisa della Rochetta — who was now in partnership with Tesio.

When Nearco went into training he was able to absorb all the work that Tesio grafted into him. However daunting the task Tesio set, Nearco, with his brilliant speed, would shrug it off. He won all of his seven two-year-old races with considerable ease, and at three was even better! He won the Premio Parioli (Italian 2000 Guineas) by six lengths, the Italian Derby by a distance and went on to win the Gran Premio d'Italia and the Gran Premio di Milano. A week later he faced his greatest challenge in the Grand Prix de Paris over 1 mile 7 furlongs. His rivals included the English Derby winner Bois Roussel, and the French Derby winner Cillas. Nearco took the lead early in the straight, and drew away effortlessly. At the line he had a length and a half to spare over the good stayer Canot, with Bois Roussel third. He was Champion of Europe.

With the dark clouds of war looming over Europe, Tesio sold Nearco four days later to the English bookmaker Martin Benson, for the then record price of £60,000. A handsome, perfectly moulded

A beautiful, symmetrical horse with a combination of quality and power, Nearco was impossible to fault.

horse now standing 16hh, he immediately made his mark as a stallion at Beech House Stud, Newmarket. For fifteen years he was in the top ten stallions. His best sons were Dante, Nimbus and Sayajirao, although Nasrullah, Mossborough and Royal Charger had a greater long-term effect on the breed. His male-line descendants include Sir Ivor, Nijinsky, Mill Reef, Roberto, The Minstrel and Shirley Heights. He was also three times leading sire of brood mares, and filled one of the first three places in every year between 1952-59.

In later years, Ribot was to put a seal on the genius of Tesio's life, but Nearco and that famous day in Paris was the highest reward of a lifetime's study and work. His dream had come true.

BIG RACES WON	
Grand Prix de Paris	1938
Derby Italiano	1938
Premio Parioli	1938
Gran Premio di Milano	1938
Gran Premio d'Italia	1938
Gran Criterium	1937
Premio Chiusura	1937

NIJINSKY

Foaled 1967
Trained in Ireland

NIJINSKY was a horse who had the best of everything. The best pedigree — his sire was Northern Dancer; the best rearing at E.P. Taylor's famous Ontario stud; the best owner in Mr Charles Engelhard; the best trainer in Vincent O'Brien, and, ultimately, the best jockey in Lester Piggott. And he was 'The Best' — certainly the best horse in Europe of his generation.

Engelhard, a multi-millionaire whose fortune was based on minerals, paid $84,000 — a Canadian record — for the Northern Dancer colt at the Woodbine Sales in Toronto. The colt was a handful from the moment he arrived at Ballydoyle. He would rear up, refuse to canter, and sweat. Vincent was concerned by his attitude. Luckily he had the best riders to call upon. When Vincent started to gallop him the stable became excited. Although a big colt, he was mature and Vincent ran him at The Curragh over six furlongs at the start of July. He won easily by half a length at 11-4 on. He was never to start odds against until the Derby. Nijinsky now won the Railway Stakes, Anglesey Stakes and Beresford Stakes, before crossing to England for the Dewhurst Stakes. Here Piggott rode Nijinsky and the big, bay horse won like a machine.

At 7-4 on, Nijinsky was the shortest-priced favourite for the 2000 Guineas since Colombo in 1934. He won comfortably by two-and-a-half lengths, but did not please everyone. The reason was that Piggott was instructed not to take any chances. He therefore lay closer to the leader Amber Rama than he would have done otherwise, with the result that Nijinsky produced less acceleration than expected. Also, he idled in front. Nonetheless, he was a firm favourite for what I have always believed was a top-quality Derby. Gyr, the giant chestnut colt, whom Etienne Pollet had postponed his retirement for a year to train, was considered unbeatable. Stintino had impressed greatly in his trial. Nijinsky was shaken up by Piggott, and flashed home by two-and-a-half lengths from Gyr and Stintino in the fastest time since Mahmoud in 1935. Gyr went on to win the Grand Prix de St Cloud with ease.

After the Irish Derby — won easily — came Nijinsky's most majestic effort in the King George VI & Queen Elizabeth Stakes. He strolled home by six lengths, with Piggott immobile. A week later came the turning point of his career. He was struck down by a virulent strain of ringworm, which caused his hair to fall out and his skin to become raw. Vincent favoured a long rest, but his owner was anxious that Nijinsky should complete the Triple Crown. The St Leger was on September 12th — too soon. Nijinsky won the St Leger, but lost a great deal of weight.

On the day of the Prix de l'Arc de Troimphe, Nijinsky was on

OPPOSITE: *Nijinsky — a magnificent, athletic Prince among thoroughbreds. But increasingly on the racecourse he overrevved.*

94

his toes in the paddock. The attentions of dozens of photographers upset him. Nonetheless, when Piggott made his move in the straight, he looked sure to win. A hundred yards from the finish he headed the outsider Sassafras, but faltered, and was beaten a head. Piggott was blamed — and still is — by Vincent O'Brien for giving his horse too much to do. But Nijinsky was calling 'enough'. The ringworm, and the St Leger, had undermined his magnificent constitution. Sadly, he ran again in the Champion Stakes two weeks later and, starting at 11-4 on, was comfortably beaten by a great inferior horse in Lorenzaccio.

Nijinsky retired to stud in Kentucky, joining Sir Ivor at the late Bill Hancock's Claiborne Farm. His success was immediate and spectacular. His European winning sons included Golden Fleece, Shadeed, Caerleon and King's Lake. In 1987 his stallion fee was $300,000. Vincent O'Brien, who had picked him out as a yearling, and trained him superbly, always rated him one of the great ones. 'For brilliance, Nijinsky. For toughness, Sir Ivor,' he would say. Brilliant he certainly was.

BIG RACES WON	
Derby	1970
2000 Guineas	1970
St Leger	1970
Irish Sweeps Derby	1970
King George VI & Queen Elizabeth Stakes	1970
Dewhurst Stakes	1969

OPPOSITE: *'Eclipse first — the rest nowhere'*

LEFT: *Oh So Sharp, the first since Meld to win the Fillies' Triple Crown*

ABOVE: *Touchstone, the 'ugly duckling' who became a mighty swan*

*Nijinsky — the first Triple
Crown winner since
Bahram in 1935*

ABOVE: *Shergar wins the Derby by a record ten lengths*

LEFT: *Mill Reef, a great racehorse and a great stallion*

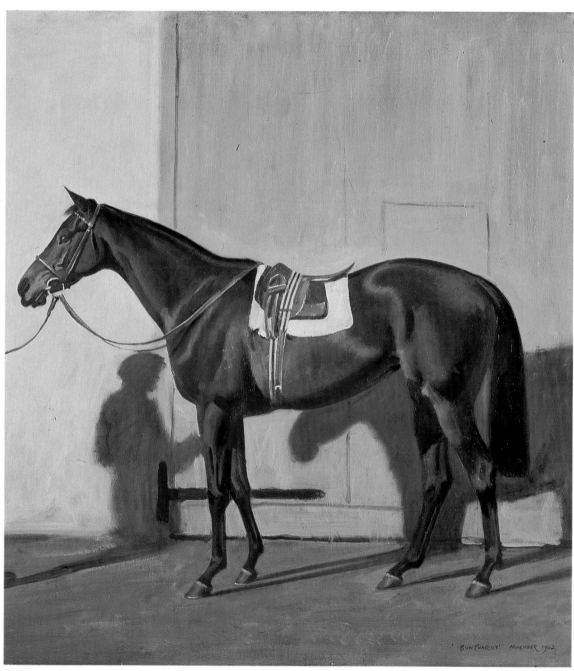

*Sun Chariot — a filly fit
for a king*

*Sir Ivor — an
international triumph*

*Park Top (Lester Piggott)
— the apple of the Duke's
eye*

NOBLESSE

NOBLESSE WAS THE easiest winner of the Oaks that I have ever seen. On that day she was a sensationally good filly.

A daughter of Mossborough out of Duke's Delight by His Grace, she was bought for 4200 guineas, by the Anglo-Irish Bloodstock Agency with whom her trainer Paddy Prendergast had close associations. The purchase was made on behalf of Mrs John Olin.

Prendergast, who trained at Maddenstown near The Curragh, until his death in June 1980, was an outstanding trainer of two-year-olds, and when Noblesse travelled to England for her first race, Ascot's Blue Seal Stakes, she was preceded by a tall reputation. She duly justified this, and went on to win the Timeform Gold Cup (now the William Hill Futurity) at Doncaster, by three lengths — the only filly to have won this race. These were her only two starts in her first season.

The following spring was the coldest since the war and there was no racing in England from December 22nd to March 8th. Noblesse, not surprisingly, did not thrive and was not ready in time for the 1000 Guineas. Her reappearance came in the Musidora Stakes at York, which she won in brilliant style by six lengths. Thereafter she became a stronger and stronger favourite for the Oaks, finally starting at 11-4 on. She won as she pleased by ten lengths.

Foaled 1960
Trained in Ireland

An oil-painting Noblesse was not — but a racing machine she was.

Noblesse was made ante-post favourite for the King George VI & Queen Elizabeth Stakes and with the Derby winner Relko, under a cloud, looked a 'good thing'. By misfortune however, she injured a hock, and was withdrawn. Instead Prendergast ran his vastly improved Irish Derby winner Ragusa, who won comfortably. It was common knowledge, however, that the filly was rated vastly superior. Noblesse came back in the autumn with the target of the Prix de l'Arc de Triomphe, but after defeat in the Prix Vermeille, her connections decided she was lacking her midsummer sparkle, and she was retired to stud in America.

Noblesse proved a successful broodmare in all too short a stud career, breeding two useful winners in America in Straight Arrow (by Nashua) and Noblesse Oblige (by Gallant Man) as well as Fughetta (by Ribot) who became a winner in France, and Carezza, trained by Bernard van Cutsem, who went on to win the Nell Gwyn Stakes. Noblesse's final foal, Where You Lead (1970) by Raise A Native, was also a good winner, and dam of winners.

BIG RACES WON	
Oaks	1963
Musidora Stakes	1963
Timeform Gold Cup	1962
Blue Seal Stakes	1962

NORTHERN DANCER

AS A RACEHORSE, Northern Dancer put Canadian racing and breeding firmly on the map. As a stallion he has become a legend.

Northern Dancer, by Neartic, a son of Nearco, was bred by the legendary E.P. Taylor at his stud in Oshawa on the outskirts of Ontario, Canada. Like his grandsire, and his son Nijinsky after him, he was a bully, and often a menace as a yearling. At the Sales he failed to reach a reserve of $25,000 and returned to Taylor's farm at Willowdale, Ontario.

In the months after being broken and before moving on to the track, the Taylor yearlings would exercise in an indoor barn as a protection against the cold Canadian winter. Northern Dancer would pull, charge through the string, bump the wall, and do everything in his power to dislodge his rider, usually with success. 'Every time that rough little guy set foot in the barn there was chaos,' recalls E.P. Taylor's vice-president Joe Thomas, in *Classic Lines*.

Northern Dancer began his two-year-old career in Canada, and won five of his seven races, including the Coronation Futurity, and the Carleton Stakes. Now it was decided that Northern Dancer was good enough to take on the best in the States. In November he flew south and promptly beat Bupers, the Futurity winner, by eight lengths over a mile at Aqueduct. Soon afterwards, his trainer Horatio Luro discovered a hairline quarter crack on the front of his near fore hoof. Northern Dancer ran and won again — at 4-1 on — but immediately afterwards Luro contacted the Californian blacksmith, Bill Bane, who had developed a technique for treating quarter cracks with heat, fusing the hoof wall. The treatment worked and Northern Dancer was not troubled with foot problems after the following February.

Northern Dancer grew to 15.3hh during the winter, but still looked a sprinter type. Ridden by Bob Ussey he lost his first race of the next season at Florida to Chieftain. Against orders, Ussey had hit Northern Dancer with the whip, and was sacked. 'This is not a stick horse,' said Luro. Bill Shoemaker rode the stocky little colt in the Flamingo Stakes and Florida Derby, winning both, and accepted the ride in the Kentucky Derby. But forty-eight hours later he decided to swap horses and rode the Californian colt Hill Rise. 'I may have made the wrong choice,' said 'The Shoe'. He had. Ridden by Bill Hartack and driven vigorously with the whip the length of the straight, Northern Dancer held off Hill Rise by a neck, in a record time of two minutes flat. In the Preakness, he increased the margin over Hill Rise by two-and-a-quarter lengths, but in the Belmont (one-and-a-half miles) he failed to stay.

Sadly, after a victorious return to Canada for the Queen's Plate,

Foaled 1961
Trained in Canada and USA

'Make way for the winner!' Owner-breeder E.P. Taylor leads in Northern Dancer after his victorious 'Run For The Roses' (Kentucky Derby).

the little colt injured a tendon at exercise at Belmont Park and was retired to stud — the greatest horse in the history of Canadian racing. Northern Dancer was syndicated for $2,400,000 and stood at the Windfield Farm in Kentucky. The sum, colossal at the time, now looks staggeringly paltry. At one stage in the 'eighties, a nomination to the great stallion changed hands for $900,000. In 1987, at the age of twenty-six, his stallion career finally came to an end. In the meanwhile, he had sired Nijinsky, Lyphard, The Minstrel, Shareef Dancer, Storm Bird, Nureyev, El Gran Senor, Try My Best, Sadlers Wells and others, to become the most influential sire of the second half of the twentieth century.

BIG RACES WON	
Kentucky Derby	1964
Preakness Stakes	1964
Flamingo Stakes	1964
Florida Derby	1964
Blue Grass Stakes	1964
Sir Gaylord Purse	1963
Coronation Futurity	1963
Carleton Stakes	1963

OH SO SHARP

Foaled 1982
Trained in England

OH SO SHARP was never a spectacular winner of races in the style of, say, Noblesse, but her achievement in winning the Fillies' Triple Crown entitles her to be considered out of the ordinary.

One of the first foals to be bred by Sheik Mohammed al Maktoum, the third son of the Ruler of Dubai, at Dalham Hall Stud, she was trained for the Sheik by Henry Cecil at Newmarket. A daughter of the brilliant miler, Kris, out of the Graustark mare Oh So Fair, she showed unexpected reserves of stamina. Her dam's previous best produce were Roussalka, Etienne Gerard and Our Home, none of whom won beyond a mile and a quarter.

While her sire, Kris, had started his career at Leicester, Oh So Sharp made her first appearance at Nottingham. She started at 2-1 on and won impressively, ridden by Paul Eddery, the stable jockey Lester Piggott having sustained a serious injury the previous week. Her next race, Sandown's Solario Stakes, marked the occasion of Piggott's return to the saddle. There were grounds for questioning Piggott's fitness to ride, but Oh So Sharp carried him to a comfortable two-length success from the colt Young Runaway. Oh So Sharp completed her two-year-old career by beating Helen Street (later to win the Irish Oaks) by a length and a half in Ascot's Hoover Fillies' Mile.

The following season, after acrimony in the stable, Piggott was replaced by Steve Cauthen as Cecil's stable jockey. Piggott was deeply disappointed to lose the ride on Oh So Sharp. 'She could be the best filly I've ever ridden,' he told me in spring 1985. The new partnership was launched in the Nell Gwyn Stakes (7 furlongs), which the filly won by a length from Bella Colora, with Helen Street third. It was a performance of sufficient merit to make Oh So Sharp 2-1 favourite for the 1000 Guineas. Her success was as spectacular as it was dramatic. Making up two lengths in the last 100 yards, she thrust her head in front on the line beating Al Bahatri and the luckless Bella Colora by two short heads. The uncertainty as to her ability to stay a mile and a half in the Oaks was made irrelevant by a slow early pace. Oh So Sharp took the lead two furlongs out and stormed away to win by six lengths from Triptych. It was the performance of her career.

The injury to Derby winner Slip Anchor resolved Henry Cecil's dilemma as to whether to run the filly in the 'King George'. Oh So Sharp was made 5-4 on favourite, but met with the first defeat of her career, after looking the likely winner a furlong from home. It has always been my contention that Oh So Sharp failed to last out the mile and a half at the end of an exceptionally fast-run race — the time was a remarkable 2 minutes 27.61 seconds — but this

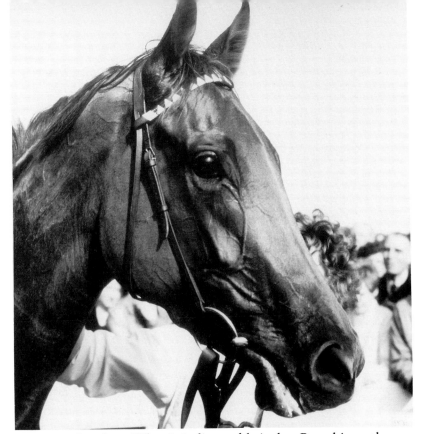

Oh So Sharp — a queen amongst fillies — and the first winner of the fillies' 'Triple Crown' since Meld.

is a minority view. What is indisputable is that Petoski ran the race of his life to win by a neck, with the subsequent Prix de l'Arc de Triomphe winner Rainbow Quest coming third. Oh So Sharp was probably feeling the effects of that race when, at 5-2 on, she failed to peg back Commanche Run in the Benson & Hedges Gold Cup. However, the following month she came back to win a sub-standard St Leger by three parts of a length. It was class and courage, rather than stamina, that enabled her to win.

During the autumn it was debated whether she should remain in training as a four-year-old, but in the end she retired to stud. Her first mate was Dunbeath. In 1987 she visited Shareef Dancer.

Oh So Sharp was a quite attractive, rather lengthy filly with a distinctive old-fashioned head. Like so many good fillies, she was inclined to be idiosyncratic, and was well served by the stable's travelling head lad George Windsor, who fell in love with her and rode her throughout the winter and spring of her three-year-old career. It would be unrealistic to suggest that she was on a par with Meld, but on Oaks day she was a very, very good filly indeed.

BIG RACES WON	
Oaks	1985
1000 Guineas	1985
St Leger	1985
Hoover Fillies' Mile	1984
Solario Stakes	1984

ORMONDE

Foaled 1883
Trained in England

ORMONDE WAS ALMOST certainly the outstanding horse of the nineteenth century. He was unbeaten, and never really extended except, perhaps, for a few strides in the Derby. He won the Triple Crown in what was considered a vintage year.

Ormonde, by Bend Or, the Derby winner of 1880, out of the Doncaster Cup winner Lily Agnes, was bred and raced by the 1st Duke of Westminster, reputedly the richest man in England. Trained by John Porter at Kingsclere, Ormonde was big and backward as a two-year-old, and was troubled by splints. Nor was he especially impressive in his slower paces. Fred Archer, who had ridden his sire Bend Or, said that until Ormonde extended himself, he felt that he was sitting on his neck. Ormonde did not race until October, whereupon he won three races at Newmarket, notably the Dewhurst Plate.

The field for the 2000 Guineas of 1886 was probably one of the finest in the history of the race. The Bard had won all his sixteen races as a two-year-old; a colt named Saraband had won at Kempton with incredible ease, while Minting, the favourite, was described by his trainer Matthew Dawson as one of the best horses he had ever known. The betting was 11-10 Minting, 3-1 Saraband, 7-2 Ormonde, 33-1 others. Fred Archer rode Saraband, with George Barrett on Ormonde. Ormonde won in a canter — and Matthew Dawson went home to his room in a sulk and did not emerge for the remainder of the meeting!

Fred Archer secured the ride on Ormonde in the Derby, and with Minting redirected to the Grand Prix de Paris, it became a virtual match between Ormonde (85-40 on) and The Bard (7-2). The little Bard ran a gallant race, but Ormonde won comfortably by a length and a half. At Ascot he won the St James's Palace Stakes and Hardwicke Stakes on successive days, beating the 1885 Derby winner Melton in the 'Hardwicke'. In the St Leger he landed odds of 7-1 in a common canter by four lengths. Odds of 25-1 were bet on him in the Great Foal Stakes at Newmarket; in the Newmarket St Leger he 'walked over'; in the Champion Stakes he landed odds of 100-1, and finally in the Free Handicap he gave two stone and an eight-length beating to a fair horse in Mephisto.

During the winter it was rumoured that he had 'gone' in the wind which proved to be all too true. Nonetheless, he remained unbeaten, winning twice at Royal Ascot, notably the Hardwicke Stakes, from his old rival Minting. Minting was, in fact, well fancied to beat him, but despite interference caused by George Barrett riding an outsider — Barrett having been replaced on Ormonde by Tom Cannon, following Fred Archer's suicide the previous autumn — Ormonde won comfortably by a neck. He was greeted amidst scenes not repeated until the era of Brown Jack.

His final appearance was over six furlongs on the Newmarket July course, where he had to be driven out to win. He retired almost certainly at just the right moment. In 1887 Queen Victoria, whose heir the Prince of Wales was now a patron of Kingsclere, celebrated her Jubilee, and at one stage it was suggested that the Duke — a fine horseman — should ride Ormonde in the Royal Procession. Instead, Ormonde came quietly to London for a garden party at the Duke's London residence, Grosvenor House. He was unboxed at Waterloo, walked deliberately across Westminster Bridge, and by special permission through Green Park. Ormonde behaved impeccably and was widely admired by guests who included the Prince and Princess of Wales, four kings, two queens, and numerous princes. Ormonde's only social gaffe was to eat the carnations presented by the Queen of Belgium.

Ormonde (Fred Archer), with trainer John Porter. Note the contrast between Archer's length of stirrup-leather and Lester Piggott's on page 14.

Ormonde spent two seasons at stud in England, and was then sold by the Duke to Argentina for £12,000. In the face of criticism, the Duke argued, quite logically, that Ormonde was a 'roarer', coming from a line of 'roarers', and that he might easily do considerable damage to British bloodstock. Ormonde ended his days in California, but was not especially fertile and died in 1904. He was almost the perfect racehorse.

BIG RACES WON	
Derby	1886
2000 Guineas	1886
St Leger	1886
Champion Stakes	1886
Hardwicke Stakes (twice)	1886-87
St James's Palace Stakes	1886
Rous Memorial Stakes	1887
Newmarket St Leger (walkover)	1886
Imperial Gold Cup	1887
Great Foal Stakes	1886
Dewhurst Plate	1885

ORWELL

Foaled 1929
Trained in England

ORWELL, TRAINED AT Manton by Joe Lawson, began his career in such spectacular style as to suggest that he might be one of the greatest horses ever to be trained at that famous stable. Bred by Lord Furness, Orwell was a bay son of Gainsborough (by Bayardo), out of a mare called Golden Hair (daughter of Golden Sun, a sprinter). Although troubled by bad feet, Orwell came to hand early, and was saddled for the Great Surrey Foal Plate at the Epsom Derby meeting.

Epsom is not an ideal course on which to introduce a two-year-old, and the combination of firm ground, inexperience and a tender ride from the veteran Freddie Fox, led to his defeat. Thereafter he was unbeaten as a two-year-old. Ridden by Bobby Jones, he won the Chesham Stakes at Royal Ascot, the National Breeders' Produce Stakes at Sandown, the Champagne Stakes at Doncaster, and then the Imperial Breeders' Produce Stakes at Kempton. This was his least impressive performance, probably attributable to the plan to run him the following week in the Middle Park Stakes. This he won comfortably bringing his seasonal prize money to a record £18,613. He was awarded joint top-weight in the Free Handicap with his stable companion Mannamead.

Beaten only once in his first season, Orwell (Bobby Jones) established a two-year-old stakes record of £18,613.

While Orwell thrived during the winter and spring, Mannamead, unluckily for the stable, met with an accident in his first gallop of 1932 and missed most of the season, with the result that Orwell became the stable's sole Classic colt. Orwell won the Greenham Stakes comfortably enough, and was made even money favourite for the 2000 Guineas. He won decisively by two lengths from Dastur.

Sadly, Orwell was a complete flop in the Derby, for which he was 5-4 favourite. It has been said that he failed to stay, but the slow early pace was all in his favour, and he was beaten soon after Tattenham Corner and finished ninth of twenty-one. He had not moved well to post, and when he returned to Manton he was found to be lame with knee trouble. This disability remained with him, and he did not race again until the St Leger. This time Orwell — again favourite — clearly failed to stay, and finished seventh. His only remaining race was in Newmarket's Great Foal Stakes, which he won by a length and a half. He pulled up extremely lame, and Jones was only just able to get him to the unsaddling enclosure.

Orwell retired to stud at King Edward's Place, Wanborough, near Swindon. His stud career was a considerable disappointment, perhaps largely as a result of his inherent unsoundness. He was, however, a very good racehorse, until Derby Day.

BIG RACES WON	
2000 Guineas	1932
Great Foal Stakes	1932
National Breeders' Produce Stakes	1931
Middle Park Stakes	1931
Imperial Breeders' Produce Stakes	1931
Chesham Stakes	1931
Champagne Stakes	1931

PARK TOP

Foaled 1964
Trained in England

IT BECOMES CLEAR very quickly to anyone making a study of the Sport of Kings that luck, above all, is the prime factor. No matter how skilful the practitioner, nor how brilliant the horse, without luck — or more important, with bad luck — the whole pack of cards collapses.

No one is more conscious of this than Andrew, 11th Duke of Devonshire. Throughout his career he has been a quite exceptionally unlucky owner. However, when he finally had the good fortune to own a good horse, the animal concerned turned out to be not just good, but great. That filly was Park Top, bought with a single bid of 500 guineas, as a yearling.

The story of the purchase underlines the 'luck' factor. The filly was by Kalydon, a good stayer but unfashionable stallion, out of Oola Hills, a half-sister to the brilliant Pappa Fourway, but a very moderate race mare. John Hislop, bidding for Bernard van Cutsem, bought the plain yearling filly for the reserve price. For a late foal (May 27th), by a non-commercial stallion, out of a non-winning mare and with bad joints, he was not surprisingly the only bidder.

Van Cutsem, who had trained Kalydon, had intended the filly for a new American patron who had offered him an open cheque. When he heard of the purchase price he was too embarrassed to contact the American. Accordingly, he telephoned his old friend Andrew Devonshire with the good news that he had bought him a 'delightful, cheap filly by Kalydon'. When the Duke was told of the dam's name, he went rigid. 'But I used to own her. She was useless,' he said icily. Nonetheless, he took the filly.

Park Top was backward as a two-year-old, and suffered a mishap to her near side hock. She also coughed. It was not until May of her second season that she saw a racecourse, winning a minor maiden event at a Windsor evening meeting. Three weeks later she ran in a mile-and-a-quarter conditions race at Newbury. I remember the evening as if it were last year. Tucked in last by a bobbing Russ Maddock, she was pulled out two furlongs from home, and swept from last to first within about 150 yards. It was electrifying ... pure class. Six days later she went to Ascot for the Ribblesdale Stakes and beat the Oaks runner-up, St Pauli Girl, by a comfortable half-length. Within a month she had gone from being 'unknown' to a Royal Ascot winner.

Her autumn campaign was interrupted by a minor injury and the Duke did not hesitate to keep her in training as a four-year-old. The campaign was not a success, at least until July. Indeed so despondent was the volatile Duke that he agreed to sell the mare to France for £30,000. Now came the next great slice of luck. The agent telephoned to ask for 15% commission at a moment when the owner had been liberally entertained by his trainer. 'Tell him to get stuffed — the deal's off,' was the Duke's reply. From here on, Park Top never looked back. She ended the season by winning the Prix d'Hédouville at Longchamp and finishing second in Ascot's Cumberland Lodge Stakes.

Her five-year-old career was a triumph. Now ridden by Geoff Lewis, she won the Coronation Cup and Hardwicke Stakes, and was odds-on favourite for the Eclipse. Here, Lewis was caught on the fence in the 'Sandown trap' and Park Top, who now liked to

Park Top and Piggott make the winning look easy. The mare's spectacular burst takes her from last to first in the 1969 'King George'.

be covered up and waited with until the last moment, was a desperately unlucky loser.

Piggott replaced Lewis in the King George VI & Queen Elizabeth Stakes and coming from last to first in the straight — on the rails — Park Top gained a spectacular success. In September she won Longchamp's Prix Foy and the following month ran a superb race to finish second to Levmoss in the Prix de l'Arc de Triomphe — flying at the finish.

At six years, she won La Coupe at Longchamps, and the Cumberland Lodge Stakes, but she was no longer quite the filly that she was and had become increasingly difficult to ride. She retired to stud the winner of thirteen races worth £136,440. Sadly, but almost predictably, with her masculine appearance, she proved a complete failure at stud, breeding one winner, of no consequence, from just three foals. Next to Meld and Petite Etoile, she was probably the best post-war middle distance filly.

BIG RACES WON	
King George VI & Queen Elizabeth Stakes	1969
Coronation Cup	1969
Hardwicke Stakes	1969
Ribblesdale Stakes	1967
Cumberland Lodge Stakes	1970
La Coupe	1970
Prix d'Hédouville	1968

PERSIMMON

PERSIMMON WAS THE first Royal winner of the Derby for 108 years. His owner-breeder, the Prince of Wales — later King Edward VII — was to win two more Derbys with Diamond Jubilee and Minoru, but Persimmon was unquestionably the best of the trio.

Foaled 1893
Trained in England

A lengthy bay colt by St Simon, Persimmon had galloped like a good horse before his first race, the Coventry Stakes at Royal Ascot. Favourite at 2-1, he made it a most agreeable meeting for the future King, winning in a canter by three lengths. His next race was at Goodwood, where he landed odds of 2-1 with ease in the Richmond Stakes, and his only other two-year-old race was in the Middle Park Stakes. Richard Marsh, his trainer, was most unwilling to run the Royal colt as he had been coughing for almost two weeks shortly before the race. However, after a 'rough' gallop in the week of the race, the Prince's manager, Lord Marcus Beresford, insisted upon his running. He was duly beaten into third place, but tenderly ridden by Jack Watts.

Persimmon grew a thick woolly coat in the winter and was exceptionally slow in coming to hand, so much so that it was decided to miss the 2000 Guineas. Three weeks before the Derby, he did a gallop so lamentable that it cast his entire entourage into deep despair. Thereafter he began to sparkle, and Marsh became extremely optimistic. The worst moment came on the eve of the race when Persimmon refused to be loaded into his rail-horsebox at Dullingham Station. Two horse specials from Newmarket had already passed through and the last was due in about a quarter of an hour. Eventually, as the crowd of onlookers grew, Marcus shouted: 'Now this horse has to go to Epsom, and he has to go into this box. To every man that helps me get him in I will give a sovereign!' A dozen volunteers sprang forward, and Persimmon was bodily lifted into the box!

St Frusquin, the three-length winner of the 2000 Guineas, was 13-8 on favourite, with Persimmon second favourite at 5-1. It turned out to be a great race with the strength and experience of Watts — who had considered retiring the previous winter — swinging the balance. Persimmon won by a neck, and horse and rider were beseiged by the public. The lugubrious, introspective Watts, who smiled rather less often than Lester Piggott, looked as doleful as ever, but forced a faint glimmer of pleasure as Marsh slapped his thigh and shouted: 'Do you know you've just won the Derby for the Prince of Wales?'

St Frusquin, receiving 3lb, gained his revenge over Persimmon in the Princess of Wales Stakes, by half a length after another great race, but then broke down leaving the St Leger at the mercy of

AFTER THE MORNINGS WORK.

IN REPOSE.

Persimmon — a day in the life of the 'High-Mettled Racer'.

Persimmon. As a four-year-old Persimmon reached his peak, winning the Gold Cup by eight lengths, and then reverting to half the distance in the Eclipse Stakes. In his autobiography, *A Trainer to Two Kings,* Richard Marsh wrote: 'A grander horse than Persimmon was as a four-year-old, especially on the day that he won the Gold Cup at Ascot, I never beheld. I would not have feared St Frusquin then, nor the greatest horse that ever walked the turf.'

Persimmon retired to the Royal Stud at Sandringham, and met with immediate success, siring the great Sceptre in his first crop. He was Champion Sire twice, and bred four Classic winners before he broke his pelvis and was put down at the age of fifteen.

BIG RACES WON	
Derby	1896
St Leger	1896
Gold Cup	1897
Eclipse Stakes	1897
Jockey Club Stakes	1896
Coventry Stakes	1895
Richmond Stakes	1895

PETITE ETOILE

PETITE ETOILE, a great filly by any standards, was one of those animals whose talents were heightened by the brilliant riding of Lester Piggott. Ridden by another rider, the grey filly would certainly have been a champion, but ridden by Piggott with his combination of confidence, charisma and ice-cool nerve, she was electrifying.

Foaled 1956
Trained in England

Bred by the Aga Khan and raced by his son Prince Aly Khan, the daughter of Petition had speed on both sides of her pedigree, but especially on her dam's side, where she traced back to Mumtaz Mahal. She was an exceptionally quirky animal and was brilliantly handled by Noel Murless. For instance, at exercise she liked to have another grey in front of her and, more important, behind her. Otherwise she sulked.

Her racing career began explosively. She was sent to Manchester Races in May, and on the way from the stables to the racecourse got loose and knocked her lad unconscious. In a two-horse race, she was beaten eight lengths by the fast northern colt Chris. Two successes at Sandown were separated by defeat at the hands of Krakenwake in the Molecomb Stakes, where she was caught sideways on at the start. Piggott felt she was unexceptional.

Her three-year-old career started well for her, but badly for Lester Piggott. Circumstances compelled Lester to ride the Queen's Short Sentence in the Free Handicap, leaving George Moore, Aly Khan's jockey in France, to ride Petite Etoile. The grey filly won impressively, under top weight, at 9-1. In the 1000 Guineas, Lester elected to ride Collyria for Sir Victor Sassoon, with Doug Smith taking the ride on Petite Etoile. Despite hitting the front too soon, Petite Etoile held on to beat the favourite Rosalba by a length, with Aly Khan's more fancied runner, the French-trained Paraguana (George Moore), third. Lester Piggott finally rode Petite Etoile in the Oaks, but with her 'fast' pedigree and exceptional acceleration, she was considered unlikely to stay, and started at 11-2. Beautifully ridden by Piggott, and bouncing off the fast ground, she won in a canter by three lengths. Murless also trained the third and fourth, Collyria and Rose of Medina.

Petite Etoile went on to win the Sussex Stakes, Yorkshire Oaks and Champion Stakes, but her brilliance continued to be matched by her volatile temperament. One evening the Aly Khan's stud manager Cyril Hall walked into her box and, prodding his finger into her neck, said: 'You're getting a bit fat, old girl!' The grey filly whirled round in a flash, sunk her teeth into his lapels, and lifted him off the ground!

As a four-year-old she returned to Epsom for the Coronation Cup — the 1959 Oaks winner against the 1959 Derby winner, Parthia.

It promised to be a famous race, but Petite Etoile won on a tight rein — a spectacle I remember vividly to this day. It was her most brilliant performance. In the King George VI & Queen Elizabeth Stakes, Petite Etoile started at 5-2 on, but was beaten in sensational fashion. A combination of soft ground, interference from Scobie Breasley's mount Sunny Court, and lack of stamina, probably all contributed to her defeat, although Piggott was widely blamed for over-confidence.

Prince Aly Khan had been killed in a car crash in June, and the great filly passed to his son Karim — the young Aga Khan — who decided to keep her in training for a further year. Although some of the old spark was missing, she won a second Coronation Cup, before reverting to a mile at Royal Ascot in the Rous Memorial Stakes (won easily). In July, Murless had no option but to run her in the newly-created Aly Khan Memorial Gold Cup at Kempton, which unfortunately was designed over a mile and a half. Sir Winston Churchill's High Hat set a terrific pace and galloped the filly into the ground. Only at Epsom, where Piggott could give her a breather at the top of the hill, did she truly stay a mile and a half. The result was a bitter disappointment for the young Aga Khan.

Petite Etoile retired at the end of the season, but her stud career was a dismal failure. She was a truly great racehorse, but Murless and Piggott were equally great components of her success.

At the start of the memorable Coronation Cup of 1960 ... Lester Piggott keeps the volatile Petite Etoile away from the two other runners — Parthia (3) (Harry Carr) and Above Suspicion (Doug Smith).

BIG RACES WON	
Oaks	1959
1000 Guineas	1959
Coronation Cup (twice)	1960-61
Champion Stakes	1959
Yorkshire Oaks	1959
Sussex Stakes	1959
Coronation Stakes	1961
Rous Memorial Stakes	1961
Free Handicap	1959

PHAR LAP

Foaled 1925
Trained in Australia

FEW HORSES IN history have been commemorated by a statue. Phar Lap, the most popular horse in the history of Australian racing, has gone one better, having recently been the subject of a compelling full-length film. In Australia Phar Lap is, quite simply, a legend.

Like so many of the best southern hemisphere horses, Phar Lap was foaled in New Zealand. Harry Telford, a fifty-one-year-old 'third division' trainer, had scoured the New Zealand Yearling Sales catalogue and was attracted by the pedigree of the chestnut colt by Night Raid out of Entreaty. He wrote to his brother Hugh in Wellington, New Zealand, and asked him to bid up to 200 guineas for the colt. The Night Raid yearling was the very last to pass through the ring, and Hugh Telford bought him for 160 guineas.

When he arrived by boat at Sydney, Harry Telford was horrified. A tall, plain, leggy colt in the first place, his purchase had suffered an appalling journey and looked a wreck. His intended owner, Mr David Davis, took one look at him and declared he wanted nothing to do with him. A compromise was reached whereby Davis paid for him and Telford leased him for three years — i.e. trained him for nothing — with Davis receiving one-third of his winnings. Telford's methods were unorthodox, and severe. On one occasion he galloped Phar Lap (Siamese for 'lightening') flat out up the sand dunes on the coast near Sydney. A less resilient horse could have been broken for life.

Phar Lap's career began modestly with four unplaced runs. His fortunes changed when he came under the care of a young groom called Tommy Woodcock. Eventually he won a six-furlong maiden race, but his jockey Jim Baker jumped off and said 'I don't think he'll stay!' In his second season he gradually moved into the Big League. He won the Rosehill Guineas, the A.J.C. Derby, the Craven Plate and the Victoria Derby — both Derbys in record time — but he was beaten in the Melbourne Cup with 7st 6lb after his lightweight jockey, Bob Lewis, had fought with him throughout the race. In the autumn, however, he won the Legers in Melbourne and Sydney, and a series of big weight-for-age races. In Adelaide he won the King's Cup with 9st 5lb.

In his four-year-old career he was better than ever, winning over various distances and a variety of courses. He also established some astonishing times. Such was his dominance that, carrying 9st 12lb, he started 11-8 *on* for the Melbourne Cup — the only time a horse has ever started odds on for Australia's greatest race. He duly won as part of a sequence of fourteen successive wins in the highest class. Before the Melbourne Cup, Phar Lap had survived an attempt on his life, when a pot-shot was taken at him from a car, at Caulfield.

Telford took Phar Lap to a secret hide-out at St Albans, Geelong, and brought him to the track with a police escort at the last moment, for the Melbourne Cup.

In his final race of the 1930-31 season, the conditions of a big race at Flemington were altered, so that a horse called Waterline, who should have met him at level weights, was in receipt of 21lb. Two days earlier Waterline had won a race under 10st 7lb. Furthermore, Phar Lap was off-colour and Tommy Woodcock pleaded with Telford not to run him. Despite everything, Phar Lap ran his rival to a neck.

Phar Lap won his first eight races the following season and was allotted 10st 10lb in the Melbourne Cup. He was not 100% fit and should not have run, but in difficult times during the recession, the Victoria Racing Club blackmailed his connections into running, to boost the attendance. Phar Lap was well beaten, and two months later was sent to race in America. On March 20th, 1932, he crossed

What the British call 'A Monkey Up a Stick!' Even by Australian standards, Phar Lap's jockey takes his 'short hold' to extremes.

the border to Mexico for the Aqua Caliente Handicap (1¼ miles). His jockey, Bill Elliott, staggered the Americans by dropping the big horse out last of the ten runners, as the front runners recorded 23.6 seconds for the first 'quarter' and 46.8 seconds for the first half-mile. At half-way, Elliott pulled his horse around the field, on the wide outside, and was in front three furlongs from home! He won with plenty to spare, in record time.

It was to be his last race. On April 5th he was found dead, poisoned at Mento Park, California. His death was sudden, mysterious and probably agonising. Many Australians, to this day, believe that he was poisoned by the Mafia. What is more likely is that he ingested some material used for spraying trees. At least the Americans had seen enough to share the Australian view that he was one of the greatest — if not the greatest — horses of all time.

He stood 17.0½hh, with a huge girth, and a heart — now preserved in the Australian National Museum — weighing 15lb, compared to the normal 8-10lb. In all he won thirty-seven out of fifty-one starts, worth £66,738. Phar Lap was — and is — a legend.

BIG RACES WON	
Melbourne Cup	1930
Aqua Caliente Handicap	1932
A.J.C. Derby	1929
Victoria Derby	1929
A.J.C. St Leger	1929
V.R.C. St Leger	1929
V.R.C. Governor's Plate	1929
A.J.C. Plate	1929
Rosehill Stakes	1929
A.J.C. Craven Plate (3 times)	1929-31
A.J.C. Randwick Plate (twice)	1930-31
W.S. Cox Plate (twice)	1930-31
Melbourne Stakes (twice	1930-31
V.R.C. King's Plate (twice)	1930-31
A.J.C. Spring Stakes (twice)	1930-31

PRETTY POLLY

Foaled 1901
Trained in England

ONE OF THE fascinating mysteries of the Turf is why great horses tend to be foaled in clusters. While Mill Reef, Brigadier Gerard and Nijinsky were foaled within twelve months of one another, so were Sceptre and Pretty Polly only separated by two years. At least another twenty years passed, and arguably forty, before another comparable filly appeared on the scene.

Pretty Polly, who was bred by her owner Major Eustace Loder, was by Gallinule — a good two-year-old, but a 'bleeder' and a 'roarer' — out of a mare called Admiration, who had been bought as a steeplechaser. A strong, robust chestnut filly, she was involved in all manner of escapades as a yearling, and on more than one occasion was lucky to escape with her life.

She was trained by Peter Purcell Gilpin who, having moved from Dorset, had recently built the Clarehaven Stables at Newmarket, which he named after a mare on whom he had won a fortune in the Cesarewitch in 1900. Pretty Polly did not impress Gilpin greatly either as an individual — she was almost too powerful and masculine — or in her work. As a result no one could believe her first outing at Sandown in June. The chestnut filly was so far clear after two furlongs that many believed it was a false start. At the line she was judged to have won by ten lengths, although many reckoned it was closer to 100 yards!

Pretty Polly went through her two-year-old career unbeaten, taking on colts and fillies alike. In the Champagne Stakes and Middle Park Plate her victims included St Amant, who went on to win the following year's Derby. She was easily the best two-year-old of either sex. Between seasons she lengthened and filled out, standing just under 16hh. She won the 1000 Guineas with ease in record time, and frightened off opposition in the Oaks to such a degree that she had just three rivals, winning by three lengths at 100-8 on. Unfortunately, but not surprisingly, she had not been entered in the Derby. Thereafter she won the Coronation Stakes, Nassau Stakes and at Doncaster, both the St Leger and Park Hill Stakes.

Now the winner of fifteen races, in none of which she had been extended, the great filly was dispatched by her owner to Paris for the Prix de Conseil Municipal. It was a journey fated from the outset. Bad weather delayed the filly at Folkestone, whereafter her horse-waggon was shunted into every siding *en route,* despite liberal remuneration to French railway employees. On the eve of the race, rain fell in torrents, leaving the ground heavy. Her usual jockey William Lane was injured, so Danny Maher rode her for the first time. The result was a sensation. The French three-year-old, Presto II, led throughout to win by two-and-a-half lengths, at 66-1. Many

Pretty Polly may have been too powerful and masculine for her trainer's taste, but she did have a pretty, feminine head — unless the artist flatters her!

excuses were put forward for Pretty Polly, principally the journey and the going. Maher claimed that despite her St Leger success, she was not a true stayer. In fact, Maher and Morny Cannon, the rider of her compatriot Zinfandel, had played cat-and-mouse and allowed Presto II far too much rope. In such appalling conditions it was impossible to recover the lost ground.

Pretty Polly's four-year-old career was a triumph. She won the Coronation Cup in a canter, in 2 minutes 33 seconds — a time yet to be surpassed. In the autumn she won the Champion Stakes, Limekiln Stakes, and Jockey Club Cup (2 miles 3 furlongs). In her five-year-old career, she met her second defeat, in the Gold Cup. Once again, different accounts have been put forward. Some adhered to Maher's judgement that she was never a true stayer; others pointed out that she was troubled by a large wart on her girth which had to be lanced within 24 hours of the race. She was reluctant to leave the paddock, but battled bravely in the race before going down by a length to Bachelor's Button. She retired the winner of twenty-two races, from twenty-four, worth £37,000.

Her stud career was a pot-pourri of success and failure. The six colts that she bred were disappointing and made no contribution to Turf history. Her four fillies, however, were all winners and established from separate successful families, from which Psidium, St Paddy and Brigadier Gerard all originate. One final observation is inescapable. If she had run in all five Classics she would almost certainly have won the lot!

BIG RACES WON	
Oaks	1904
1000 Guineas	1904
St Leger	1904
Coronation Cup (twice)	1905-6
Champion Stakes	1905
Jockey Club Cup	1905
Coronation Stakes	1904
Nassau Stakes	1904
Park Hill Stakes	1904
National Breeders' Produce Stakes	1903
Middle Park Stakes	1903
Cheveley Park Stakes	1903
Champagne Stakes	1903

RIBOT

Foaled 1952
Trained in Italy

ONE OF THE vacuums of my life is that I never saw Ribot race. I was playing in a cricket match at school when he won at Ascot and have never seen a recording of the race, as sadly it did not survive a 'purge' in the BBC Library.

It is, nonetheless, obvious that Ribot was one of the greatest horses of all time. Ribot was a final tribute to the work of Signor Frederico Tesio (described in the section devoted to Nearco) who died, sadly, in the spring of Ribot's two-year-old career. He raced in the colours of Tesio's long-time friend and partner the Marchesa Incisa della Rochetta, was trained by Ugo Penco, and ridden by the veteran Enrico Camici.

Ribot was by Tesio's good stayer Tenerani, out of a mare called Romanella, whose dam the little Italian had bought for 350 guineas at Newmarket in 1937. He was reared at the partnership's Dormello Stud, close to the south-west shores of Lake Maggiore, near Arona. Ribot was not especially eye-catching when he went into training, nor did he impress greatly on his debut, which he won by a length. After winning the Criterium Nazionale by two lengths, he came close to defeat when Penco instructed Camici to drop him out and ride him from behind. Ribot resented these tactics, and only got up to win in the last few strides.

Ribot had not been entered for the Italian Classics, having been small and apparently nothing special as a yearling, so was not severely tested until the autumn of his three-year-old career. Now, after wide-margin wins from domestic rivals, he was thrown in against the best in Europe in the Prix de l'Arc de Triomphe. Although Phil Drake, Vimy and Meld were missing, it was a strong field — and Ribot beat them comprehensively by three lengths. He returned to Italy for the Premio del Jockey Club in Milan and beat an international field by fifteen lengths.

As a four-year-old, Ribot continued to carry all before him in Italy, notably in winning the Gran Premio di Milano (1 mile 7 furlongs) by eight lengths. To seal his international reputation he was sent to England for the King George VI & Queen Elizabeth Stakes, for which he started 5-2 on. Possibly the Milan race had taken the edge off his speed, but Camici was seen to be pushing Ribot along in the heavy going to keep in his place in the early stages. Once the straight was reached Ribot lengthened his stride and won decisively by five lengths.

Ribot's second 'Arc' was gained from a stronger field than the previous year, including two challengers from America — the first in Europe for twenty years. As at Ascot, the ground was 'heavy' but this time he was never off the bit until, cruising into the lead

turning into the straight, he quickened and left his rivals for dead two furlongs from home. The winning margin was a long-looking six lengths. Only three horses previously had won more than one Arc de Triomphe and this was unquestionably one of the finest performances in the history of the race.

Retired as the unbeaten winner of sixteen races, Ribot started his stud career at Lord Derby's Woodland Stud at Newmarket, where he remained for two seasons. After a further two seasons at the owner's Olgiata Stud in Italy, he was leased for a five-year period to Mr John W. Galbreath's Darby Dan Stud in Kentucky. However, as the years progressed, Ribot became increasingly difficult to handle. In his box there was a deep furrow at a height of about ten feet where Ribot would stand on his hind legs and gnaw away at the wood. Only a strapping six-foot negro groom could handle him. Accordingly, no insurance company was prepared to take the risk of covering his journey back to Europe, and Ribot stayed at Darby Dan until his death in April 1972.

Ribot (Enrico Camici) ploughs through the Ascot mud to record a five length win in the King George VI & Queen Elizabeth Stakes.

123

His European offspring included classic winners Ribocco, Ribero, Ragusa, Long Look and Boucher, as well as Romulus and Ribofilio. He sired two Arc de Triomphe winners in Molvedo and Prince Royal II, while in America Tom Rolfe, Graustark and Art & Letters were among his best sons. Now, as his grandsons and granddaughters make their mark worldwide, his influence remains a living testimony to the genius of Frederico Tesio.

BIG RACES WON	
Prix de l'Arc de Triomphe (twice)	1955-56
King George VI & Queen Elizabeth Stakes	1956
Gran Premio de Milano	1956
Premio Emanuele Filiberto	1955
Premio Garbagnate	1956
Gran Criterium	1954
Criterium Nazionale	1954

SAGARO

SADLY, IT IS over forty years since an English Classic winner won the Ascot Gold Cup, and the days when the race was an automatic target for a Derby winner in his four-year-old career are long gone. Today's Gold Cup horse tends to be an out-and-out stayer. For this reason Sagaro was an exceptional contemporary Gold Cup winner; he was a true stayer, with a classic turn of foot at the end of two-and-a-half miles.

Sagaro was bred in Ireland by his owner, the Geneva-based financier Gerald Oldham. His sire, Espresso, had been bought by Oldham for 1000 guineas, and progressed through handicaps to win the Grosser Preis von Baden twice.

Foaled 1971
Trained in France

Sagaro (Lester Piggott) displays his notable turn of foot to win the second of his record three Gold Cups.

Sagaro was trained at Lamorlaye by Francois Boutin, and won in every season between two and six years. His first major success came in the Grand Prix de Paris, which he won by two lengths from Bustino. As a four-year-old he was a beaten favourite in the Prix du Cadran (French Gold Cup), but on firm going at Ascot was backed to reverse the placings with Le Bavard, which he duly did, by four lengths. The following season was Sagaro's best. In France he won the Prix de Barbeville and Prix du Cadran, before returning to Ascot for a second, comfortable Gold Cup win, by a length from Crash Course.

At this stage Oldham was disposed to sell his horse as a stallion, but remarkably he received barely a single offer. Reasoning that a repetition of the previous season, when his win earnings were over £63,000, would provide superior income to his first season at stud, Oldham kept him in training for a further year. His reward was a third Gold Cup success — an achievement never previously accomplished. At last Sagaro attracted a buyer in the shape of the National Stud, at £175,000. Predictably, however, he attracted predominantly modest mares and before long was moved from Newmarket to the Limestone Stud in Lincolnshire. He died in 1986 having failed to sire a Group 1 winner.

BIG RACES WON	
Gold Cup (three times)	1975-77
Grand Prix de Paris	1974
Prix du Cadran	1976
Prix de Barbeville	1976

ST SIMON

THE LAST TWENTY YEARS of the nineteenth century were a wonderful period on the Turf, and St Simon was one of a number of great horses of the era. There are those who reckon him to be the greatest of all time.

Foaled 1881
Trained in England

St Simon was a son of the 1875 Derby winner Galopin, out of a mare, St Angela, that had produced little of note at the age of sixteen. His owner-breeder, Prince Batthyany, did not enter St Simon for the Derby, but this matter became academic when the Prince died suddenly in May 1883, thus rendering all his engagements void. The Prince's horses came up for sale at Newmarket two months later and, despite rumours to the effect that he could 'go', several owners, including the Duke of Hamilton, were influenced by other rumours that he was unsound. These were triggered by a ruse devised by the Prince's trainer John Dawson, who daubed one of the colt's hocks with paint to create the illusion of a blister so as to deter bidders, as he wanted the colt for himself. His brother Matt saw through the deception, and bought the colt for his young patron the Duke of Portland for 1600 guineas.

Although quite fat when he came to Matthew Dawson at Heath House, Newmarket, it was only four weeks to the day before St Simon appeared at Goodwood for his first race. Ridden by Fred Archer, he won in a canter and reappeared the following day to beat a solitary opponent in a maiden race. After winning a nursery at Derby, he went to Doncaster to carry top weight in a field of twenty-one for the Prince of Wales's Nursery. Well clear at half-way, he won by eight lengths, pulling up — which could have been twenty lengths.

At the Newmarket Houghton Meeting, the Duke of Portland made a 500 Guineas match with the Duke of Westminster, between St Simon and a colt named Duke of Richmond. St Simon won by three parts of a length 'easily' according to Archer 'with scarcely 7lb in hand' according to the runner-up's jockey Tom Cannon. St Simon thrived during the winter, but was inclined to be highly-strung and to sweat. One morning Archer felt he was working lazily so touched him with his spur. St Simon took off at a terrifying pace, charged through another string, and ended up at the bottom of the Limekilns over a mile away. 'He's not a horse,' complained Archer, 'he's a blooming steam engine!'

St Simon was also volatile in the stable and only his groom, called Fordham, could approach him. Lads handed in their notice rather than attempt to groom him. It was also near impossible to box him to go racing. In the end it proved easiest to back him into his box. When one of Dawson's owners commented to Fordham that it must

The highly-strung St Simon. 'I have only trained one good horse in my life and that was St Simon,' his trainer claimed.

take patience to look after St Simon, the lad replied: 'Patience! Talk about Job, sir. Job's never done a St Simon!' Indeed, the only thing that ever frightened St Simon was an umbrella!

St Simon was eventually ridden by Charles Wood as a three-year-old, Archer having fallen out with the Duke. His first race was a match over one-and-a-half miles (with pacemakers), with the six-year-old Tristan, a top-class horse who had won two Hardwicke Stakes, two Grands Prix de Deauville and the Gold Cup. Tristan was set to concede 23lb — approximately weight-for-age — and St Simon won by six lengths.

Nothing opposed St Simon in the Epsom Gold Cup (now Coronation Cup), while over an extra mile in the Gold Cup he again beat Tristan — this time by twenty lengths. Further successes came at Newcastle and in the Goodwood Cup, which he won by twenty lengths from the previous year's St Leger winner Ossian.

St Simon was retired to stud the unbeaten winer of nine races worth £4671. Matt Dawson, who trained six Derby winners, claimed: 'I have trained only one good horse in my life and that was St Simon.' He was a brilliant success at stud, and was champion sire nine times, including seven in a row. His ten Classic winners included Persimmon, Diamond Jubilee, St Frusquin and La Flèche. He collapsed and died one morning at exercise at the age of twenty-seven. Over 100 years after his birth, his name remains a by-word.

BIG RACES WON	
Gold Cup	1884
Goodwood Cup	1884
Epsom Gold Cup	1884
Prince of Wales's Nursery	1883

SCEPTRE

NO HORSE IN racing history has ever won all five Classics, but Sceptre came closest. She won all bar the Derby — and was unlucky not to win that!

Foaled 1899
Trained in England

Sceptre was not only a truly great filly, she was also one of the best-bred fillies to be a top-class mare. Bred by the Duke of Westminster, she was by Persimmon (by St Simon) out of Ornament, an own-sister to the mighty Ormonde. Unluckily for the Grosvenor family, the 1st Duke of Westminster died in the winter of 1899, and his bloodstock was put up for auction the following year. The Duke's trainer, John Porter, knowing the family and admiring the individual, was anxious that the young Duke should buy the Persimmon filly. But they met a formidable opponent in the adventurer and gambler, Bob Sievier, a former bankrupt who was currently on what the Americans call a 'high roll'. Sievier bid 10,000 guineas — a record at the time — and sent her to be trained by Charlie Morton at Wantage.

Sceptre ran three times as a two-year-old, winning the Woodcote Stakes at Epsom and the July Stakes at Newmarket. In the Champagne Stakes she had 'gone' in her coat, and ran indifferently. During the autumn, Morton accepted an offer to become private trainer to Mr J.B. Joel, whereupon Sievier decided to train his own horses and leased a yard belonging to John Porter at Shrewton in Wiltshire.

In 1902, Sceptre was subjected to the most demanding season ever faced by a high-class filly. Intent on landing a gamble, Sievier backed her to win £30,000 for the Lincoln Handicap. While he was away in Paris on business, his new American assistant galloped her flat out over a mile on four successive days. She arrived at Doncater tucked-up, edgy and off her feed. Carrying 6st 7lb, and ridden by an apprentice called Hardy, she was slowly away and badly ridden, but was still only caught in the final stride, and beaten a head. Remarkably, she came home and ate up — and began to thrive. (The American had been sacked on Sievier's return from Paris.) Sievier now decided to aim her at both the 2000 *and* 1000 Guineas. Ridden by the former amateur, Herbert Randall, she won the '2000' easily in the record time of 1 minute 39 seconds. Two days later she collected the '1000' even more easily despite racing with only three plates, and being slowly away.

Sceptre was now aimed at the Derby, but ten days before the race she bruised a foot, and went to Epsom short of one gallop. Furthermore, Randall rode an appalling race, getting left at the start, rushing the filly up the hill and 'bursting' her. In the end she was only fourth to Ard Patrick. Two days later, however, she won the

Oaks in magnificent style, returning to an ovation. Not content with this, Sievier sent her to Paris for the Grand Prix. Here Randall rode an even worse race, giving the outside to nobody, and finishing unplaced. Back at Royal Ascot, the Coronation Stakes proved a repetition of the Derby, and Randall was finally sacked. The following day, ridden by Hardy, she won the St James's Palace Stakes easily.

Rested until Goodwood, she 'blew up' in the Sussex Stakes on the first day, was galloped on the following two days, and won the Nassau Stakes on the Friday in a canter! With Ard Patrick an absentee, Sceptre won the St Leger by three lengths, but two days later was beaten in the Park Hill Stakes. At the end of the season, Sievier was short of money and submitted the filly to public auction, but she failed to make her reserve. The following spring, Sievier again trained her for the Lincoln, hoping that a successful gamble would keep his creditors at bay. But carrying 9st 1lb she could finish only fifth, and soon afterwards Sievier was compelled to sell his great filly to Sir William Bass for 25,000 guineas.

Sceptre was now to be trained by Alec Taylor at Manton. Sievier's

Sceptre with the rascally Bob Sievier ... a queen who was treated like a selling plater.

advice to the great trainer was: 'Treat her like a selling plater'. Taylor saddled her to win the Hardwicke Stakes, but in a famous race for the Eclipse, she was beaten a neck by Ard Patrick, with the Triple Crown winner Rock Sand a moderate third. Thereafter, Sceptre was unbeaten in 1903, winning the Jockey Club Stakes, Duke of York Stakes, Champion Stakes and Limekiln Stakes. As a five-year-old, Sceptre ran three times without regaining her best form.

At stud she produced one colt and seven fillies, four of whom won. None was a champion on the racecourse, but Maid of the Mist, in particular, established a celebrated blood-line. In her prime, Sceptre was a magnificent filly, standing 16.0½hh, with power and substance. She was tough, brave and in the right hands would have very probably swept the board. As it is, she established a record that remains unsurpassed.

BIG RACES WON	
Oaks	1902
2000 Guineas	1902
1000 Guineas	1902
St Leger	1902
Hardwicke Stakes	1903
Jockey Club Stakes	1903
St James's Palace Stakes	1902
Duke of York Stakes	1903
Nassau Stakes	1902
Champion Stakes	1903
July Stakes	1901

SEA BIRD II

Foaled 1962
Trained in France

'WHAT WAS the greatest horse you have ever seen?' The question is often asked — and never easy to answer. It is to the author's everlasting regret — as explained earlier — that he never saw the great Ribot. So the answer must rest between Mill Reef, Nijinsky and Sea Bird II.

Sea Bird II was certainly the easiest winner of the Derby, although his finest hour was reserved until the Prix de l'Arc de Triomphe. He was a freak of breeding. His sire Dan Cupid — a son of the brilliant but volatile American horse Native Dancer — was inconsistent and unpredictable, and his best distance hard to define. His dam Sicalade by Sicambre, was not only a non-winner, but so also were her four female predecessors on Sea Bird's maternal side. If mares had to take a 'means test', Sea Bird II would have never been foaled!

Sea Bird II was a chestnut with a pronounced white blaze and two white stockings behind. He was not especially prepossessing and he turned out his off-fore leg. If he had gone to the yearling Sales it is unlikely that he would have fetched more than £2000-£3000. In fact he was raced by his breeder, M. Jean Ternynck, a wealthy textiles magnate from Lille in north-east France, and had the good fortune to be trained by the brilliant Etienne Pollet.

As a two-year-old, Sea Bird II did not run until September 2nd, when he won by a short head over seven furlongs at Chantilly. A fortnight later he won the Criterium de Maisons-Laffitte by two lengths and then took on his stable companion Grey Dawn II — the season's top two-year-old — in the Grand Criterium. Partnered by Maurice Larraun and ridden very much like a second string, Sea Bird II was beaten two lengths by his favoured stable companion. It was the first and only defeat of his career.

The following spring, after a comfortable success in the Prix Greffuhle, Sea Bird II put up a spectacular performance in the Prix Lupin, beating Diatome by six lengths. Now declared an intended runner for the Epsom Derby, Sea Bird II was immediately established a short-priced ante-post favourite. The ease with which Sea Bird II won the Derby had to be seen to be believed. Ridden with astonishing confidence by the Australian Pat Glennon, Sea Bird II coasted up to the leader I Say, a furlong and a half from home, and was gently eased into the lead. Fifty yards from the post, Glennon dropped his hands: Sea Bird II had treated his rivals with contempt. He also took in the Grand Prix de Saint-Cloud — once again eased well before the line — before his late summer break.

The 1965 Prix de l'Arc de Triomphe was a classic. In a vintage year for French three-year-olds, Sea Bird II was now to meet the

French Derby winner Reliance II for the first time. Reliance II, an own brother to Match III, and half-brother to Relko, was unbeaten. In addition to the Prix du Jockey Club, he had also won the Grand Prix de Paris, and Prix Royal Oak (French St Leger). Also in the field were Diatome, the Russian champion Anilin, the Irish Derby and 'King George' winner Meadow Court, and Tom Rolfe, winner of the Preakness Stakes and American Derby, and rated the best three-year-old in America. Sea Bird was favourite at 6-5, with Reliance II next best at 9-2 and Diatome 15-2.

It was a warm sunny day, and in the parade Sea Bird II simply poured sweat. The race was magnificent to watch. In the straight the Russian colt led briefly for a few strides until Sea Bird II glided majestically by with Reliance II in his slip-stream. For a brief moment it looked like being a race. Then, for the first time, Glennon asked for his all. Within a matter of strides Sea Bird II opened up a gap and despite veering violently to the left, stormed clear to win by six lengths from Reliance II, with Diatome five lengths away third. It was a performance that explained implicitly the concept of trying to make one horse run faster than another.

The range and power of Sea Bird II (Pat Glennon) on his way to post for the 1965 Derby.

Sea Bird II was received with a rapturous ovation, and showered with superlatives. No one claimed to have seen a better horse, with only the possible exception of Ribot. To set a seal upon the performance, Diatome travelled to America a month later and won the Washington D.C. International.

Sea Bird II retired to stud in America under a similar five-year agreement to that which enticed Ribot. He returned to France in 1972, but unhappily died in March 1973 of an intestinal blockage. He was by no means a success at stud, his best offspring being Allez France, Gyr, and, in England, Sea Pigeon. It is hard to imagine a horse that would have beaten Sea Bird II on the day of the 'Arc'.

BIG RACES WON	
Derby	1965
Prix de l'Arc de Triomphe	1965
Grand Prix de Saint-Cloud	1965
Prix Lupin	1965
Prix Greffuhle	1965
Criterium de Maisons-Laffitte	1964

SEATTLE SLEW

JUST AS THE early 'seventies (with Nijinsky, Mill Reef and Brigadier Gerard) was one of the great eras of horseracing in Great Britian, so was the later 'seventies the 'Golden Age' of American racing. Secretariat, in 1973, was a tough act to follow, but Seattle Slew, in one respect at least, trumped 'Big Red' by becoming the first ever unbeaten winner of the US Triple Crown. The story of Seattle Slew was one of the great bitter-sweet romances of the American Turf. It had its down-side, with dramas, acrimony and sackings, but like all good fairy stories it came up with a happy ending.

Seattle Slew, a dark brown colt by Bold Reasoning out of a mare called My Charmer, was a first foal of his dam by a first-season stallion — rarely a successful formula. He was bought for a bargain $17,000 at the Fasig-Tipton Summer Sales in Kentucky, by a young couple called Mickey and Karen Taylor, on the advice of a friend, the distinguished New York veterinarian Dr Jim Hill. Hill recommended that the colt be sent to a promising young former steeplechase trainer, Billy Turner. This youthful team, together with their jockey, the French-born Jean Cruguet, were to be hailed by the New York Press as the 'Slew Crew'.

'The Slew' didn't race until September as a two-year-old, but in three runs would catch up by winning New York's richest juvenile race, the one mile Champagne, by nine-and-three-quarter lengths, in a race-record time of 1 minute 34.25 seconds. That success won him the Eclipse Award for two-year-olds.

The Slew had three races in the Spring of 1977 *en route* to the Triple Crown. He won a small seven-furlong race at Hialeah in a track-record 1 minute 20.6 seconds leading up to Hialeah's top race, the 1 mile 1 furlong Flamingo Stakes, which he won easily. Back in New York he took in Belmont Park's Wood Memorial, which proved little more than a $100,000 training session. So The Slew went to Louisville unbeaten — and history was about to be made. He won the Derby by one-and-three-quarter lengths, after missing the 'break'; the Preakness by one-and-a-half lengths, and the Belmont by four lengths. The third leg drew 71,026 people to Belmont Park, the fourth largest crowd in New York history. They cheered the new champion to the echo. It was the Slew Crew's finest hour.

As so often happens, success brought problems. The Slew was now big box-office, and tracks all over the USA dreamed up amazing schemes to lure the Triple Crown hero. The fame and adulation had a big effect on the young owners. They hired an advertising agency, and began to promote The Slew with flak jackets, T-shirts, stickers and all the gadgetry of the Drug Store. Billy Turner, who had traditional standards, was offended by the gimmickry, and

Foaled 1974
Trained in USA

especially when the owners insisted that The Slew fly to California for the Swaps Stakes at Hollywood Park. The track had boosted the purse to $300,000 to hook the Triple Crown winner. The Slew had a totally unsuitable preparation. He had been tranquillized for the trip, and tranquillized for a commercial promotion. Although he went off at 5-1 on, he was outpaced and outpointed by the former Murless-trained J.O. Tobin, who clocked an amazing 1 minute 58.6 seconds for one-and-a-quarter miles. At last the bubble had burst.

The Slew didn't race again in 1977, but in the autumn the owners split with Billy Turner. 'I hated to give up that horse,' Turner said later, 'but I couldn't stay. It was a matter of different style.' The colt's new trainer was Doug Peterson, a twenty-six-year-old from Colorado. Within six weeks he almost had a dead horse on his hands. The Slew, who had been syndicated for $12 million, went down with colitis, an inflammation of the colon, or main part of the large intestine. For long days and nights he was nursed back to health by his devoted owners, sitting up twenty-four hours a day. Only after two weeks was it certain that he would pull through. Four months later The Slew was back on the track at Aqueduct winning a minor allowance race. Now a further problem loomed — a minor leg injury. An autumn campaign was planned, with his first target the $300,000 Marlboro Gold Cup. On the way he was caught and beaten a neck by the top sprinter Dr Patches, over nine furlongs at Meadowlands. Cruguet stated: 'The Slew wasn't the horse he once was.' Peterson blamed Cruguet. They fell out, and after a fortnight of soul-searching by the Taylors, Cruguet was sacked.

Angel Cordero was The Slew's new jockey. He went in at the deep end. The Marlboro was a head-to-head between The Slew and the current season's Classic hero Affirmed (ridden by Steve Cauthen). It was the first-ever meeting between two winners of the Triple Crown. Cordero, a brilliant front-rider, made every yard on The Slew, quickening and quickening, to win by three lengths in a sensational 1 minute 45.8 seconds for the 1 mile 1 furlong. In the Woodward (1¼ miles), The Slew hit his peak, beating the ex-European Exceller by four lengths in two minutes flat, equalling Kelso's record.

Now came one of the greatest races in New York's history. In the Jockey Club Gold Cup (1½ miles) the three great horses came together again. Seattle Slew was favourite at 5-3 on; Affirmed 11-10, and Exceller almost 4-1. After a furlong Cauthen's saddle slipped on Affirmed and the big chestnut ran out of control. Such was the pace of the two front-runners that Exceller was over twenty lengths adrift after half a mile. Shoemaker, on Exceller, began to 'creep'. Incredibly, in the straight he caught The Slew on the inner and went half a length up. The favourite, who had run the first half-mile in 45.5 seconds, was out on his feet. Somehow he dredged up a reserve

of courage and battled back. With every stride he pulled back an inch ... two inches. The crowd roared as they had never roared. Could The Slew possibly — impossibly — get back up? At the line Exceller had it by just a head, with the third horse fourteen lengths back. It was The Slew's bravest hour.

He retired a month later, the winner of fourteen from seventeen starts, worth $1,208,726. For some reason Seattle Slew was regarded by some as a 'freak' and unlikely to make a stallion. He proved the 'experts' very wrong. Within six years, next to Northern Dancer, he was America's most valuable stallion.

Seattle Slew (Jean Cruguet) wins the Kentucky Derby on his way to becoming the first unbeaten winner of the Triple Crown.

BIG RACES WON	
Kentucky Derby	1977
Preakness Stakes	1977
Belmont Stakes	1977
Marlboro Gold Cup	1978
Woodward Stakes	1978
Wood Memorial	1977
Champagne Stakes	1976

SECRETARIAT

Foaled 1970
Trained in USA

EVERY NOW AND then one sees something on a racetrack that is impossible to believe. For someone who loves the sport, such a moment brings a tear to the eye, and an embarrassing lump to the throat. It happened to the author on the occasion of the Belmont Stakes on June 9th 1973. I was not at Belmont Park, but was standing by a videotape machine at Television Centre in London. So long as I live I shall never forget that moment.

Secretariat had already won the Kentucky Derby and the Preakness. In the Derby, coming from behind, he beat Sham by two-and-a-half lengths at 1 minute 59.4 seconds, beating Northern Dancer's record by 0.6 seconds. It was sweet revenge, for Sham had beaten 'Big Red', as Secretariat had become affectionately known, in the Wood Memorial, when the big chestnut had been suffering from an abscess on the upper lip. The Preakness saw a repetition except that Secretariat took the lead after only two furlongs. At the line, not only was the 1-2-3- identical to the finishing order at Churchill Down — Secretariat, Sham and Our Native — but also the winning distances, at two-and-a-half lengths and eight lengths.

Thus was the stage set for the greatest performance I ever saw. Sham was again in the field — there were only five runners — and took his only chance to take on Big Red. For the first six furlongs he raced with Secretariat leading him by a neck, even half a length. The two of them clocked 1 minute 9.8 seconds for the first six furlongs — in a one-and-a-half mile race! (To put this in perspective, the course record for six furlongs at Ascot is 1 minute 13.29 seconds.) And suddenly the 'race' was over. Sham cracked, dropped out and Secretariat ran further and further away. It was astonishing … it simply had to be seen to be believed. Here was a horse who had gone so fast that he was entitled to pull up to a walk — and he seemed to be going faster! Now it was merely a race against the clock. Roared every inch of the way by the huge New York crowd, the big colt with the blue and white checked blinkers was eight lengths clear at the one mile in 1 minute 34.2 seconds; 20 lengths clear in 1 minute 59 seconds at the one-and-a-quarter mile; and finally, at the line, was a staggering thirty-one lengths clear in a world-record 2 minutes 24 seconds. Hardened horsemen shook their heads in disbelief. Only Citation was mentioned in the same breath. 'The most tremendous horse I ever saw race,' was said time and time again.

Secretariat's career was not without its blemishes. On August 4th he was beaten at 10-1 on at Saratoga, having previously drawn an estimated 5000 people to a morning work-out. The crowd were stunned. Thereafter, American hype took over. A $250,000 match

was proposed between Big Red and his older stable-companin, Riva Ridge. When the stewards refused to sanction the event, it transformed into the Marlboro Cup, a $250,000 invitation race over 1 mile 1 furlong. Big Red had picked up a virus at Saratoga, and to the sponsors' horror it seemed impossible for him to be fit. Lucien Laurin got him to his peak in the nick of time, and the race was memorable. In the straight Big Red drew away to win by three-and-a-half lengths from Riva Ridge and Cougar — both 'millionaires' — in a world-record 1 minute 45.4 seconds. Another baffling defeat followed in the Woodward before Secretariat bowed out in sensational style in the Man O'War, and, finally, the Canadian International Championship. Secretariat retired the winner of sixteen races, worth $1,316,808, but the sensations of his career were far from over.

The magnificent Secretariat with his remarkable 76" girth, devours the ground in his paddock.

Syndicated for $6 million, prior to his three-year-old career, the massive 16.2hh colt, with the incredible 76″ girth, now retired to Seth Hancock's Claiborne Farm in Kentucky. To the horror of the farm and the horse's shareholders, Big Red was reported to be afflicted with spermatogonia, i.e. sperm that was immature. For an awful few months it seemed that Big Red was far from likely to be a 'Big Daddy'. In the end, to everyone's relief, his fertility reached an acceptable level and in America, at least, he achieved a reasonable degree of success. But above all Secretariat was a King of the Track — a sporting phenomenon that put the Sport of Kings on the front page. And I, for one, will never forget that 'Belmont'...

BIG RACES WON	
Kentucky Derby	1973
Preakness Stakes	1973
Belmont Stakes	1973
Man O'War Stakes	1973
Canadian International Championship	1973
Champagne Stakes	1972
Laurel Futurity	1972
The Garden State	1972
Hopeful Stakes	1972
The Futurity	1972

SHERGAR

Foaled 1978
Trained in England

THE STORY OF SHERGAR is a very personal one for me. Many of his greatest moments I shared, at least in spirit. Even on the awful day that his theft by terrorists was announced, I played an indirect role: it was not until watching my broadcast on BBC TV's 'Sportsnight' programme that the terrorists realized the horse was the property of a syndicate, and not of the Aga Khan. Within forty-eight hours they were aware that their ransom demands were unlikely to be met.

Great horses, in general, fall into two categories. Some, from their very first faltering steps as a foal, have an aura of star quality. Others, like Alycidon, Ribot and most recently Dancing Brave, do nothing in their formative months and early training to suggest they are anything out of the ordinary. Such a horse was Shergar. It is meant as no disrespect to either Shergar or my wife — a fair judge of a riding horse — when I recall her initial comment on seeing Shergar: 'Ah, that would make me a nice hunter!' In the precocious world of modern-day racing, Shergar was inconspicuous as a two-year-old amongst Michael Stoute's magnificent and imposing string.

Bred and owned by the Aga Khan, whose horses tend to arrive late from the stud and, indeed, are often not named until mid-summer, Shergar did little serious work until the autumn. When he did start his fast work, he impressed Michael Stoute's senior work-rider, Cliff Lines. He became one of 'Cliff's horses', and I suspect that the shrewd former jockey furnished himself with some enticing ante-post vouchers for the 1981 Derby!

Shergar first ran at Newbury on September 19th, in a one-mile maidens-at-closing event. Ridden by Lester Piggott and favourite at 11-8 in a field of twenty-three, he won easily by two-and-a-half lengths in course-record time. It is very rare that Stoute progresses a horse directly from maiden to Group 1 company, but so much did Shergar please him in the following week, that the William Hill Futurity Stakes was chosen as Shergar's second race. Enjoying far from the best of runs, Shergar finished second to Beldale Flutter, beaten by two-and-a-half lengths.

During the spring of 1981, Shergar made exceptional progress. On Saturday morning April 18th, I happened to watch Shergar galloping on the Waterhall Line Gallop. Unextended, he finished at least ten lengths clear of his galloping companions. Shergar was a 33-1 shot for the Derby, but not for long! A week later, Shergar made his seasonal reappearance in the Guardian Classic Trial at Sandown. He won the race as easily as he had won the gallop — by ten lengths. Just ten days later he went north for the Chester Vase. This time he won by twelve lengths. He was the biggest

Shergar (Walter Swinburn) on the lawn at Beech Hurst. 'I was just a passenger on a very good horse,' claimed Walter.

'certainty' for the Derby I have ever known. Yet the bookmakers still offered 9-2.

Derby Day dawned to the splash of wheels and squelch of hooves. So hard and persistent was the June rainfall that racing at Salisbury the previous day had been abandoned. Shergar, proven in soft ground, was now firm favourite at 11-10 on. The 1981 Derby was not so much a race as a procession. Shergar took the lead three furlongs out and drew further and further away. The winning distance was ten lengths — the widest margin in the history of the race.

Walter Swinburn, 19, who had shared the glory at Epsom, was suspended for the period of the Irish Sweeps Derby, which Shergar won by an effortless four lengths in the hands of Lester Piggott. Walter was back on board for the King George VI & Queen Elizabeth Stakes in which he galloped his rivals relentlessly into the ground, to win by the same margin. Shergar's autumn target was the Prix de l'Arc de Triomphe, and some experts expressed surprise when the St Leger was chosen as his pre-Paris objective. There were rumours that Shergar was lacking some of his earlier sparkle on the gallops, and the great horse was opposed in the market. In the event Shergar ran the first and only moderate race of his life, finishing fourth, nine lengths behind Glint of Gold, whom he had beaten by ten lengths in the Derby.

Shergar was retired shortly afterwards to the Aga Khan's Ballymany Stud in Co. Kildare, Ireland. On February 9th, 1983, he was taken from his stable by Irish Republican terrorists, and within a week he was slaughtered. The criminals responsible for this obscene crime have never been brought to justice, although they may have faced retribution from within their own ranks.

BIG RACES WON	
Derby	1981
Irish Sweeps Derby	1981
King George VI & Queen Elizabeth Stakes	1981
Chester Vase	1981

SIGNORINETTA

Foaled 1905
Trained in England

THE STORY OF SIGNORINETTA is one of the great romances of the Turf. Owned, bred and trained by an eccentric and rather excitable Italian, Chevalier Odorado Ginistrelli, Signorinetta will always be remembered as the Derby winner who was the result of a 'love match'!

Ginistrelli, born in Naples, began his racing career at Portici, in Italy. After a violent quarrel with a rival owner, he left Italy and arrived with a handful of horses and brood mares at Newmarket. Despite being regarded as a rather bizarre and comical character, he acquired a nomination to St Simon for his best mare, Star of Portici, and bred an outstanding filly called Signorina, who won all her nine races as a two-year-old. Unfortunately, his star filly proved an extremely shy breeder, and was barren for ten years in succession. Anyone else would have written her off, but the Chevalier

Signorinetta and, on the left, Chevalier Ginistrelli wearing his infamous panama hat.

had an extreme affection for Signorina and persisted. Finally, his stubbornness was rewarded when the mare was successfully covered by a stallion called Best Man. The resultant colt, Signorino, was placed in the 2000 Guineas and Derby. Signorina was then barren for a further two seasons, and the Chevalier was again in despair.

It so happened that Signorina's paddock bordered on a neighbouring stud, where a nine-guinea stallion called Chaleureux was led out each morning. Signorina would gallop to the paddock rails to greet her friend and Chaleureux, on one occasion, got loose and attempted to jump into her paddock. The Chevalier — like many Italians, a romantic — decided to try to mate the pair, 'on the boundless laws of sympathy and love'. Signorina, now eighteen, immediately fell in foal — and the produce was Signorinetta.

As a two-year-old, Signorinetta appeared moderate. She was unplaced in her first five outings and finally won a nursery at Newmarket from five indifferent opponents. Nor did her three-year-old season begin with promise. She was well down the field in the 1000 Guineas and unplaced at 25-1 in the Newmarket Stakes. But the Chevalier was determined to run her in the Derby. Despite having no top-class horses to work with, he was thrilled by her gallops, and tried unavailingly to persuade his friends to back her at 100-1.

The 1908 Derby was not a vintage affair, but Signorinetta, ridden by William Bullock, had the race won fully two furlongs from home. While the crowd was totally stunned, they were quickly brought back to life as the Chevalier danced out onto the course to greet his winner, wearing an old Panama hat! Two days later, Signorinetta won the Oaks by the same margin of two lengths. This time the King sent for the Chevalier and led him to the front of the Royal Box, where the excited Italian was cheered to the echo.

The remainder of Signorinetta's career was totally undistinguished, as was her career at stud. But the Chevalier, at the age of seventy-five, had made his dream come true. It is a dream that has remained elusive to thousands since.

BIG RACES WON	
Derby	1908
Oaks	1908

SIR IVOR

Foaled 1965
Trained in Ireland

SIR IVOR WAS THE most exciting, enervating winner of the Derby since the Second World War. The 1968 Derby was a magnificent race to watch, and Sir Ivor and Lester Piggott represented everything that is best in racing — a magnificent thoroughbred, with superb temperament and brilliant acceleration, ridden by a master of his craft.

Sir Ivor was Vincent O'Brien's second Derby winner, and like his first, Larkspur, was owned by the Virginian Raymond Guest. He was bought by the renowned 'Bull' Hancock, of Claiborne Farm, for $42,000 at Kenneland Sales. His breeder was Mrs Alice Chandler, a descendant of the famous hunter, Daniel Boone. At the time, the Sir Gaylord colt was tall, lanky and, in the words of his breeder, 'rather lop-sided'.

Sir Ivor was broken in Kentucky, and sent to Vincent O'Brien in November. He struck Vincent as a backward type of horse and Vincent warned his owner, who had been appointed US Ambassador to Ireland, to be patient. Sir Ivor was already a very big colt, but luckily in the spring he thickened out, rather than grew upwards. To Vincent's surprise he was ready for his first race at the end of June. That day, he was beaten into fourth place; but it was his only defeat as a two-year-old. A brilliant campaign was climaxed by his success, ridden by Lester Piggott, in France's Grand Criterium. 'He quickened so fast he nearly ran out from under me,' Lester grinned.

After Sir Ivor's first success his owner struck a bet of £500 each way at 100-1 for the Derby with William Hill. This much publicised wager became an obsession with the famous bookmaker as Sir Ivor went from strength to strength. The bookie's problem was almost solved during the winter. Vincent, always innovative, tried the experiment of sending his Classic horses to the mild, Mediterranean climate of Pisa, on the Gulf of Genoa. It was a fraught expedition. Sir Ivor had an infected foot, which lasted for three weeks; then one morning he unseated his rider and was within feet of falling into a deep dyke!

Back at Ballydoyle, Sir Ivor began to work lazily. It was a foul Spring, with persistently heavy ground, and Vincent decided to complete his preparation for the 2000 Guineas from the Links Stables at Newmarket. The author remembers vividly a brilliant work on racecourse side. Piggott had chosen to ride Sir Ivor in preference to the unbeaten Petingo, trained by his father-in-law, Sam Armstrong. Petingo, likewise, was sparkling in his work. In one of the great 2000 Guineas, Sir Ivor won brilliantly by one-and-a-half lengths.

William Hill, and others, now contended that Sir Ivor, with his brilliant speed and mile-and-a-quarter pedigree, was unlikely to stay

Poetry in motion ... Sir Ivor and Lester Piggott cruising like a well-oiled machine.

the distance of the Derby. Piggott and O'Brien gave the matter deep thought. The outcome was one of the most audacious rides in the history of the Derby. Lester waited and waited, and for an awful moment looked unable to pull out. Ice cool, he switched at the last possible moment, balanced the big colt, and thrust for the line. The result was spectacular, and heart-stopping. Incredibly, he beat Connaught by one-and-a-half lengths, having hit the front less than fifty yards from the line.

Vincent's Irish jockey Liam Ward was back on Sir Ivor in the Irish Sweeps Derby, and riding an orthodox race, leading two furlongs from home, was caught and beaten by Ribero — ridden by Piggott. A week later Sir Ivor was beaten again, by Royal Palace, and Taj Dewan, in a great race for the 'Eclipse'. Sir Ivor returned to Ireland badly jarred up. In the autumn he met a champion — and a true stayer — in Vaguely Noble in the Prix de l'Arc de Triomphe, but came back to his best distance of one-and-a-quarter miles for the Champion Stakes, which he won easily.

The American-owned colt bowed out in the land of his birth in the Washington D.C. International (1½ miles) at Laurel Park. Ridden with superb artistry by Piggott, in horrible going, he came

147

from behind to beat Czar Alexander and Fort Maroy by three parts
of a length, in the last fifty yards. Sir Ivor and Lester were covered
with mud, and the colt was exhausted. 'I've never seen a horse so
tired after a race,' says Lester. 'He had given everything.'

Raymond Guest, whose only misfortune was in missing the Derby
because of official duties in Ireland, allowed his great colt to stand
for one season at stud in Ireland, before returning to America. For
no obvious reason, Sir Ivor's daughters have enjoyed considerably
more success than his sons, notably Ivanjica, Godetia, Lady Capulet
and Optimistic Gal. His best colt, Bates Motel, was very backward
and late in coming to hand. Sir Ivor was great all right — but then
so too was Piggott.

BIG RACES WON	
Derby	1968
2000 Guineas	1968
Champion Stakes	1968
Washington D.C. International	1968
Grand Criterium	1967
National Stakes	1967

SUN CHARIOT

Foaled 1939
Trained in England

OF THE 4,870 WINNERS ridden by Sir Gordon Richards there can be no doubt that Sun Chariot's Oaks gave the great man more pleasure than any — bar one! Sun Chariot, bred at the National Stud, raced in the colours of King George VI. Although the country was at war, the King's successes in 1942 were hugely popular and in all he won four Classics, only the Derby proving elusive, through the defeat of Big Game.

Like so many great fillies, Sun Chariot, a daughter of Hyperion, was temperamental to the point of distraction. Only one man, a groom called Warren, could persuade her to comply with his wishes and Fred Darling allowed the stable lad to ride her in most of her work. Gordon Richards did not ride her as a two-year-old, missing most of the season with a smashed ankle. Languishing in hospital, Gordon sent his friend Tom Reece, the billiards professional, to Newbury to back the Royal filly in her first race. Soon after Reece had left for the races, Gordon had a visit from Bud Flanagan and Chesney Allan. Dick Perryman had been to the 'Crazy Gang Show' the previous night at the Victoria Palace and told Flanagan and Allan to back what he stated was the best two-year-old he had ever ridden, at Newbury the next day. A quick glance at the newspaper told Gordon that Perryman's 'flyer', Perfect Peace, was in the same race as Sun Chariot. In a panic, Gordon arranged for a telegram to be sent to Newbury telling Reece to back Perfect Peace and not Sun Chariot. When the evening paper arrived, Gordon's face fell. Sun Chariot had won at 11-4, Perfect Peace was third! When Reece returned from the races, Gordon explained what happened. 'What!' he exploded. 'You've been riding horses for twenty years and you still take notice of what a couple of bum actors tell you!'

Harry Wragg rode Fred Darling's horses while Gordon was injured and the filly completed the season unbeaten. In the Middle Park Stakes, she beat Ujiji by three lengths, becoming the first of her sex to win the race since 1921. Gordon was fit again in 1942, but started the season disastrously and was still awaiting his first winner when he rode Sun Chariot over six furlongs at Salisbury. Gordon tried to impose his will and drop the filly in behind two others. This did not suit Sun Chariot and she refused to take hold of her bit. The outcome was her first and only defeat.

In the 1000 Guineas, Sun Chariot was on good behaviour, despite swishing her tail, and sprinted away to win by four lengths — from Perfect Peace! Fred Darling allowed himself a rare smile having already won the 2000 Guineas for His Majesty with Big Game. The week before the Derby and Oaks, the King and Queen travelled to Beckhampton to see the two classic horses gallop. Sun Chariot

'Call yourself a racehorse?'
Sun Chariot (right) eyes
her Royal stable
companion the 2000
Guineas winner Big Game,
on the eve of the Derby
and Oaks.

was in one of her very worst moods. Finally, the head lad gave her a tap with his riding crop, and Sun Chariot took off — straight into the middle of a ploughed field. Thereupon, she got down on her knees, and roared like a bull! Gordon was terrified.

In the Oaks she was at her worst and ruined three starts. Finally the starter released them and Sun Chariot charged off to the left, losing all of ten lengths. According to Gordon in his book *My Story*, the other runners had travelled a furlong by the time he had gone fifty yards. After a mile, Sun Chariot had caught the others and a furlong later joined the leaders. A furlong from home she struck the front and, despite idling, held on to win by a length. 'It was one of the most amazing performances I have ever known,' Gordon said later. The King, wearing R.A.F. uniform, led in his filly with immense pride, whilst Gordon's reaction was one of overwhelming relief! Sun Chariot's final race was the wartime St Leger, which she won in brilliant style — again coming from last — by three lengths from the Derby winner, Watling Street.

Sun Chariot was a lovely type of filly and at stud she bred seven winners, including Landau, ironically the last horse that Gordon rode in public. The following year, the King presented Gordon with a Munnings painting of Sun Chariot, with Gordon up, which the great man treasured until his death.

It was ironic that Big Game was beaten in the Derby. The one thought that always nagged Gordon was that Sun Chariot, given the chance, could have won this elusive race!

BIG RACES WON	
Oaks	1942
1000 Guineas	1942
St Leger	1942
Middle Park Stakes	1941
Queen Mary Stakes	1941

TANTIEME

Foaled 1947
Trained in France

1950 WAS ONE OF the great years in the history of the French Turf. During that famous season, horses owned and bred in France won four of the five English Classics, while M. Marcel Boussac headed both the English winning Owners' and Breeders' list. It was also an era when many French horses were doped to the eyeballs. One St Leger winner was re-loaded onto an aeroplane with unseemly haste, pouring with sweat, and with his eyes still popping out of his head. Such an accusation is not relevant to Tantième, however, whose trainer, the former Cavalry officer, François Mathet, was always beyond reproach despite the controversy surrounding Relko in 1963.

Tantième, bred by his owner M. François Dupré, was champion two-year-old of his year, winning the Grand Criterium by a head in a three-way photo finish, having made up five lengths in the straight. As a three-year-old Tantième had met with a single defeat — at the hands of Scratch II in the Prix du Jockey Club. This was a most controversial affair. In 1950 Chantilly was the only racecourse in the Paris region that had no photo-finish camera. Scratch II and Tantième both finished extremely fast, with Scratch on the far rails and Tantième towards the centre of the course. In the pre-photo era, a judge was invariably inclined to favour the horse furthest from him, and the Comte de Kergorlay duly made Scratch II the winner by a short head. As Tantième was favourite, pandemonium broke out, and Mathet never accepted the verdict.

In July, Tantième travelled to Britain for the Queen Elizabeth Stakes — the predecessor to the 'King George' — and beat the 1949 'Arc' winner, Coronation V, by a head. On the day of the Prix de l'Arc de Triomphe, Tantième was greatly fancied to gain his revenge on Scratch II. Nonetheless, he was not favourite since Scratch II and Coronation V were both owned by M. Boussac and coupled for betting purposes. There was so little between the pair that a coin was tossed to decide which one Rae Johnstone should ride. Johnstone called 'heads', was right, and chose to ride Scratch II; Charlie Elliott was on Coronation V. It was a warm, sultry day, after rain, and Tantième sweated profusely. The pace was fast, which suited Tantième, and Jacques Doyesbère was always perfectly placed with his hands full. A furlong and a half from the finish, he went for home and the race was won. Scratch II ran better than Coronation V, but finished only fourth. Three-year-olds filled the first six places, underlining that it was a vintage Classic year.

Tantième stayed in training as a four-year-old and his only defeat was in the Festival of Britain Stakes — the 'interim' race between the old Queen Elizabeth Stakes, and the following year's King

A free sweater and poor traveller, Tantième shows the signs of a hard season.

George VI & Queen Elizabeth Stakes. The French colt was a poor traveller, and in none of his three British sorties did he reproduce his French form. In the 1951 Prix de l'Arc de Triomphe he was clear favourite at 17-10, and his success was more easily gained than in the previous year. So confident was Doyesbère of winning that he had arranged a dinner party for twelve at Maxim's some days before the race!

Tantième proved a good sire of stayers, his best sons being Reliance II and Match III. He was certainly the best colt of his generation, and only Ribot and Alleged share his achievement of winning two post-war Arcs.

BIG RACES WON	
Prix de l'Arc de Triomphe (twice)	1950-51
Poule d'Essai des Poulains	1950
Coronation Cup	1951
Queen Elizabeth Stakes	1950
Prix Lupin	1950
Prix Ganay	1951
Grand Criterium	1949
Prix de la Forêt	1949

THE FLYING DUTCHMAN

THE FLYING DUTCHMAN won one of the most famous races of the nineteenth century — the match, for £1000 a side, against Voltigeur at York in May 1851.

Foaled 1846
Trained in England

'The Dutchman' was owned by one of the most popular aristocrats of his time, the 13th Earl of Eglinton. Lord Eglinton, who succeeded to the title whilst still at Eton, came into racing at the age of nineteen. His first Classic winner was Blue Bonnet in the 1842 St Leger, whom he had backed to win £30,000 (the equivalent of over £1 million now), during the week of the race. The filly, who had never raced previously, won by a length. Five years later, Lord Eglinton won the St Leger with Van Tromp. Afterwards, he made an arrangement with the colt's breeder, Colonel Vansittart, that he would buy for 1000 guineas every 'correct' foal out of Van Tromp's dam, Barbelle. Her foal the previous year, by Bay Middleton, met the requirements, and became The Flying Dutchman.

The Dutchman was trained at Spigot Lodge, Middleham, by John Fobert. He was unbeaten as a two-year-old, winning notably the July Stakes at Newmarket and the Champagne Stakes at Doncaster. As a three-year-old, his first race was the Derby. In a field of twenty-six and starting joint favourite at 2-1, he beat Hotspur, a half-bred, by a hard fought half-length. The ground was heavy, which did not suit him, and his jockey Charles Marlow used the whip for the first and only time in their association. The St Leger proved a far easier task, The Dutchman winning as he pleased by two lengths.

As a four-year-old, he won the Emperor of Russia's Plate (now the Ascot Gold Cup) by eight lengths, and the Goodwood Cup by ten lengths. Now came his first meeting with Voltigeur, in the Doncaster Cup. Voltigeur had won the Derby comfortably, but had only landed the St Leger after a dead-heat and run-off with the Irish-bred Russborough. The Cup came two days after this ordeal. But The Dutchman was no better prepared. For the first time in his life he was off his feed, yet on the morning before the race, Fobert subjected him to a gallop the like of which no one had witnessed before. On the day Fobert instructed Marlow to hold up The Dutchman until the Red House (six furlongs from home). Marlow, the worse for drink, shouted: 'I'll show them what I have got under me today,' and set off at a suicidal gallop. Nat Flatman, on Voltigeur, bided his time to the distance, where Marlow found to his horror that The Dutchman had nothing in reserve. The great horse, at 6-1 on, met with his first and only defeat. His backers were stunned: Lord Eglinton leant, pale as ashes, against the Jockey Club stand, while the wretched Marlow, now stone-cold sober, stood weeping bitterly by the weighing room.

The Flying Dutchman beats Voltigeur by a 'short length' in their famous match at York.

The great match between The Dutchman and Voltigeur was arranged over two miles at York the following spring. The weights, appointed by Admiral Rous, were The Flying Dutchman 8st 8½lb, Voltigeur 8 stone. The jockeys were again Marlow and Flatman. The crowd at the Knavesmire was said to have been the largest since Eugene Aram was hanged there in the previous century! The betting was evens throughout. This time Voltigeur made the running, leading by three lengths. The ground was heavy and it was only courage that enabled The Dutchman to wear his rival down. In the end he won a desperate struggle by a short length.

The Dutchman retired to stud after this famous race, with reasonable success, though he was exported to France in 1858. Less fortunate was the wretched Marlow, 'honest as the day, but drunken and improvident', who ended his days in poverty and died in a workhouse.

BIG RACES WON	
Derby	1849
St Leger	1849
Emperor of Russia's Plate	1850
Goodwood Cup	1850
Champagne Stakes	1848
July Stakes	1848

THE TETRACH

Foaled 1911
Trained in England

THE TETRACH was a 'freak'. He was probably the fastest horse in the history of the Turf, but he looked like a rocking horse, and gave the impression of being big, backward, and likely to end up as a hunter! In fact, he was a racing machine. Steve Donoghue, his jockey, always swore that he had been on this earth before. He knew instinctively what to do.

From the outset, 'The Spotted Wonder', as he was dubbed, was a contradiction. His sire, Roi Herode, was an out-and-out stayer who was second in the Doncaster Cup. When Atty Persse paid 1300 guineas for the big grey as a yearling, one or two fellow trainers wondered if he had taken leave of his senses. Far from it, Persse had seen the distinctive colt running rings round the other yearlings at his breeder's stud in Ireland: indeed according to his breeder, Mr Eric Kennedy, he was the only yearling who could keep up with the deer! Atty Persse passed The Tetrach on to his cousin Major Dermot McCalmont, who agreed that the big colt should be given time to mature. He was very nearly gelded and turned away.

One morning, because he was getting above himself, Persse jumped him in with his most forward two-year-olds expecting him to finish tailed off. To everyone's complete astonishment, The Tetrach won the gallop doing hand-springs. The shrewd trainer was not averse to a tilt at the ring, so to ensure that the gallop was not a fluke, Persse now subjected The Tetrach to a series of astonishing trials. The most severe was against a seven-year-old called Captain Symons with whom he galloped on terms 60lbs worse than weight-for-age — the equivalent of giving twenty lengths' start. The Tetrach won the gallop in a canter, with another two-year-old, Land of Song, receiving 2lbs, beaten out of sight. Land of Song went on to win the Windsor Castle Stakes at Royal Ascot from the following year's 1000 Guineas winner, Princess Dorrie.

So when The Tetrach went to the races for the first time he was one of the greatest certainties ever to look through a bridle — and won like it! Remarkably, Persse's stable security was so good that he was returned at 9-2. It was the only time he ever started at odds against. He won with the greatest of ease at Epsom and by ten lengths at Royal Ascot. Only in the National Breeders' Produce Stakes did he face defeat. Anticipating the start, he went up with the tapes and lost almost fifty yards, but amazingly he caught the leaders in the nick of time, and won by a neck. Many racegoers, unable to see the start because of mist, felt that the grey freak was in decline. They soon learnt the reverse. The Spotted Wonder trotted up at Goodwood — where he was mobbed after the race on Trundle Hill — at the Derby, and at Doncaster in the Champagne Stakes.

155

Sadly that was his last race. He rapped his off-fore fetlock joint, and was pin-fired. The following spring he knocked the same joint, and that was that. During the winter, he was favourite for the Derby, but Steve Donoghue, no doubt correctly, took the view that he would not have stayed a mile and a half in a horse box.

At stud The Tetrach proved a most shy breeder, and produced only 130 foals. Nonetheless, eighty of them won races including four Classic winners, the best of them Tetratema. He was also champion sire when his first crop were three-year-olds. In 1926 he became completely sterile, and when his death was announced in 1935, few people knew that he was still alive. In his prime, however, he was a wonder horse and a machine... in fact one of racing's glorious flukes.

BIG RACES WON	
National Breeders' Produce Stakes	1913
Coventry Stakes	1913
Champagne Stakes	1913
Rous Memorial Stakes	1913
Woodcote Stakes	1913
Champion Breeders' Foal Stakes	1913

TOUCHSTONE

Foaled 1831
Trained in England

TOUCHSTONE WAS THE best horse owned and bred by the 1st Marquess of Westminster, whose grandson, the 1st Duke of Westminster, was to own Ormonde. He was a very late developing horse — as a foal he was so weak and weedy that his owner tried, unsuccessfully, to give him away. Eventually, he grew into a powerful individual, although he was never tall. Differing reports estimate his height between 15hh and 15.2hh. He was exceptionally wide behind, an attribute probably inherited from his mother's family. His second dam, Boadicea, was a hunter mare, who was once swapped for a cow!

The Classic colts of 1834 were above average, and Plenipotentiary was a highly regarded winner of the Derby. Accordingly he was made an odds-on favourite for the St Leger, but was ruthlessly doped, and finished tailed off. Touchstone was a rank outsider at 50-1. He had proved difficult for John Scott to train, with a persistent problem surrounding his near-fore joint. At home he was lazy, but on the racecourse he was a hard puller. He was also liable to swerve violently if shown the whip. He was not entirely sound on Leger day, and his usual jockey, the trainer's brother, William Scott, 'got off' him to ride a filly called Lady de Gros. George Calloway came in for the ride, and to William Scott's great chagrin, Touchstone won comfortably by two lengths.

Touchstone established his reputation as a four and five-year-old. He won the Doncaster Cup in 1835 and 1836, and the Ascot Gold Cup in 1836 and 1837. Tom Dawson, one of the great northern trainers of the time, stated many years later that he regarded Touchstone as superior to West Australian and The Flying Dutchman — the top horses of the 1850s.

It was as a stallion that Touchstone made his greatest mark. He sired 343 winners of 738 races worth £223,000 — almost the equivalent of £8 million today — including three Derby winners. He lived to the age of thirty-one, and was buried in the main yard at the Duke of Westminster's Eaton Stud.

BIG RACES WON	
St Leger	1834
Ascot Gold Cup (twice)	1836-37
Doncaster Cup (twice)	1835-36

Touchstone — a weak, unimpressive foal, who grew into a magnificent colt.

TROY

Foaled 1976
Trained in England

*Troy (Willie Carson) wins
the 200th Derby by a
remarkable seven lengths.*

TROY WAS AN entirely suitable winner of the 200th Derby. He won by the widest margin for fifty-four years, and went on to prove himself an exceptionally good colt. Troy was owned in partnership by Sir Michael Sobell and Sir Arnold (now Lord) Weinstock. On the death of Miss Dorothy Paget in 1960, the late Sir Gordon Richards persuaded Sir Michael — a relative newcomer to Flat Racing — to buy Miss Paget's bloodstock lock, stock and barrel. The Ballymacoll Stud, at Co. Meath in Ireland, flourished in its new ownership, and soon produced top-class horses in Reform, Sallust, Sun Prince and Homeric.

In 1971, on Sir Gordon's retirement, Dick Hern was appointed Sobell's trainer. Soon afterwards, Sobell and Weinstock bought the West Ilsley stables. Troy was the culmination of their racing and breeding involvement. By Petingo out of a mare called La Milo, by Hornbeam, he represented the best Ballymacoll blood on his dam's side. A top-class staying two-year-old, he reached his peak in the weeks leading up to the Derby. At Tattenham Corner, he was badly placed on the rails, and some way off the pace. Even three furlongs out the situation seemed hopeless. Eventually, Willie Carson pulled him off the rails, and running almost diagonally, manoeuvred him to the wide outside. Two or three smacks with the whip produced a sensational response. Within a furlong and a half he had come from six lengths adrift to seven lengths clear. He was a hugely popular winner, although the stable had also saddled the Queen's colt Milford, ridden by Lester Piggott.

Troy now went from strength to strength. In the Sweeps Derby, he again beat the Epsom runner-up, Dickens Hill — this time by four lengths. In the 'King George' he beat the French four-year-old Gay Mecene by a length and a half, but in the Benson & Hedges Gold Cup he ran lazily and won by only three parts of a length. After a six-week break he came back in the autumn for the Prix de l'Arc de Triomphe, but failed to reproduce his summer form and finished third to the filly Three Troikas.

Troy was syndicated at a valuation of £7.2 million, and made a most encouraging start at stud. Tragically, however, he died in May 1983 from a perforated intestine.

BIG RACES WON	
Derby	1979
Irish Sweeps Derby	1979
King George VI & Queen Elizabeth Stakes	1979
Benson & Hedges Gold Cup	1979
Lanson Champagne Stakes	1978

TUDOR MINSTREL

Foaled 1944
Trained in England

TUDOR MINSTREL was the horse that persuaded Gordon Richards that he was probably never going to win the Derby! He was, without doubt, one of the best one-mile horses this century. Certainly Gordon stated that he was the best he had ever ridden. Trained by the great Fred Darling who was suffering from extreme ill-health at the time, Tudor Minstrel was unbeaten in four races as a two-year-old, and topped the Free Handicap.

His 'prep' race for the 2000 Guineas was at Bath where he had just two opponents, one of them a stable companion called Greek Justice. He won comfortably and went on to the Guineas a firm favourite at 11-8. Petition was well fancied to beat him, but reared over at the start, hurt his back and made no show. Tudor Minstrel sprinted away to win by eight lengths, and was hailed by some as 'horse of the century'.

Tudor Minstrel was now odds-on for the Derby, but two weeks before the race Gordon had a nasty shock. Fred Darling would always gallop his Derby horse on a special left-hand gallop he had laid out at Beckhampton, as a facsimile of the Derby course. To Gordon's horror, although the colt had won at Bath, he now found that Tudor Minstrel could not 'act' left-handed. 'This fellow's action is all *right*,' he told Darling. 'He can't get on to the other leg. If he does he's all at sea!' Whether or not Gordon kept his fears to himself, Tudor Minstrel remained the warmest favourite for the Derby in living memory at 7-4 on.

The race was the greatest nightmare of Gordon's career. When Gordon tried to catch hold of Tudor Minstrel and drop him in, the powerfully-built brown colt fought him. If Gordon let him go he shot off to the right. The result was a spectacle so bizarre that it haunted poor Gordon thirty years later. Tudor Minstrel tugged and fly-jumped all the way up the hill, throwing his head in every direction. He was in front at Tattenham Corner, but eventually his exertions took their toll and he finished a leg-weary fourth. Gordon was shattered, and for once his loyal public turned against him. He received letters, telegrams and even telephone calls galore, accusing him of pulling the horse's head off.

Tudor Minstrel reverted to a mile at Ascot, and going right-handed over his best distance, won in a canter. But in the Eclipse, on watered going, he was outstayed by Migoli. At stud he sired Sing Sing, Tudor Melody and the Kentucky Derby winner Tomy Lee, amongst a host of top-class winners. He was exported to America in 1959. He was the last great horse trained by the brilliant Fred Darling. At the end of 1947, Darling retired and sold the Beckhampton stables to Mr J.A. Dewar.

BIG RACES WON	
2000 Guineas	1947
St James's Palace Stakes	1947
Knights Royal Stakes	1947
National Breeders' Produce Stakes	1946
Coventry Stakes	1946

Tudor Minstrel gives Gordon Richards a foretaste of the ride he was going to experience in the Derby.

TUMBLEDOWNWIND

Foaled 1975
Trained in England

'GREAT' IS A subjective term. The ownership of Tumbledownwind was the greatest good fortune the author has ever enjoyed in racing. For a horse who cost 4,800 guineas in an age of six-figure yearling purchases, he was certainly a very great bargain.

Tumbledownwind was bought for me at the Newmarket Houghton Yearling Sales by my trainer for over twenty years, Bruce Hobbs. Because I was taking a short holiday in Paris after the Grand Criterium, I prepared a list of three yearlings for Bruce to look at on my behalf. One was by Sun Prince, the second by Morston, and the third by Tumble Wind, an American stallion recently arrived in Ireland, of whom, to be truthful, I had never heard until three weeks before when I happened to see a most attractive yearling by him at Liz Burke's Stackallan Stud.

On the evening of October 15th, Bruce rang me in Paris: 'I've bought you a yearling, and I think you'll be pleased,' he stated. 'Just within your limit!' Evidently, Teddy Underdown, the actor and former amateur rider, was staying with Bruce, and had fallen in love with the colt. Bruce suggested we call him 'Tumbledown' — Teddy's nickname. The name wasn't available, so he became 'Tumbledownwind'.

Racing is a game governed by vicarious twists of fate, in which one's very survival is often dependent upon the results of a horserace. For several weeks I had been backing a filly of Bruce's called Welsh Flame to win a substantial sum in the Cambridgeshire, from 33-1 downwards. In the end it was very important that she won. She didn't. The upshot was that I had to ask Bruce to take a half-share in my colt. This situation led, in due course, to my welcoming as partners two delightful friends of Bruce's, Joe Farmer and Norah Hunter Blair. We were to share some moments none of us will ever forget.

Tumbledownwind, a bonny, athletic little colt, rather in the Mill Reef mould, came quickly to hand and was the stable's first two-year-old runner. After finishing second at the Newmarket Craven Meeting, he won by six lengths at the Guineas meeting. He won without being extended at Haydock — and now it was next stop Royal Ascot! We decided to go for the Chesham Stakes (6 furlongs), rather than the New Stakes (5 furlongs). On the eve of the race, my wife and I dined with Willie Carson and Suzanne Kane. 'You want to sell that horse of yours you know,' said Willie. 'You'll get £15,000 for him'. 'He might be a good horse,' I ventured. 'Rubbish,' said Willie, 'his future's behind him!' Tumbledownwind was beaten at Ascot, by a filly called Sookera who went on to win the Cheveley Park Stakes.

OPPOSITE: *Tumbledownwind (Geoff Lewis) after his first success at the Newmarket Guineas meeting. Cheer up, Geoff!*

The little colt, who had been 'wound up' for Ascot now had a rest. The author at the time was especially fond of Goodwood, and requisitioned that his pride and joy should run at the July meeting. Tumbledownwind came to the meeting 'undercooked', having only done two pieces of work since his break. The trainer and jockey, Geoff Lewis, were racing at Newmarket. Geoff Baxter rode Tumbledownwind for the first time — and won by four lengths, in course record time.

The Gimcrack Stakes at York is one of England's great traditional races. The names of famous horses like Bahram, Petition, Palestine, Bebe Grande, Petingo and Mill Reef, appear on the Roll of Honour. The winning owner is invited by the Anciente Fraternite of York Gimcracks to speak at the famous Gimcrack Dinner. It is, in fact, a big deal. Tumbledownwind won the Gimcrack despite a deluge of rain, which made the going unsuitable. He was brave, and would not be beaten. The author has vivid recall, having described the race on BBC Radio. The little colt met with his third defeat in the Mill Reef Stakes. It was a case of a good, big one (Formidable) beating a good little one (Tumbledownwind). Formidable was very good, and went on to win the Middle Park Stakes.

A month later, at the author's instigation, Tumbledownwind was sold for a substantial sum to the Marquesa de Moratella. The following spring he was trained for the 2000 Guineas. In April, on his way to post for the Ascot 2000 Guineas Trial (at Newmarket) he coughed and was withdrawn. For two days before the 2000 Guineas, the rain fell with such intensity that the roof of the bedroom in which I was sleeping caved in. Nonetheless, Tumbledownwind led to within 150 yards of the finish. It was an heroic effort, on ground he hated.

Eventually the brave, little colt was sold on to become a stallion in New South Wales, Australia. He was a wonderful horse, with a marvellous temperament, and a heart as big as a lion. He changed one man's life, and that man will always be indebted to him, and to his wonderful trainer Bruce Hobbs. For me, he was 'The Greatest'.

BIG RACES WON	
Gimcrack Stakes	1977
Rous Memorial Stakes	1977

VAGUELY NOBLE

IT WAS ONE of racing's — and life's — great ironies that the best colt ever bred by the late Major Lionel Holliday should have been foaled in the year of his death. Major Holliday, a blunt, irascible Yorkshireman, with a substantial dyes and textile business in Huddersfield, was a fine judge of a foxhound and a thoroughbred — perhaps in that order.

He was certainly the most substantial English owner-breeder in the twenty years following the Second World War, and enjoyed some outstanding success. But he never achieved his life's ambition to win the Derby. The closest he came was when Hethersett was brought down on Tattenham Hill when favourite in 1962. In 1964 the Major mated his Lancashire Oaks winner, Noble Lassie, with Sir Winston Churchill's horse Vienna. The produce was an unexceptional bay colt to be called Vaguely Noble.

Some eight months after Noble Lassie and Major Holliday's other twenty-odd pregnant mares foaled, the Major died. The majority of his mares, foals and horses in training were sent to the December Sales the following year. Vaguely Noble was retained, and raced as a two-year-old in the colours of his son, Mr Brook Holliday.

Foaled 1965
Trained in England and France

Vaguely Noble first ... the rest nowhere! The Holliday colt wins Ascot's Sandwich Stakes by twelve lengths.

But, as a relatively plain colt, by an increasingly unfashionable stallion, he was not entered in the Classics.

Vaguely Noble, trained by Walter Wharton, the last of a long line of trainers employed by the opinionated Yorkshireman, began his career with two defeats at Newcastle and Doncaster. His third race, in soft going, at Ascot in the Sandwich Stakes, was truly spectacular. Ridden by Bill Williamson he drew away to win by twelve lengths. Two weeks later he put up an even more staggering performance in the Observer Gold Cup to win by seven lengths. The key on each occasion was yielding ground.

Vaguely Noble, although leased to Brook Holliday, was the property of the late Major's executors. The family was faced with substantial death duties on the Major's estate and reluctantly it was decided Vaguely Noble would have to be sold. The auction was as spectacular as his recent performances. Amidst glitz, TV lights, and general pandemonium, he was bought for a sensational 136,000 guineas by Dr Robert Franklyn, an American plastic surgeon. The price was a new world record for public auction.

After a brief spell with Paddy Prendergast, Vaguely Noble went to be trained by Etiènne Pollet in France. The strategy was twofold: firstly, the well-watered French racecourses would suit Vaguely Noble, and secondly, the most important European race open to him, in the absence of Classic entries, was the Prix de l'Arc de Triomphe. Vaguely Noble's only defeat in 1968 came in the Grand Prix de Saint Cloud, where his jockey, Jean Deforge, who had become prone to exaggerated waiting tactics in the autumn of his career, left him with too much to do in the relatively short straight.

This defeat had the beneficial effect of re-uniting Vaguely Noble with the outstanding Australian Bill Williamson. Williamson rode a copy-book race in the Prix de l'Arc de Triomphe, which the Vienna colt won in magnificent style by three lengths from Sir Ivor. Amongst those behind in an outstanding 'Arc' were Ribero, La Lagune, Roselière and the winners of the French and German St Legers. Suddenly, 136,000 guineas looked a bargain price!

Vaguely Noble's career at stud has been exceptional. His big winners include Dahlia, Lehmi Gold and Exceller — all of whom won $1 million — Empery, Nobiliary, Noble Decree, Gay Mecene, Ace of Aces and many others. At the age of 22, his stallion fee in 1987 was lowered to $100,000! He was certainly one of the outstanding post-war winners of the Arc.

BIG RACES WON	
Prix de l'Arc de Triomphe	1968
Observer Gold Cup	1967

VOLTIGEUR

Foaled 1847
Trained in England

NOWADAYS THE WINNER of the Derby is almost without exception bred in Ireland, Kentucky or the environs of Newmarket. Voltigeur was bred near Hartlepool. Nor was this an unusual eventuality: this was the great era of Yorkshire racing and breeding. John Scott, the Dawsons, John Fobert and John Osborne — all Yorkshire based — were trainers at the peak of their profession. Between 1835 and 1857, Yorkshire stables won the Derby nine times. John Scott, who trained at Whitewall Stables, Malton, won the race five times, and the St Leger no less than sixteen times. Now, Dante's wartime Derby apart, it is over 100 years since a northern horse won the Blue Riband.

The Hartlepool breeder, a Mr Robert Stephenson, sent his brown colt by Voltaire to Tattersalls' Yearling Sales with a reserve of £350, but failed to receive a bid of £100. The Earl of Zetland's private trainer, Robert Hill, took a liking to the colt, and tried to persuade his patron to buy him privately, but the peer would have none of it. The following spring, however, encouraged by his brother-in-law, a Mr Williamson, Lord Zetland changed his mind and bought him for 1000 guineas with a further 500 guineas to be paid if he won the Derby.

Voltigeur with his heavy, crested neck, and unusually flat feet, awaits the next assault by the stable cat!

Voltigeur ran only once as a two-year-old, winning at the now-defunct Richmond (Yorkshire) racecourse, close to his owner's Aske Estate. Throughout the winter, money from Yorkshire poured onto Voltigeur. At the end of May he travelled south, but on his arrival at Epsom failed to impress the touts, and his price receded to 16-1. On the eve of the race, Lord Zetland was on the point of scratching his colt. On arrival in London he was advised by the Keeper of the Match Book that forfeits of £400 were due from the colt's nominator. (The system of entry was rather different in those days.) When the news reached Aske Hall, the staff and tenants on the estate were horrified. Almost everyone within miles had plunged their maximum, and would lose their money if the horse were withdrawn. A deputation from the staff was dispatched to Mr Williamson, who was successful in explaining to his brother-in-law the implications of his decision. The forfeits were paid, Voltigeur ran, and ridden by Job Marson, beat his twenty-three rivals by a comfortable length. Lord Zetland, who was not a gambler, won £600 in bets, while his coachmen won £200 — a sum almost certainly in excess of his year's salary!

Voltigeur was 13-8 on for the St Leger, but during the race was repeatedly interfered with by a horse called Chatterbox, so that Marson struck the front earlier than intended. To his supporters' horror, he faltered in the last furlong, and was caught in the final stride by Chatterbox's stable companion, Russborough, a 20-1 shot. The Judge awarded a dead-heat. According to custom, the two horses were pulled out again two hours later for the deciding heat. After a grim struggle, Voltigeur narrowly mastered his opponent.

Two days later, the hardy colt was saddled again to take on The Flying Dutchman in the Doncaster Cup. After a famous race, in which his rider Nat Flatman dropped his whip passing the stands, Voltigeur beat the great 'Dutchman' by half a length. (The story of this race and the re-match appear earlier.)

Voltigeur was a medium-sized colt, with the heavy, rather crested neck characteristic of his sire's stock, and rather flat feet. Every one of the thirty-two sires and dams in his pedigree traced directly to the Godolphin and Darley Arabians. He would stand for hours in his box with the stable cat perched happily on his back. At stud, he enjoyed considerable success and was the great grandsire of St Simon.

BIG RACES WON	
Derby	1850
St Leger	1850
Doncaster Cup	1850
Flying Dutchman Handicap	1852

WAR ADMIRAL

IT IS CUSTOMARY nowadays to dispatch top-class thoroughbreds to stud with unseemly haste, maximising all the while their potential stallion value. When the great Man O'War retired to stud in America, after a truly sensational racing career, quite the reverse was the case. His owner, Samuel Doyle Riddle, was either exceptionally selfish, or misguidedly protective — probably the latter. After building the equine equivalent of a shrine to Man O'War, he restricted his horse to twenty-five mares a year — mostly owned by himself, his close friends or his nephew-by-marriage, Walter Jeffords. Possibly by luck rather than good judgement — and any credit goes to Walter Jeffords who bought the great granddam — Man O'War finally bred a champion in War Admiral.

War Admiral was a very different individual to his sire, the original

Foaled 1934
Trained in USA

War Admiral (Charley Kurtsinger), smothered by the traditional garland after the Kentucky Derby.

'Big Red'. He was a brown colt, standing no more than 15.2hh — a full four inches less tall than his sire — and weighing less than 1000lbs. He had a mercurial temperament and, like his father, was impatient at the starting gate. By good fortune he was trained by George Conway, who had been assistant trainer to Louis Feustal while Man O'War was racing.

While as a two-year-old he was good, without looking a champion, his three-year-old career was spectacular. He won the Triple Crown in brilliant style, equalling the US record for one-and-a-half miles in the Belmont Stakes. It was a performance all the more remarkable since he had sliced off a square inch of his hoof while playing up at the start. At the end of the season he was unbeaten in eight races, winning three in the autumn after a four-and-a-half month break because of his foot injury.

His four-year-old career was a triumph with one blemish. One horse in America had comparable charisma to War Admiral — a five-year-old called Seabiscuit. Seabiscuit was foaled 'on the wrong side of the tracks'. As a two-year-old it took him eighteen races to win a minor event and at one point he was beaten by a virtual pony in a claiming race. The following season he was claimed for $7500 in a superior 'claimer'. From here on he went from strength to strength. The American public clamoured for a match between the two horses and after a couple of 'false alarms' — when Seabiscuit's owner Charles S. Howard withdrew him at the last moment — it finally took place over nine-and-a-half furlongs at Pimlico in the autumn of 1938.

Depending upon the individual's viewpoint, the match was magnificent — or a fiasco! According to one writer of the period, War Admiral, the favourite at 4-1 on, was 'badly managed, trained, and ridden'. Another contemporary scribe, Grantland Rice, wrote of Seabiscuit: 'A little horse with the heart of a lion, and the flying feet of a gazelle, yesterday proved his place as the gamest thoroughbred that ever raced over an American track. In one of the greatest match races ever run in the ancient history of the Turf, the valiant Seabiscuit not only conquered the great War Admiral, but ran the beaten son of Man O'War into the dirt and dust of Pimlico'. The opposing view was that War Admiral's jockey, Charley Kurtsinger, was palpably out-manoeuvred by Georgie (Ice Man) Woolf on the winner. However, since the winner made every yard of the running in a new track record of 1 minute 56.6 seconds, it was hardly a 'tactical' race.

War Admiral ran twice more and redeemed his reputation. Eventually he stood at stud alongside his illustrious father and was leading sire in 1945. He was also the maternal grandsire of Buckpasser and Never Say Die. But he was never a patch on the old man...

BIG RACES WON	
Kentucky Derby	1937
Preakness	1937
Belmont Stakes	1937
Jockey Club Gold Cup	1938
Washington Handicap	1937
Pimlico Special	1937
Widener Handicap	1938
Queen's County Handicap	1938
Wilson Stakes	1938
Saratoga Handicap	1938
Saratoga Cup	1938
Whitney Stakes	1938
Rhode Island Handicap	1938

WEST AUSTRALIAN

Foaled 1850
Trained in England

WEST AUSTRALIAN WAS the first horse to win the Triple Crown. He was certainly one of the great horses of the nineteenth century, and was described by John Scott, who won forty-one Classics, as the best horse that he ever trained. Nonetheless, he won the 2000 Guineas by only half a length, and appears to have been all out to win the Derby by a neck — although one contemporary account states that he won 'very easily — as a reference to Weatherby [the Racing Calendar] shows'.

West Australian was the fourth Derby winner to be owned by Mr John Bowes, of Streatham Castle, Co. Durham. Mr Bowes was the elder son of the Earl and Countess of Strathmore, but did not succeed to the title because of — in the polite terminology of the age — a 'delayed marriage' on the part of his parents. In fact, they did not marry until nine years after his birth. Bowes was described as a shy and retiring individual, despite serving as a member of parliament for sixteen years, and marrying a French actress, for whom he hired a leading Parisian theatre to display her limited talents. Regardless of this personal indulgence, he was a successful businessman, and increased his inheritance substantially. He was also a shrewd backer of his horses.

West Australian did not race until the autumn of his two-year-old career, but in August, John Scott had tried him so highly that John Bowes travelled to London to back him to win the following year's Derby for £30,000. After a narrow defeat in the Criterion Stakes at the Newmarket Houghton Meeting, he turned the tables on his conqueror, Speed the Plough, later in the week in the Glasgow Stakes. West Australian started 6-4 on for the 2000 Guineas, and won by half a length from the Duke of Bedford's Sittingbourne. It is hard to evaluate how much he had in hand as his jockey, Frank Butler, a grandson of Samuel Chifney, liked to ride from behind and come with the legendary 'Chifney rush'.

His success in the Derby was also at the expense of Sittingbourne. In a field of twenty-eight, he started favourite at 6-4. If artistic record is accurate, it is easy to surmise that West Australian, through his confirmation, would not have been suited by the course.

In the month leading up to the St Leger, there was surprising opposition to West Australian in the market. John Scott and Mr Bowes's racing manager, Isaac Walker, were advised that a consortium of professional gamblers, including the legendary ex-prize fighter John Gully, had bribed Frank Butler to stop 'The West'. Isaac Walker's suspicions had begun when Butler declared that if the colt won 'by the length of his arm, it would do'. Lord Derby was chosen as spokesman for the stable to warn Butler what would

happen to him if West Australian was beaten in controversial circumstances. Within days, The West's odds shortened dramatically, and he duly won in a canter by three lengths.

As a four-year-old, West Australian won the Ascot Gold Cup narrowly, and a race at Goodwood by twenty lengths. On retirement he was sold as a stallion to Lord Londesborough for £4750, and latterly became the property of the Emperor Napoleon in France, but was not a success.

Henry Alken Jnr's portrait of West Australian (Frank Butler), the first-ever winner of the Triple Crown.

BIG RACES WON	
Derby	1853
2000 Guineas	1853
St Leger	1853
Ascot Gold Cup	1854

WINDSOR LAD

Foaled 1931
Trained in England

WINDSOR LAD'S DERBY — in which Colombo was beaten favourite — was one of the most controversial in the history of the race. But although the Maharajah of Rajpipla's colt was considered a lucky winner at the time, he finished his career with the reputation as one of the outstanding middle-distance colts of the pre-war era.

1934 was an important year in horseracing. The thoroughbred industry was beginning to climb out of the doldrums of the Great Depression. Neville Chamberlain cut income tax from 5/- to 4/6d in the £1, and bloodstock values surged by up to 50%. At the start of the season, Colombo was regarded by many as the best colt since Isinglass, the Triple Crown winner of 1893. Windsor Lad, by contrast, had appeared no more than a promising stayer as a two-year-old, and was allotted 8st 3lb in the Free Handicap, 18lb less than Colombo. During the winter, Windsor Lad thrived physically, and quickly showed himself to be a true stayer by winning the Chester Vase (1½ miles 85 yards) and Newmarket Stakes (1¼ miles). It was generally considered that if there were a flaw in Colombo's stamina then Windsor Lad, ridden by Charlie Smirke, would be one of the colts most likely to take advantage.

The story of Windsor Lad's Derby appears under the section devoted to Colombo. It remains the author's personal view that Windsor Lad was the best stayer on the day. The result was a triumph for Charlie Smirke, back in the saddle after five years warning off for allegedly preventing an 11-4 on shot from starting in a race at Gatwick. During his absence from racing, Smirke had worked as as salesman and beach hand at Brighton for 35/- a week. By 1933 he was almost destitute, and would occasionally sleep on the beach.

While Rae Johnstone was branded the villain of the Derby, it was Smirke's turn to earn widespread castigation for his ride on Windsor Lad in the Eclipse. Like so many jockeys before and since — notably Geoff Lewis on Park Top — Smirke found himself shut in on the rails and could only extricate himself all too late. Windsor Lad finished third to the four-year-old King Salmon and Umidwar, who had been fifth in the Derby. Smirke described it as the worst race he had ridden in his entire career. Fifty yards past the post he was three lengths in front. Within the next ten days Rajpipla, who was convinced that Smirke had 'pulled' Windsor Lad, had sold him to the bookmaker Martin Benson for £50,000. Benson kept the horse with Marcus Marsh and re-engaged Smirke. Windsor Lad was never beaten again. He won the Great Yorkshire Stakes in a hack canter, and the St Leger by two lengths.

As a four-year-old Windsor Lad side-stepped a clash with the

outstanding French colt, Brantome, in the Gold Cup, but was a brilliant winner of the Coronation Cup from Easton and, despite falling lame during the race, was a gallant winner of the Eclipse from the three-year-old Theft. Sadly, after three years at stud, he developed chronic sinus trouble and was finally destroyed in 1943. No one rued his passing more than Charlie Smirke. Over thirty years he was the only horse who brought tears of emotion to the ebullient Cockney's eyes.

Windsor Lad and a cheerful Charlie Smirke after the dramatic Derby of 1934. Owner 'Pippy' looks in another world — while you-know-who in the feather proclaims: 'White man for pluck … black man for luck!'

BIG RACES WON	
Derby	1934
St Leger	1934
Eclipse Stakes	1935
Coronation Cup	1935
Chester Vase	1934
Newmarket Stakes	1934
Great Yorkshire Stakes	1934
Rous Memorial Stakes	1935

NATIONAL HUNT

ALDANITI

WHEN RED RUM won his third Grand National in 1977, it was impossible to conceive a more emotional occasion at Aintree. Incredibly, within five years the impossible had happened. The success of Aldaniti — once regarded as a hopeless cripple — and cancer victim Bob Champion brought tears to the eyes of the strongest, least emotional of men.

Foaled 1970
Trained in England

Aldaniti was bred by Mr Thomas Barron at the Harrogate Stud, near Darlington in Yorkshire. His sire, Derek H., a tough handicapper on the flat, was a Hunter's Improvement Society stallion, standing at Harrogate. His dam, Renardeau, had been narrowly saved from the knacker's yard. Josh and Althea Gifford bought Aldaniti — much on the advice of Althea's father, George Roger-Smith — as an untried four-year-old at Ascot Sales in May 1974. The price — 3200 guineas — was considerably more than Gifford intended to pay. The big, strong, four-year-old gelding was already named. Tommy Barron had composed the name from those of his four grandchildren, Alastair, David, Nicola and Timothy.

By the autumn, Gifford had still not found a buyer for the big, backward horse, with so little speed in his pedigree. The Findon trainer decided to take a chance, and give him a run in his wife's colours. To the astonishment of all, he won a useful novices' hurdle at Ascot at 33-1, beating the Queen Mother's Sunyboy. The following morning he was sold privately to Nick and Valda Embericos, long-established owners of Josh's and who live at nearby Barkfold Manor, Kirdford.

Aldaniti did not win again over hurdles and twelve months later in January 1976, he went lame for the first time, after running at Sandown, and was fired on both forelegs. His return to action thirteen months later was over fences. He won at Ascot, Uttoxeter and Leicester before finishing third, in November 1977, in the Hennessy Cognac Gold Cup. Once again he was found to be lame, having chipped two pieces of bone from his off-hind leg near the fetlock joint. This injury entailed seven months spent in his box.

He returned to action in December 1978. In March he finished a distant third in the Gold Cup, and the following month a good second in the Scottish Grand National. In November 1979, be broke down again — as before on the off-fore leg. This time it looked hopeless. Meanwhile, in August 1979, his jockey Bob Champion was told he had cancer. Unless he underwent immediate chemotherapy treatment he had no more than eight months to live. The story of how Aldaniti and Bob regained their fitness, and won the 1981 Grand National, became the subject of the popular movie *Champions*.

Aldaniti and cancer victim Bob Champion jump the last fence in the 1981 Grand National clear of Royal Mail (Philip Blacker).

Aldaniti's success brought immense credit upon the Giffords, their staff, the Embericoses, their head groom Beryl Millan, the vet Mike Ashton and, of course, Bob himself. In 1987 Aldaniti, now seventeen, embarked upon a 250 mile walk from Buckingham Palace to Aintree, ridden by a different individual each mile, to raise funds for the Bob Champion Cancer Trust, and the Royal Marsden Hospital where Bob was treated. The project raised a remarkable £820,000.

BIG RACES WON	
Grand National	1981
Whitbread Trial Chase	1981
Alanbrooke Memorial Handicap Chase	1979

ARKLE

ARKLE WAS THE MOST exceptional racehorse with whom the author — or anyone else lucky enough to see him — has ever come into contact. He was proud, brave, kind, gentle and exceptionally intelligent. He was quite simply the greatest steeplechaser that ever lived.

Foaled 1957
Trained in Ireland

Arkle was bred by Mrs Mary Baker, of Malahow House, near Naul, Co. Dublin. His sire, Archive, was a forty-eight guineas stallion, while his dam, Bright Cherry, was a fair two-mile race mare. To Arkle's considerably good fortune, he was bought for 1150 guineas, as an untried three-year-old at Ballsbridge by Anne, Duchess of Westminster. Formerly Nancy Sullivan, from Co. Cork, the Duchess was not only a fine horsewoman herself, but the most sympathetic and sporting owner imaginable. Her horses come first, regardless of any other considerations. It was also Arkle's good fortune that he was trained by the late Tom Dreaper, a man of indefinable but instinctive genius, and ridden by one of the finest horsemen of the post-war era in Pat Taaffe.

Arkle was named after a mountain facing the Duchess's house by Loch Stack in Sutherland where the author has spent many happy hours fishing. From the moment he won his first hurdle race as the stable's 'neglected' at 20-1, Arkle was always destined for greatness. On his first visit to Britain he won the Honeybourne Novices' Chase at Cheltenham in November 1962, and on his next he won the Broadway (now Sun Alliance) Chase at the Cheltenham Festival.

His first great race was against Mill House in the 1963 Hennessy Gold Cup. Mill House had won the Cheltenham Gold Cup and was set to concede Arkle 5lb. Pat Taaffe was confident of success until Arkle slipped on landing at the final ditch. Mill House won easily with Arkle third. It was a misty day, and many of those in the stands — the author included — were unable to see what had happened.

It proved an expensive misfortune when the pair re-met in the 1964 Gold Cup, the greatest steeplechase of the past forty years. Mill House, with some justification, had established a reputation as the finest steeplechaser since Golden Miller, and was odds-on. In the last mile and a half, Mill House galloped as fast as he could and flew his fences. But between the last two fences Arkle surged past him, jumped the last a length in front, and drew away up the hill to win by five lengths. The Irish were ecstatic and Mill House's supporters totally stunned.

Mill House and Arkle had several further encounters, but despite increasing weight advantages, Mill House was never able to beat him again. In the end Mill House was a broken horse. Arkle, meanwhile, went from strength to strength. Two further Gold Cups were won, while in handicaps not even receipt of two stone could enable the next-best horses to match him. So great was his superiority that the Irish handicapper was instructed to prepare two handicaps for races in which Arkle was entered — one with Arkle, and one without! In England his domination led to the introduction of 'extended' handicaps, so that the weights could be increased substantially if Arkle was an absentee.

In the Hennessy Gold Cup of 1966, Arkle met with a rare reverse when Stalbridge Colonist, receiving 35lb and brilliantly ridden by Stan Mellor, beat the great horse narrowly. The following spring, in Arkle's absence, Stalbridge Colonist came within three parts of a length of winning the Cheltenham Gold Cup, at level weights.

Experts sought to analyse the reasons for Arkle's greatness. Two factors were undoubtedly his exceptionally low heartbeat, and his manner of overlapping his forelegs with his hind-legs, in the style of a greyhound. He was also a phenomenally accurate jumper, who never fell on the racecourse.

Arkle's career ended all too soon when he broke a pedal bone during the King George VI Steeplechase at Kempton on Boxing Day,

Arkle (Pat Taaffe) flicks over a fence at National Hunt racing's great theatre, the Cheltenham Festival.

1966. Despite an operation, and rest, he was never sufficiently fit to resume his career and on October 9th, 1968 he was officially retired to the Duchess's farm at Bryanstown, near Maynooth, Co. Kildare. In 1969 he travelled to England for the Horse of the Year Show and took part in the Parade of Personalities. He thrived on adulation, helped himself to apples and pears from a costermonger's cart and munched up the hydrangeas. But the following spring his stiffness — either rheumatism or brucellosis — became more acute. Eventually, despite his pride, he could scarcely stand. The Duchess had to make the saddest decision of her life. On May 31st, 1970, the vet, James Kavanagh, gave Arkle his final injection. Arkle lay down in his box and went to sleep for ever.

No one who saw what he achieved — and how he achieved it — could ever expect to see his like again.

BIG RACES WON	
Gold Cup (3 times)	1964-66
King George VI Chase	1965
Irish Grand National	1964
Hennessy Gold Cup (twice)	1964-65
Whitbread Gold Cup	1965
Leopardstown Chase (3 times)	1964-66
SGB Chase	1966
Gallaher Gold Cup	1965
Thyestes Chase	1964
Broadway Novices' Chase	1963
Power Gold Cup	1963
John Jameson Gold Cup	1963

BATTLESHIP

Foaled 1927
Trained in USA and England

BATTLESHIP WAS THE smallest horse ever to win the Grand National. He was also an entire horse, wearing blinkers, and was ridden by the tallest and youngest jockey ever to win the race!

Battleship was owned by the American heiress Mrs Marion du Pont Scott. On the death of her father, William du Pont, in 1927, she inherited a 5000-acre sporting estate in Orange County, Virginia, with its eighteenth-century country house, a racecourse, stud farm, pack of hounds and a stable of fighting cocks. She was married to the Hollywood movie star Randolph Scott, but was far from a tinseltown lady. An out-and-out sportswoman, she developed a fierce determination to win the Grand National, and Battleship, despite his limitations in size, and his stallion status, was the horse that she chose to fulfil her ambition.

Battleship's pedigree was more suited to winning the Derby than the Grand National. He was by the great Man O'War out of a Classic French filly called Quarantine by Seasick. Mrs du Pont Scott bought Battleship as a two-year-old in 1929. In 1935 he won the American Grand National. The following year Battleship was sent to England to be trained by Reg Hobbs at Lambourn, with the specific objective of winning the 1937 Grand National.

In those days the Grand National fences were big, black, stark and upright. They were certainly not ideal for a pint-sized stallion — Battleship never grew an inch above 15.2hh. For months Reg Hobbs did everything in his power to deter the owner from running Battleship in the National. Finally, after Cheltenham, he wired Mrs du Pont Scott stating that he had scratched Battleship because he was 'inclined to jump on his head a little when landing over his fences in heavy going'.

The following year Hobbs embarked on a similar campaign of deterrence, but this time the owner was quite adamant. 'He will be returning to Virginia the following week in any case, so you had better get him to Aintree,' she stated. As the stable's other entry, Flying Minutes, had broken down, Hobbs demurred. Reg's son, Bruce, already a top jockey at the age of seventeen, was offered £300 to ride the little horse. Reg still had misgivings, and lengthened the reins by eighteen inches so that Bruce could slip them that much further at the big drop fences.

Battleship was easy to back at 40-1. Bruce had his first bit of good fortune at the seventh fence, where Battleship, carrying 11st 6lb, jumped to the right, and Bruce was disappearing out of the side-door. Fred Rimell grabbed him by the seat of the pants, and pulled him back. 'Where are you going matey?' laughed Fred. Three fences from home Battleship made a bad mistake, and almost went.

Bruce gave him a breather and jumped the last three lengths behind Royal Danieli. A loose horse carried Battleship wide, while Dan Moore, on Royal Danieli, hugged the far rails. The two horses raced thirty feet apart and flashed past the post together. After a long delay, the Judge called Battleship's number by a head. To the day he died, Dan Moore swore that if there had been a photo finish he would have won, although newsreel evidence does not support his view.

Battleship was retired immediately and returned to America as foundation stallion at Mrs du Pont Scott's jumping stud. He was leading jump stallion five times and sired the 1956 American Grand National winner, Shipboard. He was the last entire horse to win the great race — an achievement unlikely to be repeated.

BIG RACES WON	
Grand National	1938
American Grand National	1935

BULA

Foaled 1965
Trained in England

BULA, AT HIS PEAK, was a quite exceptionally brilliant hurdler. When he turned his attention to chasing he was probably the best three-mile chaser on the park courses. The Gold Cup on heavy ground was not his race.

Bula was one of the many great horses who gave no previous indication of ability at home. On his first appearance at Lingfield, he was ridden by Stan Mellor. Paul Kelleway, Fred Winter's stable jockey, had been injured in the previous race and Richard Pitman, who was at the meeting, could not be found! Stan was told to give him a nice race, and find out if he was any good. Accordingly, Stan dropped him out, changed his hands and gave him a kick at the second last, and was staggered to find Bula sprinting past his rivals to win easily.

Bula (John Francome) — now the accomplished steeplechaser, after a spectacular hurdles career.

Paul Kelleway, who had been apprenticed to the 'Head Waiter' Harry Wragg on the flat, was a great believer in relaxing horses and switching them off at the back of the field. These were clearly the tactics that suited Bula who showed himself to be possessed with remarkable speed. Bula went for thirteen races without defeat, with the controversial Kelleway, whose tactics infuriated the traditionalists who believe a jumping 'trier' should always be racing in the first four, riding some brilliant races. More than once, notably in Sandown's Benson & Hedges Hurdle, Kelleway's critics were convinced that the waiting tactics had been overdone, but unfailingly the ice-cool rider had the last laugh.

Bula won two Champion Hurdles in brilliant style, but in 1973 his fire had fizzled out. Fred Winter launched him upon a chasing career, and he proved an outstanding recruit. By 1975, ridden now by John Francome, he had graduated to Gold Cup class, and he ran a brave race in appalling conditions to finish third to Ten Up. The following year he was favourite to become the first ever to win the Champion Hurdle and Gold Cup, but ran a most disappointing race behind Royal Frolic.

In 1977 he reverted to two miles in the Champion Chase and in equally abominable conditions, fell heavily damaging his shoulder muscles so badly that soon afterwards he was put down. In all he had won thirteen steeplechases and a total of thirty-four races from fifty starts. Without doubt, Paul Kelleway, more than anyone else, was responsible for how his career evolved.

BIG RACES WON	
Champion Hurdle (twice)	1971-72
Welsh Champion Hurdle	1971
Ackermann Skeaping Hurdle	1971
Benson & Hedges Handicap Hurdle	1970
Black & White Whisky Gold Cup	1973
Blue Circle Cement Chase	1975

CAPTAIN CHRISTY

Foaled 1967
Trained in Ireland

CAPTAIN CHRISTY at his best was a truly outstanding steeplechaser. His most brilliant performance was his thirty-length defeat of Bula in the 1975 King George VI Chase. Few horses, since the war, would have beaten him that day. But his career was chequered by performances both erratic and inconsistent.

As a young horse he was owned, trained and ridden by Major Joe Pidcock. At the age of sixty-two, the sporting Irish-based amateur rode Captain Christy in the three-mile hurdle at Cheltenham where, despite limited assistance from the saddle, the 'Captain' ran exceptionally well. During the summer the five-year-old was bought by Mrs Jane Samuel and sent to Pat Taaffe to be trained. The Captain immediately struck form and won five of his seven races the following season, notably the Sweeps Hurdle and Scottish Champion Hurdle.

The Captain's first season of steeplechasing was spectacular and dramatic. After a brilliant start in Ireland, he unseated his rider two out in the Black & White Gold Cup at Ascot, fell when almost a fence clear in the Wills Premier Chase Final at Haydock — and then, as a seven-year-old relative novice, won the Cheltenham Gold Cup. This was a personal triumph for Bobby Beasley. Two years earlier his riding days appeared over, following problems induced by increasing weight, alcoholism and a series of bad falls. Now, at the age of thirty-seven, he was able to climax a superlative career, fifteen years after his first Gold Cup success on Roddy Owen.

The following season The Captain won the King George VI Chase by eight lengths from Pendil, who had been brought down while cruising in the Gold Cup. But back at Cheltenham he ran a lifeless race in soft ground in the Gold Cup and was pulled up. That autumn saw his second and most spectacular 'King George', but two months later he was beset by tendon trouble from which he never properly recovered. Like the 'little girl with the curl', when he was good, he was very, very good.

BIG RACES WON	
Gold Cup	1974
King George VI Chase (twice)	1974-75
Sweeps Hurdle	1972
Scottish Champion Hurdle	1973
Power Gold Cup	1974

*Bobby Beasley slips
his reins to the
buckle-end as Captain
Christy blunders at the
last fence in the 1974
Gold Cup, while The
Dikler (Ron Barry)
breathes down his neck.*

CRISP

Foaled 1963
Trained in Australia
and England

NO ONE WHO SAW Crisp's sensational front-running performance in the 1973 Grand National will ever forget it. It was the most extravagant, enthralling exhibition of jumping that the Grand National has ever seen. Crisp achieved what no other horse in my lifetime has ever accomplished. He made the Grand National fences look easy.

Crisp was a big, strong, brown almost black gelding, bred by his owner Sir Chester Manifold in Australia. He had won on the flat, over hurdles, and over fences before he came to Britain in 1970. His steeplechase wins included the Melbourne Cup Chase and in America, the Carolina Hunt Cup at Camden. Crisp's first race in England, where he was trained by Fred Winter, was a two-mile handicap chase at Wincanton. Carrying automatic top weight of 12st 7lb he won in brilliant style by fifteen lengths. At Cheltenham the following month, despite dead going which was considered unlikely to suit him, he won the two-mile Champion Chase by a spectacular twenty-five lengths. Suddenly chasing had a major new star — although a suggestion at this stage that he was a Grand National horse in the making would have been met with hilarity.

The magnificent power-house Crisp, greeted by Australian owner-breeder Sir Chester Manifold on the eve of his historic Grand National attempt.

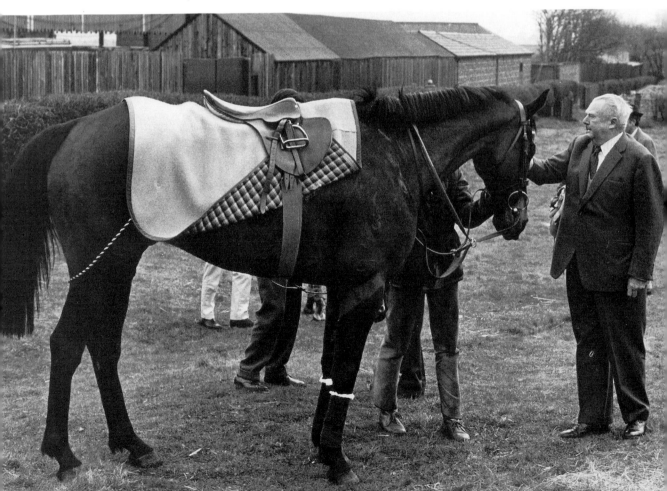

By the following February, Fred Winter had built him up to racing over three miles. At Kempton he gave weight and a beating to The Dikler and Kinloch Brae and was made favourite for the Gold Cup. But soft going, and three-and-a-quarter miles at Cheltenham proved too demanding, and the big horse weakened over the last two fences to finish fifth.

The following spring an amazing strategy was planned. Crisp would revert to two miles at the Cheltenham Festival, and eighteen days later step up to four-and-a-half miles — more than double the distance — in the Grand National. At Cheltenham, Crisp, held under restraint early in the race, was outpaced by Inkslinger and Royal Relief in the Two Mile Champion Chase. At Aintree he led for four miles 850 yards in the world's toughest steeplechase. Passing the author at Bechers Brook second time round, he was almost a fence clear and jumping, as they say, from fence to fence. His jockey, Richard Pitman, was allowing him to do what he did best — jump with extravagent splendour. It was magnificent, enthralling, but Aintree is a cruel task-master. When the jumping is over, there remains a gruelling, soul-destroying slog of 494 yards on the flat. Crisp was so tired he staggered to almost a walk in the last strength-sapping 100 yards. Suddenly a lead of twenty lengths had been whittled to fifteen... to ten... to five lengths. Now his lead was being snuffed like a candle. Red Rum was coming... and coming... and coming. Five cruel strides from the post he had caught, and beaten, the magnificent Crisp.

Under twelve stone, Crisp had helped lower the course record from 9 minutes 20.4 seconds to 9 minutes 1.90 seconds. The other horses were almost 100 yards away.

Crisp won two more races the following season, but then developed leg trouble and was eventually retired to the hunting field. For Richard Pitman, and everyone who watched the 1973 Grand National objectively, he provided the thrill of a lifetime.

BIG RACES WON	
National Hunt Two Mile Champion Chase	1971
Carolina Hunt Cup	1970
Geoffrey Gilbey Memorial Chase	1973

DAWN RUN

Foaled 1978
Trained in Ireland

DAWN RUN made National Hunt racing history, and was killed, all within three months. In March 1986, she became the first horse, after repeated attempts by other great horses, to complete the Champion Hurdle/Gold Cup double. On June 27th, in the Grande Course de Haies at Auteuil, she fell and was killed almost instantly.

Like another great National Hunt horse, Persian War, Dawn Run's destiny was very much entwined with that of her owner. Mrs Muriel Hill bought the Deep Run filly as a yearling for 5800 guineas at Ballsbridge. Now in her late fifties, she was determined to continue her riding career, which had started at the age of forty. When Dawn Run was sent to be trained by Paddy Mullins at Goresbridge, Co. Kilkenny, Mrs Hill would travel wherever possible to ride her mare in the morning. Some of their exercise was unconventional. The Deep Run mare showed herself to be strong and wilful.

Dawn Run began her career in 'bumper' (N.H. Flat) races, ridden by the owner, now in her sixty-second year. Two major events happened almost simultaneously. Mrs Hill won her first race on Dawn Run; and the stewards of the Irish National Hunt Committee refused to renew her licence to ride. Dawn Run paid two visits to England in her first season over hurdles. She finished second to Sabin du Loir in the Sun Alliance Hurdle (2½ miles) at Cheltenham, and three weeks later won the 2 miles 5 furlongs handicap hurdle at Liverpool by ten lengths carrying 11st 10lb.

The following season saw the increase in the mare's allowance from 3lb to 5lb. It was a controversial move, but a most timely one for Dawn Run. On her reappearance in England, she was ridden for the first time by Jonjo O'Neill at Ascot. She won in the last stride, by a short head. The extra 2lb made an all-important difference. Her season progressed unbeaten to the Champion Hurdle which she won by three parts of a length from the outsider Cima. Once again she had less than 2lb in hand. A brilliant campaign ended in triumph in the Grande Course de Haies at Auteuil worth £41,254. Many critics raised their eyebrows at this expedition, at the end of a long, hard season, and while other horses were enjoying the Irish summer grass, but on this occasion there was a happy ending...

Mrs Hill was now determined that Dawn Run should win the Gold Cup, although Paddy Mullins had misgivings over the mare's ability to adjust her style. Her first race over fences at Navan in November 1984 was successful, but was followed by thirteen months' absence from the racecourse because of a worrying leg ailment.

She reappeared at Punchestown on December 14th, 1985, now ridden by the trainer's son Tony Mullins, and won by eight lengths.

OPPOSITE: Dawn Run (Jonjo O'Neill) on the way to their historic Gold Cup triumph.

Dawn Run was back. Now history was to repeat itself. Just as Mrs Hill had insisted on an experienced jockey for Dawn Run in her Champion Hurdle campaign, now it happened again after Mullins was unseated by Dawn Run at Cheltenham in January. Jonjo O'Neill was booked for the Gold Cup, but to the concern of all, a freeze-up throughout February and early March prevented Jonjo from riding the mare over fences in public before the big day. So Dawn Run came to the Gold Cup with experience of just four steeplechases, in one of which she had unseated her rider.

The outcome of that famous race at Cheltenham is now part of steeplechasing lore. The mare's superb courage, combined with Jonjo's exceptional strength, made for the most exciting and evocative race in the history of the Gold Cup. Her last gasp win, in a course record time, lifted her earnings to an all-time National Hunt record, but it was a day when statistics took second place to emotion.

Less than three weeks later, she came to Liverpool for a re-match with the Gold Cup runner-up, Wayward Lad, but fell at the first fence. The Irish contrived a match for IR£25,000, between herself and the Two Mile Champion Chaser, Buck House, over two miles at Punchestown, which she won comfortably. Then came the fateful campaign in France. Tony Mullins was 'sacked' again; Jonjo had retired, so the veteran French jockey, Michel Chirol, was invited to ride. The outcome was the death of the most popular National Hunt mare since the war.

BIG RACES WON	
Gold Cup	1986
Champion Hurdle	1984
Grande Course de Haies	1984
Wessel Cable Champion Hurdle	1984
Sandeman Aintree Hurdle	1984
Ladbroke Christmas Hurdle	1983

EASTER HERO

EASTER HERO was the first of the new breed of steeplechaser. Until his era, the chasing world favoured strong, robust individuals, with considerable bone, and the size to carry fifteen stone across country. Easter Hero was a horse of a different calibre. He was medium-sized, handsome, and full of quality. He was also full of character. As a young horse in Ireland, he was ridden at exercise by the subsequent Royal jockey, Danny Morgan. Day after day, he would get the better of Danny until finally the great Irish horseman discovered the secret. If he dropped the reins the elegant chestnut would immediately pull up and trot back to where his trainer was standing.

His owner-trainer at the time was Mr Frank Barbour, a wealthy but eccentric linen manufacturer with a big estate at Trimblestown, Co. Meath. Every autumn he would take a ferry-load of horses via Liverpool to the stable yard of a pub near Tarporley. From there he would raid the big meetings at Manchester, Liverpool and Cheltenham in March. Easter Hero won the Molyneux Chase (2¼ miles) at Liverpool in November 1926, and the following autumn the Becher Chase (2½ miles).

In March 1928 he had won six races in a row in England, and become a leading public fancy for the newly created Cheltenham Gold Cup. On the eve of the race, to the astonishment of the racing world, it was announced that he had been sold and would not run at Cheltenham. The buyer turned out to be Captain Lowenstein,

Foaled 1920
Trained in England

Easter Hero, the first of a new breed ... handsome, full of quality, and seldom out of the headlines.

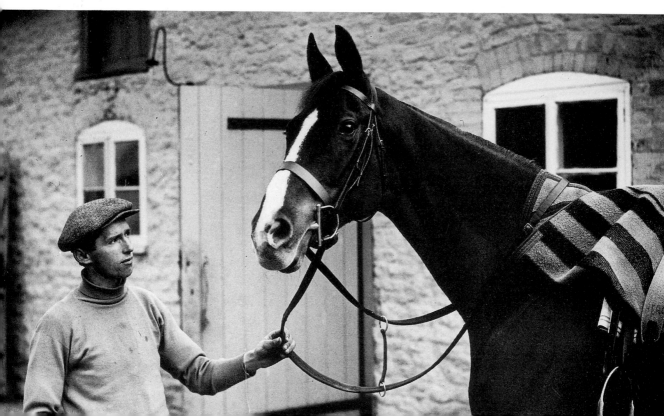

a Belgian financier, who had recently come into racing. The price was a staggering £7000 — the equivalent nowadays of over £250,000 — with a contingency of £3000 should he win the National.

The 1928 Grand National was one of the most sensational in the history of the race. Easter Hero, widely admired, went straight into the lead jumping magnificently. By Bechers he was clear, and treating the fences with contempt. The Canal Turn, in those days, was a Open Ditch. Easter Hero completely misjudged it and landed on top of the fence. Within seconds three-quarters of the forty-two-strong field had been taken out of the race. Only nine horses jumped Valentines and in the end only one horse — the 100-1 outsider Tipperary Tim — completed the course without mishap.

Easter Hero was never far removed from sensation, and in July his new owner, Captain Lowenstein, vanished whilst flying to Brussels over the North Sea. It was assumed he had fallen out of the aircraft, but his body was never found. Accordingly, Easter Hero was sold again — this time to the American millionaire sportsman, Mr John Hay Whitney. His new trainer was Jack Anthony.

In 1929, Easter Hero did run in the Gold Cup and, ridden by Fred Rees, won in brilliant style by twenty lengths.

In the Grand National he was allotted 12st 7lb. The going was heavy, and Easter Hero set off in his usual flamboyant style, delighting the crowd with a spectacular leap at the Water. He led to the second last, but his efforts had taken their toll, and Gregalach, receiving 17lb, caught him and beat him by six lengths. After the race he was found to have severely twisted a plate, probably knocked loose at Valentines. The following season Easter Hero gained a second twenty-length success in the Gold Cup, but missed the National because of a tendon sprain.

In 1931 he again carried 12st 7lb at Aintree and started favourite at 5-1, but was knocked over at Bechers on the second circuit. The following day he could only dead-heat with an inferior animal in the Champion Chase Cup (2 miles) and was promptly retired.

There is no doubt he was one of the greatest chasers between the wars leaving aside his ill-fortune at Liverpool, and on Park courses he was unbeaten between November 1926 and February 1931. On retirement he was hunted by his owner over post-and-rails in Virginia, and lived with celebrity status until the age of 28.

BIG RACES WON	
Gold Cup (twice)	1929-30
Champion Chase (d.h.)	1931
Molyneux Chase	1926
Becher Chase	1927

FLYINGBOLT

IF FLYINGBOLT HAD not been a contemporary of Arkle — and, even more ironic, in the same stable — he might easily have proved himself one of the great National Hunt horses of all time.

Foaled 1959
Trained in Ireland

Flyingbolt was bred by Mr Robert Way at the Hall Stud, Burrough Green, a village five miles from Newmarket. His sire Airborne, the 1946 Derby winner, was standing at Hall Stud, but was a failure as a flat-racing sire. His dam Eastlock, by Easton, had been bought by Way for fifty guineas at Lord Glanely's dispersal sale in 1941. She was nineteen when Flyingbolt was foaled, and he was her last foal. He was also the last thoroughbred bred by Robert Way, who sold the Hall Stud in 1958.

Robert Way sent his tall, angular, pale chestnut Airborne colt to the Newmarket Yearling Sales, where he was bought by Delma Harty of the famous Co. Limerick family and passed out of his breeder's life. The next he heard of him was when a friend told him at a cocktail party six years later: 'Do you know that you bred the best steeplechaser in Ireland?' By now he was the property of Mrs T.G. Wilkinson, wife of a retired Lieutenant Colonel in the Durham Light Infantry and M.F.H. of the North Kilkenny. Like Arkle, Flyingbolt was trained by Tom Dreaper.

Big, ugly, raw-boned — but what a machine! Flyingbolt (Pat Taaffe) makes the Cheltenham fences look easy.

Flyingbolt was unbeaten in his first season over hurdles, winning his division of the Gloucester Hurdle with ease. The following season he switched to chasing and was again unbeaten. His biggest triumph was a runaway success in what is now the Sun Alliance Chase. In autumn 1965, as a six-year-old, he began to be compared with Arkle. He won the Massey Fergusson Gold Cup by fifteen lengths under 12st 6lb, with pools of water lying on the course.

While Arkle was winning his third Gold Cup, Flyingbolt won the Two-Mile Champion Chase by fifteen lengths. The following day he was pulled out again for the Champion Hurdle and was made 15-8 favourite. He led over the last, but was outpaced by Salmon Spray and Sempervivum. He ended a remarkable season by winning the Irish Grand National under 12st 7lb, conceding 40lb to the runner-up Height O'Fashion.

Now the entire jumping world was clamouring for a meeting between Flyingbolt and Arkle. Collateral form-lines suggested there was little, if anything, to choose between them. But Tom Dreaper and Pat Taaffe were determined it should never happen. In his autobiography *My Life and Arkle's*, Pat Taaffe recalls how one morning the two horses were hacking upsides, when Flyingbolt looked over at Arkle, seemed to curl his lip, and suddenly took off with his rider Paddy Woods. Not to be outdone, Arkle took charge of Pat, burst after Flyingbolt, and with their riders just helpless passengers, the two great horses flew neck-and-neck flat out over four schooling fences.

Pat recalls: 'Paddy and I held on to them for dear life, and waited for the fires to die down. Well, they cleared the fences alright, but it was a bit close for comfort. And Mr Dreaper never allowed them to be schooled together again.' Pat went on: 'In character they were the night and day. A small child could walk into Arkle's box with absolute safety. No child, no man, would ever willingly step into Flyingbolt's ... at least not twice. He'd kick the eye out of your head!'

Sadly, Flyingbolt was to fall victim to a rare virus which affected his withers and limbs and despite constant specialist veterinary treatment, he never truly recovered his full powers after 1966. He was certainly the best steeplechaser never to win the Gold Cup.

BIG RACES WON	
Irish Grand National	1966
Two-Mile Champion chase	1966
Massey Fergusson Gold Cup	1965
Black and White Gold Cup	1965
Broadway Novices Chase	1965
Thyestes Chase	1966
Gloucester Hurdle	1964

FREDDIE

FREDDIE WAS A brave and courageous steeplechaser, who epitomized everything that is best in British National Hunt racing.

The handsome dark brown gelding was reared, broken, hunted, trained and raced by the sporting and immensely likeable Berwickshire farmer, Mr Reg Tweedie. As an amateur rider Tweedie won the Foxhunters' Challenge Cup at Cheltenham and the Valentine Chase at Liverpool, on his father's horse Ballybrack. Now, thirty years on, there came into his hands not only probably the best, but certainly the most popular hunter chaser since the war.

Freddie made his first appearance in public in the Hunt race at the Buccleugh Point-to-Point as a five-year-old. He finished second. The following spring, ridden by Alan Mactaggart, he went through the hunter chase season unbeaten, and unextended. In 1964, such was his reputation after running away with the Foxhunters' Chase at Cheltenham, that he was given top weight in the Scottish Grand National — an unthinkable accolade for a hunter chaser. Nonetheless he ran, and failed by only half a length to concede 22lb to the experienced Popham Down.

Foaled 1957
Trained in Scotland

Freddie (Pat McCarron) leads from Kellsboro Wood (Johnnie Haine) and Kapeno (Nick Gaselee) on the first circuit of Sandown's Gallaher Gold Cup.

His days as a hunter were now over, and his target for 1965 was the Grand National at Aintree. At the same time an ambitious plan was conceived to bring the winner of the Maryland Hunt Cup, Jay Trump, to England, with a similar objective. The BBC producer, Tony de Lotbinière, launched an imaginative project to film both horses over the six-month period prior to the great race. Freddie was shown rounding up sheep on Reg Tweedie's Borders farm; Jay Trump was shown being put through his paces with his American rider Tommy Crompton Smith, by first-season trainer Fred Winter.

The project achieved success to a degree that no one could have dreamt. The two horses dominated the last mile of the Grand National with the advantage passing from one to another. Freddie, the 7-2 favourite was carrying 11st 10lb but had the assistance of the top professional jockey, Pat McCarron. Jay Trump, receiving 5lb, was ridden by a man with no experience of Aintree and only a handful of rides in Britain to prepare him. Jay Trump won a famous battle by three parts of a length, but Freddie, drawing on deep reserves of courage, was immensely gallant in defeat.

Freddie came back in the autumn as fresh as new paint. He finished second to Arkle in the Hennessy Gold Cup and won the Great Yorkshire Chase, a race in those days of immense prestige. His task in the Grand National, where he carried 11st 7lb, was made substantially more difficult by a miserable misty day, with pouring rain. Twenty-two horses came to grief and a further twelve were pulled up in the searching conditions, while the outsider Anglo (ten stone) came home alone. Freddie battled on bravely to finish second.

The following season Freddie was as good as ever, winning four of his seven races, including the valuable Gallaher Gold Cup at Sandown. This time he had 11st 13lb in the National — top weight was the subsequent Gold Cup winner, What A Myth — but this was Foinavon's year ... Pat McCarron recollects that he was 'hunting' around happily in mid-division when, as he put it, 'the curtains were drawn'. Freddie finally cleared the twenty-third fence at the fourth attempt, but Foinavon, and the rest, were gone beyond recall.

Freddie's last race was in November 1967. He sustained tendon strain and was retired to the green grass of the Border country. He lived for almost twenty years in retirement, and was always looked upon as part of the Tweedie family.

BIG RACES WON	
Great Yorkshire Chase	1966
Mildmay Memorial Chase	1965
Gallaher Gold Cup	1966
Foxhunters Challenge Cup	1964

GOLDEN MILLER

GOLDEN MILLER was not only one of the two greatest steeplechasers in the history of racing, he was also the focus of more drama and controversy than any other great horse in the last sixty years. Two full-length books have been written about 'The Miller', but still the mysteries of his career remain. Nor will it ever be possible to gauge how close, at his peak, he was to the greatness of Arkle.

Foaled 1927
Trained in England

His was a story peopled by larger-than-life characters: his owner, the wealthy and capricious Miss Dorothy Paget, daughter of Lord Queensborough, whose shabby clothes and bizarre lifestyle made her one of racing's most remarkable eccentrics; his trainer, the highly-strung but gifted Old Etonian Basil Briscoe, who put up with Miss Paget's extraordinary behaviour until the fateful Grand National of 1935, but finally cracked; his jockey — at least the important one — Gerry Wilson, champion jockey a record seven times, but whose integrity was impugned when The Miller developed his bizarre 'kink'.

Like so many great horses, Golden Miller made little impact when he first arrived at the stables of Basil Briscoe at Longstowe, near Cambridge. Bred in Ireland, he had been bought for 500 guineas out of a field by the Northamptonshire hunter-dealer Captain Dick Farmer. On the gelding's arrival, Briscoe telephoned Farmer and reminded him that he had wanted a likely chaser, 'not a three-year-old carthorse'.

Briscoe chose the name Golden Miller from his parents' names, Goldcourt and Miller's Pride. 'What a good name for a bad horse,' commented the head lad Stan Tidey. Golden Miller's first owner was Philip Carr, a stockbroker, whose son Arthur was Captain of Nottinghamshire C.C. and had led England against Australia in the 1926 Test series. Within six months The Miller had staggered his stable by winning two races, and earning the accolade from the experienced Bob Lyall of 'one of the best three-year-olds I have ever ridden'.

Philip Carr decided to sell his horses in the summer of 1931 and, sadly, was to die soon afterwards. The Miller needed a new owner. A telephone call from the Hon. Dorothy Paget, whom Briscoe had met socially in London, solved Briscoe's problem. Asked if he knew of any good hurdlers or chasers for sale, Briscoe replied that he could offer her 'the best steeplechase horse in the world, and also the best hurdle racer in the country'. It was not an idle boast. The hurdler was the four-year-old Insurance, who won the Champion Hurdle in the following two years, while the steeplechaser was to win a record five Cheltenham Gold Cups. Miss Paget paid £10,000 for the pair.

Golden Miller (Gerry Wilson up), a record five-times winner of the Gold Cup — and the most controversial loser of the Grand National.

The Miller's first Gold Cup was in 1932. After only four steeplechases, three of which he had won, he was third favourite at 13-2 behind Grakle, the 1931 Grand National winner, and Kingsford. Grakle unseated his rider, and Kingsford fell, leaving Golden Miller, ridden by Ted Leader, to win by four lengths.

The Miller won his first five races of the 1932-33 season, including his second Gold Cup. Now came his supreme test — his first Grand National at the age of six. It should be recalled that in this era the Gold Cup was merely a stepping-stone to Liverpool. The Gold Cup was worth £670 to the winner, the Grand National £7345. Carrying 12st 2lb and ridden by Leader, The Miller jumped hesitantly at first and on the second circuit began jumping to his right. At Bechers he ploughed through the fence, leaving as large a hole as was ever seen. Remarkably, Leader rushed him back towards the front-runners, jumping the Canal Turn on the inside, but The Miller hit the fence and failed to turn. It was the first and only fall — albeit only partial — of his life. Leader returned full of depression. 'He'll never make an Aintree horse,' he reported.

It was now that Gerry Wilson came into the story. As Ted Leader was starting to train, and his other jockey Billy Stott was injured in a car crash, Gerry Wilson was retained to ride The Miller in all his races. The 1934 Gold Cup was won easily by six lengths, and despite the forebodings of Ted Leader, The Miller was again directed to Aintree. As in 1933, he was set to carry 12st 2lb. Golden Miller was on edge on arrival at Aintree, seeming to remember his unhappy experience twelve months earlier. But this time, with his tendency to jump right ironed out by the supreme horseman Wilson, his only mistakes were at Bechers on each circuit. At the last fence, The Miller jumped past Delaneige and stormed home by five lengths in a new record time of 9 minutes 20.4 seconds — the first horse to complete the Gold Cup/National double.

Golden Miller's fourth Gold Cup was one of the greatest races ever seen. Opposed at the last minute by Thomond II, a small but hugely courageous chaser, owned by Mr Jock Whitney, Golden Miller found himself in a ding-dong, neck-and-neck battle over the last three fences. It was only 100 yards from the finish that The Miller mastered his rival, and won by three parts of a length. The time for the race — 6 minutes 30 seconds — beat the existing record established by Easter Hero by twenty-seven seconds. Afterwards Thomond's jockey, Billy Speck, said to Gerry Wilson over a quiet drink: 'Well done mate! Well here's one thing — when we are old and grey, sitting back and enjoying a drink, we can tell them how we did ride at least one great horse race, one day in our lives'. Billy Speck was never able to do that. A month later, at the Cheltenham April Meeting, he broke his back in a fall in a selling race, and died six days later.

There were just fifteen days from Cheltenham to the Grand National, and what proved to be the most sensational race in Golden Miller's career. By now, The Miller was a national hero, and even with 12st 7lb, the staggering weight of public money forced him to favouritism at 2-1 — the shortest price in the history of the race. Bookmakers had collossal liabilities, and a week before the race Basil Briscoe received a visit from a leading lawyer who warned him that a conspiracy was afoot to prevent The Miller from winning. What happened in the race has been argued over for fifty years.

Gerry Wilson had been suffering from a damaged shoulder for several weeks, and could only ride with pain-killing injections. On the eve of the race he failed to appear on the course to ride The Miller at work. Gossip from Newmarket suggested that The Miller had been subjected to incredibly severe gallops by Briscoe, despite his hard race in the Gold Cup. 'The Ring' was convinced that Golden Miller would not win: there was too much at stake — someone would have 'dealt' with it. Above all, the going was firm. The Miller had always preferred give underfoot. Unlike in the previous year, Gerry Wilson elected to jump off on the inside, and The Miller appeared to jump well over the first nine fences. At the Ditch, two fences after Valentines, Golden Miller suddenly froze. He stuck his toes in, almost stopped, somehow jumped the fence to the left, shooting his rider into the air, landing crooked, and losing Gerry Wilson over his left shoulder. The aftermath was pandemonium. Miss Paget accused Briscoe of overtraining the horse. Briscoe accused

Wilson (not to his face) of 'jumping off'. Wilson stated the horse was lame. The awful consequence was that, against Wilson's advice, the trainer insisted on running the horse the following day in the Champion Chase. Golden Miller crashed into the first fence, screwed, shuddered and unseated Gerry Wilson for the second day running.

Many years afterwards, in his public house, The Marquis of Granby near Newbury, Gerry Wilson gave me his version of the Grand National incident. 'I'm convinced,' he told me, 'that The Miller was frightened by what seemed like a mirror glinting in his face. As he came to the fence something startled him — I was conscious of it myself. He seemed to freeze, and he never forgot that experience whenever he came to that fence.' The 'mirror' was in fact a flare put down by a newsreel company to prevent a pirate camera crew from operating on the far side of the course. A flash of sunlight could well have 'blinded' a horse or jockey.

Although Golden Miller won a fifth Gold Cup in 1936, his career was now spasmodic. Basil Briscoe asked Miss Paget to remove her horse from his yard within a week of the 1935 National, as she continued to blame him for the entire episode. Gerry Wilson was sacked after The Miller had swerved and run out in a race at Newbury in February, 1936.

Golden Miller ran twice more in the Grand National. In 1936, ridden by Evan Williams and 5-1 favourite, he was brought down at the first fence, was remounted, and refused at the same eleventh fence. In 1937, now ridden by Danny Morgan and 8-1 favourite, he refused again... at the eleventh fence. His last race was on February 23rd, 1939. He retired the winner of twenty-eight races from fifty-two starts.

Many years later, chatting to Sir Fancis Cassel, Miss Paget's secretary and confidant for many years, the subject of a comparison with Arkle arose. 'Ah, but you must remember that Golden Miller was asked to do remarkable things,' he said. 'If Miss Paget was in trouble [betting], The Miller was the horse she looked to to get her out. So he was never treated like a good horse.' Miss Paget would think nothing of bets of £20,000 — the equivalent of almost £200,000 today.

Golden Miller lived to the age of thirty in contented retirement. Gerry Wilson died in 1969. 'A straighter man never drew breath,' recalls his contemporary Bruce Hobbs. 'He was my hero.' The Miller, moreover, was the hero of a generation.

BIG RACES WON	
Gold Cup (five times)	1932-36
Grand National	1934

HATTON'S GRACE

THE EXTRAORDINARY ACHIEVEMENTS of Hatton's Grace in the autumn of his career, were a remarkable testimony to the genius of his trainer, the thirty-one-year-old Vincent O'Brien. In November 1947, at the age of seven, Hatton's Grace was down-the-course carrying 10st 11lb in a £222 handicap hurdle at Naas. Within eighteen months, at the age of nine, and now trained by Vincent O'Brien, he was winning the first of his three Champion Hurdles.

Hatton's Grace was bred at the Victor Stud in Co. Tipperary, and initially changed hands for eighteen guineas. As a six-year-old he came to be trained by Barney Nugent, and was owned by Mrs Moya Keogh, whose husband Harry was a fearless gambler. It is clear from Hatton's Grace's record during the 1947-48 season that he was a 'gambling' horse. After his defeat at Naas at 100-8, he was a well-backed favourite and comfortable winner at Leopardstown in his next race. Furthermore, he caried a 10lb penalty to success at Naas the following week.

Hatton's Grace came to Vincent O'Brien in the summer of 1948. A commission agent called Nat McNabb was betting for both Keogh and O'Brien at the time, and knowing the success that O'Brien was

Foaled 1940
Trained in Ireland

Hatton's Grace (near side) on the way to his third win in the Champion Hurdle. The last-flight photo is almost identical to the previous year's with National Spirit (Dennis Dillon) about to fall.

enjoying persuaded Keogh to move his horses to O'Brien's stable. Hatton's Grace did not excite O'Brien's staff on his arrival. He was a small, rather mean-looking, light bay with a weak neck, and little or no presence. It was easy to understand why he had changed hands for eighteen guineas. His first two runs over hurdles for O'Brien were clearly 'educational'. In the second of them, at Naas in January, he was unplaced in a £202 handicap hurdle, starting at 20-1. In his third run, in a similar race at Naas the following month, he started 7-4 favourite and won comfortably. It is staggering what the Irish stewards were prepared to overlook at the time!

The following month — on his next outing — he won the Champion Hurdle at 100-7, beating the 5-4 favourite and previous dual-winner, National Spirit. But nothing was impossible for O'Brien in this period and now Vincent decided to train Hatton's Grace for the Irish Lincolnshire Handicap on the flat, in the first week of April. Incredibly, he won easily.

In the autumn O'Brien planned a massive coup in the Irish Cesarewitch. The stable ran Hatton's Grace, ridden by Martin Molony and Knock Hard, a previous winner of the Irish Lincoln, and later to win a Cheltenham Gold Cup, ridden by Herbert Holmes. Both were owned by Harry Keogh. After early money for Hatton's Grace, Knock Hard was backed sensationally from 10-1 to even money, while Hatton's Grace drifted back from 3-1 to 8-1. Unluckily for the stable, Holmes disobeyed his riding orders on Knock Hard, and Molony had no option but to go on and beat him.

The two horses had a re-match over hurdles at Leopardstown on December 27th. This time Hatton's Grace, conceding a stone, was favourite at 3-1 on, with Knock Hard 7-1. In a desperate finish, Hatton's Grace got up to beat Knock Hard by a head. The following March he won his second Champion Hurdle, this time favourite at 5-2. National Spirit led till the last flight, but overjumped leaving Hatton's Grace to win gamely by a length and a half.

In 1951, Hatton's Grace was eleven years old. No horse had won three Champion Hurdles, nor had any won the 'Champion' at his age. At the last flight the picture was almost identical to the previous year's. National Spirit was in front narrowly, but blundered badly and fell. Hatton's Grace battled up the hill to great Irish cheers.

Remarkably, the little horse finished his career by running in four races over fences, the last of which he won. After that achievement he was retired, to live out his days at Ballydoyle.

ABOVE OPPOSITE: *Ribot and groom — Susan Crawford's classic final tribute*

BELOW OPPOSITE: *Arkle — the greatest*

BIG RACES WON	
Champion Hurdle (three times)	1949-51
Irish Lincoln	1949
Irish Cesarewitch (twice)	1949-50

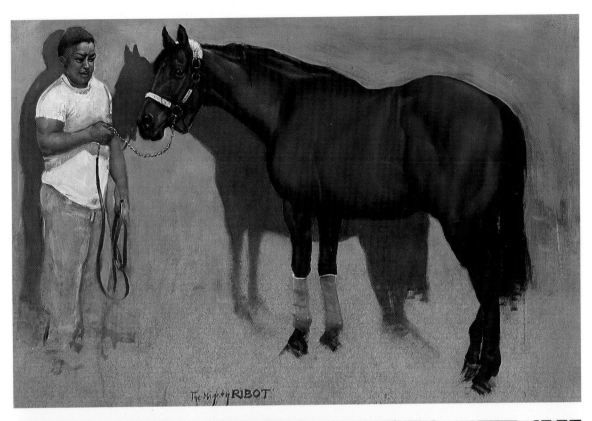

The Mighty RIBOT

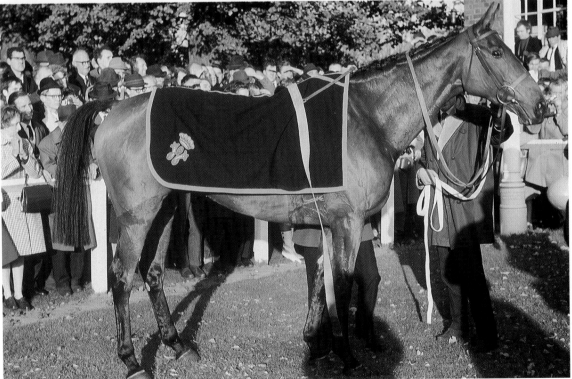

ABOVE: *Brigadier Gerard —
unbeaten in his first fifteen
races*

ABOVE OPPOSITE: *St Simon —
the stallion who became a
legend*

BELOW OPPOSITE: *Carbine —
an Australian legend*

ABOVE: *Crisp — mightier even than Bechers Brook*

OPPOSITE: *Mill House — early morning at Lambourn*

OVERLEAF: *Monksfield (left) and Night Nurse — dead level at the last flight ... and at the line*

JAY TRUMP

THE TRIUMPH OF Jay Trump in the 1965 Grand National was one of the great stories of the Turf. It is a tale of ambition, dedication, and single-minded determination. Unlike so many tales of the Turf, it is a fairy story with a happy ending.

The story began when Crompton ('Tommy') Smith, an American amateur rider, was asked by a friend of his mother's to find her a timber horse. The owner was Mrs Mary Cunningham Stephenson. Until now her stable had been confined to hunters and polo ponies. Now, after a visit to the Maryland Hunt Cup, she was determined to be involved in steeplechasing. Tommy Smith decided to buy a cheap gelding off the flat. He moved into a motel at Charles Town, West Virginia, and spent the mornings leaning on the rail at the local racetrack. Tommy looked at horse after horse, and was astonished to find so many semi-cripples in one barn. Finally, he saw a notice on the bulletin board: 'For Sale ... Jay Trump ...' By now it was almost his last resort, and the track secretary was far from encouraging. 'Couldn't get out of his way on the dirt ... and a rogue. Last year he ran into a light post and nearly killed a boy. You can't get a jockey to ride him.' Nonetheless, Tommy went to see the horse — and it was *almost* love at first sight.

It took Tommy several days to take the plunge. The big colt's appalling accident as a two-year-old, when he had jumped the rails and crashed into the metal light post, had left a hideous scar from the top of his right fore-arm to his knee. He was 16.2hh, but plain, lanky, with hip bones prominent and his ribs showing. Finally, Tommy bought him for $2000 cash — and a legend was about to unfold.

Under Tommy's care, Jay Trump thrived. He was gelded and hunted in Maryland as a three-year-old. His first race was a Ladies' Point-to-Point, in March 1962. There were two runners — and Jay Trump was second, beaten by a distance. His rider, a family friend, Patty Boyce, reported: 'He'll never amount to anything'. It did not take long to prove her wrong. Over the next two months, ridden by Tommy Smith, he won four races in a row.

The following spring he was prepared for his first Maryland Hunt Cup. On a memorable day, Jay Trump's jumping was breathtaking, and he won with ease in a new record time. Already the Grand National was at the back of Tommy Smith's mind, but Mary Stephenson insisted they wait a further year. It was a triumphant season. Jay Trump and Tommy won the Maryland 'Big Three' — the My Lady's Manor, the Maryland Grand National, and the Hunt Cup. Now he was ready for Aintree...

Jay Trump and Tommy Smith arrived at Fred Winter's stables

Foaled 1957
Trained in USA and England

OPPOSITE: *Red Rum soars over Bechers on the way to his second Grand National*

209

The moment that made it all worthwhile, Jay Trump (Tommy Smith) beats Freddie (Pat McCarron) in one of the great Grand Nationals.

at Lambourn, Berkshire, on July 16th, 1964. Winter had been a special hero of Tommy's ever since he saw a recording of his incredible win on Mandarin in the Grand Steeple-Chase at Auteuil. Now he was in his first season's training and Tommy was to be his pupil. Not a single detail was overlooked by Smith, either before his arrival (shortly after his honeymoon), or in the following eight months leading to Aintree. There was however a period of adjustment. On his first morning, Tommy Smith arrived from the village pub, wearing worn corduroys, old cowboy boots, and a felt sombrero. 'Mr Smith,' Winter greeted him, 'it is now 8.05. We always start at eight o'clock.'

Over the months Tommy, with his new wife Frances, settled into a routine of riding in the morning, and sleeping, or sight-seeing, or antique hunting in the afternoon. Jay Trump's programme began at Sandown in October. Because of firm ground there were only three runners and Jay Trump looked big and well, but somehow one felt that the big timber horse would need the race, or the experience, or both. In the event he won with considerable ease, having jumped superbly. He was Fred Winter's first runner — and first winner. More important, he was now qualified for the National.

Jay Trump's programme continued smoothly, and in February

the American horse became ante-post favourite for the National at
14-1. For his part, Tommy was running mile after mile, bicycling
and watching films of past Grand Nationals. Bryan Marshall
coached him in riding a finish.

Now a new drama erupted. Every yard in Lambourn was struck
down by a coughing virus. Within days, all but two of Winter's
horses had gone down. The two — Jay Trump and Solbina — were
isolated. Jay Trump ran at Worcester the following week. On the
morning of his race, Solbina coughed. Jay Trump did not cough,
but ran like a 'dead' horse. Suddenly, just a fortnight away from
the race, the dream seemed shattered. Jay Trump remained in
isolation, and no one but Tommy was allowed near him. Tommy
beame tense, lost weight, and couldn't sleep. Each morning he
prayed against hearing the one sound that he dreaded most. Jay
Trump drifted to 25-1.

The race for the 1965 Grand National was one of the greatest
in its 125-year history. Tommy Smith took the Fred Winter route
on the inside, where the drops are steepest on the landing side. Jay
Trump jumped superbly. Tommy was elated. At the thirteenth fence,
the little northern horse Phebu was brought down by a loose horse.
Jay Trump landed almost directly on jockey Jimmy Morrissey.
Tommy felt sick, but Jay Trump recovered. By second Bechers he
was perfectly placed. At the Canal Turn he made a brilliant diagonal
jump on the inner, and made several lengths. At the twenty-sixth
fence Rondetto fell in his path. In mid-air Jay Trump made a
spectacular flying change of direction, and missed Rondetto's
crumpled body and tangled legs by inches. Jay Trump crashed
through the last and there followed 494 yards of pure drama.
Between Jay Trump, Tommy and their dream lay the formidable
shape of the favourite, Freddie, ridden by the professional Pat
McCarron. The great race swayed in one direction, and then
another. Half way up the run-in, Tommy Smith switched his whip
to his right hand. It was almost fatal. Ever since his pitiful days
on the Flat, Jay Trump hated to be hit on the right flank. By instinct
Tommy put down the whip. Jay Trump gathered himself, and thrust
forward with a final surge. Freddie fought back and Pat McCarron
rode like a demon. But the American's will to win was irresistible.
At the post, Jay Trump had won by three parts of a length. It was
as fine an achievement by man and horse as the great race has ever
seen.

BIG RACES WON	
Grand National	1965
Maryland Hunt Cup	1963-64
Maryland Grand National	1964

JERRY M

Foaled 1903
Trained in England

JERRY M WAS A real, old-fashioned, Aintree horse, big and strong with a long back and massive, powerful quarters. Bred in Co. Limerick, he was bought as a young horse by Mr Joe Widger, who had won the Grand National in 1894 with Wild Man of Borneo. Widger named him after Jerry Mulcair, a local horse-breeder.

Jerry M won four races in his first season, and attracted considerable attention from a number of English trainers. However, each time a deal became imminent, Jerry M was 'spun' for his wind. No one admired him more than the Findon trainer Robert Gore, who was looking for a likely National horse for his patron Mr Charles Assheton-Smith, one of the richest men in England at the time. Formerly known as Duff, the quarry owner had won the National with Cloister in 1893. Now, in expectation of a baronetcy, he had changed his name by Royal Licence in 1905 to that of his maternal grandmother.

Assheton-Smith sent his vet *twice* to Ireland to inspect Jerry M. After his second visit the vet was quite insistent that he 'made a noise'. Bob Gore was determined to have him, and bearded his owner at Claridges.

'If you don't have this horse you will not have another chance,' he stated. 'He will be sold within two hours.'

'Who will buy him?' his owner enquired.

'Mr Paul Nelke,' replied Gore. (This was another owner in his stable.)

'He won't have him, he's a Jew,' declared Assheton-Smith. 'I'll tell you what I'll do. I'll toss you for him.'

Bob Gore won the toss, and Assheton-Smith reluctantly paid £1200 for what was to be one of the finest steeplechasers of the first half of the twentieth century.

Gore's judgement was quickly vindicated in his first season in England. In March 1908 he won the New Century Chase at Hurst Park and twelve days later in the Stanley Chase at Liverpool was the only runner to complete the course without mishap. In November 1908 he returned to Liverpool for the Becher Chase, which he won, but between December and April he was missing from the racecourse. Presumably, this absence heralded the start of his training problems.

That summer he travelled to France for the Grand Steeple-Chase de Paris where, after a two-hour delay caused by a stable lads' strike and a riot, Jerry M jumped brilliantly to lead for most of the four-and-a-quarter miles. In the end he was a brave second to the favourite St Caradec.

The 1909-10 season began with a win at Liverpool in the

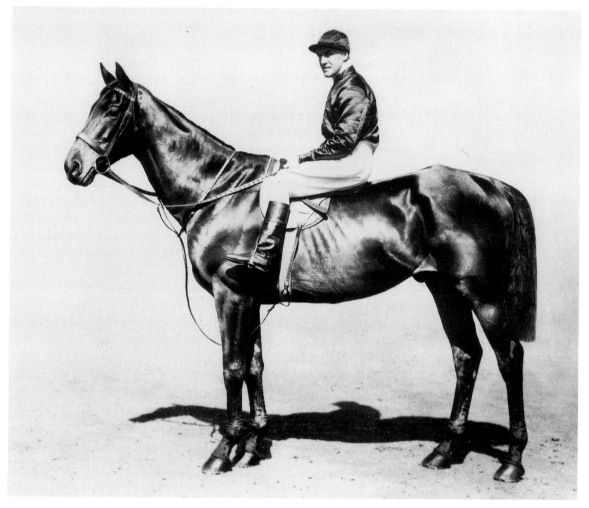

Valentine Chase, after which he started at 20-1 on in a two-horse race at Newbury, only to fall. Now it was time for his first attempt at the National. Carrying 12st 7lb as a seven-year-old, he made a valiant bid to make most of the running, but was collared between the last two fences by Jenkinstown, who was receiving 30lb.

Jerry M was now prepared for a second visit to Paris for the Grand Steeple-Chase. The prize of £6360 made it by far the richest jumping race in the world. This time there was no St Caradec (who was lame) and, starting favourite at 5-2, Jerry M won by three lengths. In the new spirit of the *entente cordiale,* the big Sussex-trained gelding returned to a magnificent reception from the Parisians.

After this, Jerry M did not race for eighteen months. His owner claimed that he withdrew him from the Grand National as a protest against the savage handicapping of Mr Topham, who once again allotted him 12st 7lb. However, since he ran with 12st 7lb in 1910 and 1912, it seems more likely that this was a smoke-screen to disguise lameness, or some other physical disability.

Jerry M ridden by Ernie Piggott, grandfather of Lester. His performance in the 1912 Grand National was one of the greatest ever.

In 1912 the Grand National was almost cancelled because of the coal strike. Rail services were restricted, and Jerry M's journey from Findon entailed travelling to London, spending the night at Knightsbridge Barracks, walking across Hyde Park amongst the riders on Rotten Row, and taking the train from Marylebone to Liverpool.

He had a new jockey in Ernie Piggott, having previously been partnered since November 1908 by Ernie Driscoll. The County Stand at Aintree was unusually empty, but the Silver Ring and course enclosures were chock-a-bloc with miners! Jerry M was joint-favourite at 4-1 despite having run just once in the past twenty-one months. Jerry M jumped superbly. At the Canal Turn he encountered an unusual hazard in the form of a loose horse straddled across the fence. According to Piggott, Jerry M jumped straight over him. Led over the last by Bloodstone, the top weight cruised past him to win on the bridle by six lengths.

It was one of the finest National-winning performances ever — and it was Jerry M's swan-song. He injured some muscles in his back, and during his further enforced lay-off, his wind degenerated. His success was a collossal tribute to Bob Gore, who claimed that Jerry M had the speed to win over six furlongs on the flat. Such a claim has the ring of another great Master of Findon fifty years later!

BIG RACES WON	
Grand National	1912
Grand Steeple-Chase de Paris	1910
Prix des Drays	1909
New Century Chase	1908
Stanley Chase	1908
Becher Chase	1908
Valentine Chase	1909

L'ESCARGOT

WHEN L'ESCARGOT WON the 1975 Grand National, he achieved the ultimate fulfilment of one man's sporting dream. Raymond Guest, an old-fashioned, feudal American, born and reared in the southern State of Virginia, is a man with a great sporting heritage. Like so many traditional Virginians, Guest is a dyed-in-the-wool anglophile.

Foaled 1963
Trained in Ireland

OVERLEAF: *'If I don't win this year, I'll eat my hat!' L'Escargot finally makes it in the Grand National — at the fourth attempt.*

His great ambitions were to win the Derby and the Grand National.

In 1962 he won the Derby with Larkspur, and six years later achieved an even more memorable success with Sir Ivor. The Grand National proved more elusive. Guest had become captivated by the race in 1928 when Billy Barton came from American and was one of only two survivors from a field of forty-two, at the last fence, only to be knocked over by a loose horse.

Guest's first serious assault on the National was with a mare called Flying Wild in 1964. She fell at the first fence. After several other attempts — often with two runners — Guest decided to take the advice of a friend and 'go for it' with his best horse. So L'Escargot, the Gold Cup winner of 1970 and 1971, was programmed for the Grand National. It took four years — but in 1975 the dream came true.

L'Escargot was bought for Raymond Guest as a three-year-old at Ballsbridge by Tom Cooper of the British Bloodstock Agency (Ireland). His first appearance on a racecourse was as a four-year-old in a 'bumpers' (amateur riders) race at Navan. Ridden by Ben Hanbury, and starting at 100-7, he won easily, landing a huge starting-price coup in Northern Ireland. Arthur Moore, his trainer's son, adds: 'His only weakness was donkeys. He had a phobia about them!' Hanbury recalls: 'I broke him myself and he was always brilliant. He had a wonderful temperament, and did everything right. From the first time he worked you knew he was going to be something special.'

The following season he won his division of the Gloucestershire Hurdle on only his second run over hurdles. Raymond Guest was always inspired by a challenge, and at the end of his first season's steeplechasing, L'Escargot was sent to America where he won the Meadowbrook Chase. He returned to America in October to run third in the Temple Gwathmey Chase at Belmont Park.

In January 1970, back in Europe, he won the first running of the W.D. & H.O. Wills Premier Chase at Haydock. Within eleven months of jumping his first fence in public, L'Escargot was now aimed at the Gold Cup. Starting at 33-1, he battled bravely up the Cheltenham hill to beat French Tan by a length and a half. The following season, in ground that was barely raceable, he won his second Gold Cup, for what was his only success of the season. In 1972, after finishing fourth in the Gold Cup, he made his first attempt at the National. Top weight, and favourite at 17-2, he was knocked over at the third fence.

OPPOSITE: *L'Escargot's Grand National dinner — how many completed the course? Amongst the guests — Arthur and Mary Moore, and jockey Tommy Carberry. Was he the 'Plaisir des Dames ...'?*

The pattern was the same in 1973 ... fourth again in the Gold Cup, followed by a distant third to Red Rum and Crisp at Aintree. In 1974 he crept closer. Now wearing blinkers he finished second to Red Rum beaten seven lengths. And so to 1975. This time he came to Aintree, at the age of twelve, having won one race in the

Grand National Night

Gala Dinner Dance

Menu

~

Cocktail de Crevette Rose de Mai
Natives de l'Ocean Sur Leur Lit de Glace
Saumon d'Ecosse Fumé au Citron

~

Consommé Yvette au Paillettes Parmesan
Crème de Champignons

~

Délice de Sole Becher's Brook

~

Filet de Bœuf Melling Road
Suprême de Volaille Aintree

Boutons de Bruxelles Limousine
Courgette Provençale
Pommes Sefton

~

Vacherin Valentine
Plaisir des Dames

~

Café

~

ADELPHI HOTEL :: LIVERPOOL

Saturday 5th April, 1975

past four seasons. As a result he had dropped to 11st 3lb in the handicap. Not even Red Rum could concede him 11lb, and L'Escargot won easily by fifteen lengths, becoming the first horse since Golden Miller to win the Gold Cup and the National.

Raymond Guest was elated by his success, and retired L'Escargot on the spot. As a token of his appreciation he gave the old horse to Dan and Joan Moore who had trained and campaigned him so successfully. Unhappily, the matter ended in misunderstanding. So well was L'Escargot in the autumn that the Moores decided to run him in the Kerry National where he was beaten a head. On hearing the news, Guest immediately sent for the horse and shipped him to Virginia, where he lived in contented retirement until his death in November 1985.

BIG RACES WON	
Gold Cup	1970-71
Grand National	1975
W.D. & H.O. Wills Premier Chase	1970
Meadowbrook Chase	1969
Gloucestershire Hurdle	1968

MANDARIN

THE BRILLIANT RIDING of Fred Winter converted the gutsy little French-bred Mandarin from a 'nearly' horse to a racing legend. Mandarin was brave... Winter was brilliant. Their combined talents on a June day at Auteuil wrote a page of steeplechasing history.

Mandarin was a top-class and hugely popular horse over six seasons. But as a young horse he was such a moderate jumper of hurdles that Fulke Walwyn almost sent him back to France, where he had been bred by his owner Mme Peggy Hennessy. Although Dave Dick was Fulke Walwyn's stable jockey, and Fred Winter had won on Mandarin over hurdles, it was Michael Scudamore who transformed the erratic young jumper from an unenviable ride over hurdles to a more than adequate jumper of fences.

Scudamore, a fine and fearless nagsman, ironed out Mandarin's bad habits and taught him to jump off his hocks. By the end of his first season he had won the Broadway Novices Chase with Scudamore up, and been beaten in a photo, ridden by lightweight Gerry Madden, in the newly devised Whitbread Gold Cup. Gerry Madden, the twenty-six-year-old Irishman, now became Mandarin's regular rider, and in the autumn of 1957 they won the Hennessy Gold Cup and King George VI Chase.

Over the next two seasons, Mandarin experienced bad luck and injury. He completed a hat-trick of 'seconds' in the Whitbread Gold Cup — most memorably in 1959 when Done Up, ridden by the hurdles jockey Harry Sprague, beat him by a short head. In December 1958 he fractured a fibula bone in his hind leg, while a year later, after winning his second 'King George', he developed tendon trouble. The following season was his most disappointing. From seven outings, he won a £491 at Sandown when his chief rival fell at the last. It was also the last season in which Madden rode him.

It was in 1961 that Fred Winter became stable jockey to Fulke Walwyn, and took over on the ten-year-old 'has-been'. Fred steered the little horse to a confidence-boosting win at Ludlow, but then, ironically, broke his collar bone so that Willie Robinson took the ride in the Hennessy Gold Cup. Mandarin won a magnificent, emotional race to keep the cognac in the family for the second time, and Fred wondered if he had lost the ride.

The King George VI Chase was snowed off, and Mandarin's next big target was the race that had always eluded him — the Cheltenham Gold Cup. Fred was back on board, and Mandarin was a well-backed third favourite behind Pas Seul (ridden by Dave Dick) and Fortria (Pat Taaffe). It was a magnificent triumph by horse and rider. Climbing the hill with a mile to race, Mandarin was off the bit and getting nowhere. At the top of the hill Winter gave him

Foaled 1951
Trained in England

Mandarin and Gerry Madden were a formidable team in the autumn of 1957, winning the Hennessy Gold Cup and King George VI Chase.

a couple of smacks and he started running. Fred drove his willing partner up Fortria's inner at the second last, and drew level at the elbow. On the run-in, it was Winter against Taaffe... the little battler against the Irish former two-miler. Mandarin simply would not be beaten and to cheers and tears, won the great race by a length.

Three months later, on June 17th, came the famous journey to France for the Grand Steeple-Chase de Paris — at almost £20,000, worth three times the value of the Gold Cup. Fred Winter, who had to ride Beaver II at 9st 11lb later in the day at Auteuil, was drained and exhausted. Beset by a stomach upset the previous evening, he had spent an almost sleepless night after a week of wasting.

The Paris course is varied and confusing, with many obstacles that Mandarin had never experienced before. Mandarin jumped the first two well, but landing over the third his rubber bit snapped, leaving Fred with no brakes or steering — and three-and-a-half miles to cover! Thanks to a combination of good luck, and willing assistance from the French jockeys, notably Jean Daumas, Fred managed to guide Mandarin round the tortuous course, often just by pressure with his knee and shifting his weight. The crisis came at the fourth last when, having raced diagonally, the horses take a sharp right-hand turn, and steer a middle course. Mandarin threatened to turn too far to the right and Fred desperately threw all his weight to the left. Mandarin straightened but became unbalanced and broke down. Nonetheless, Fred was able to drive the little hero into the lead in the home straight. Mandarin jumped the last two in front, but now the effort and his injured leg took their toll. Mandarin's stride shortened, and the French horse Lumino started to close. Fred drove with body, legs and every ounce of energy his exhausted and weakened body could dredge. The two horses flashed past the post together. Mandarin had won by a head! He had pulled up within a few strides. He was lame and exhausted, but he had won one of the greatest races in steeplechasing history.

Mandarin was always a delicate horse and his success was a notable tribute to the skill of his trainer Fulke Walwyn. Never a good 'doer', his diet was supplemented by a daily bottle of Mackeson stout. After his third defeat in the Whitbread Gold Cup, Colonel Bill Whitbread ordered him two bottles of Mackeson for life, to be delivered from his 'local' in Lambourn.

BIG RACES WON	
Gold Cup	1962
Grand Steeple-Chase de Paris	1962
King George VI Chase	1957,1959
Hennessy Gold Cup	1957,1961
Broadway Novices' Chase	1957

MANIFESTO

Foaled 1888
Trained in England

UNTIL THE ARRIVAL of Red Rum, Manifesto was widely regarded as the greatest Grand National horse of all time. Many would still claim that the title was his due. At a time when the Aintree fences were substantially more upright and formidable than today, his record reads won two, third three times and fourth once, from eight starts. Red Rum's record was three wins and two seconds from five attempts.

Manifesto was a big, plain, old-fashioned bay horse by Man O'War, a stallion who — like his American counterpart thirty years later — was, at the least, mercurial. In fact he was savage and dangerous. He was the resident stallion at Mr Harry Dyas's stud near Navan, Co. Meath. Dyas was a shrewd owner-breeder-dealer in the Irish tradition. Any horse was for sale, preferably after it had landed a substantial 'touch' for the stable.

Manifesto was lightly-raced as a young horse. Around Christmas he was ferried with a string of horses to the north of England for a spring campaign, which in 1894 yielded an unexpected success in the valuable Lancashire Chase at Manchester. His first National attempt was as a seven-year-old in 1895. Carrying 11st 3lb he led for much of the way, until tiring and finishing fourth to his compatriot Wild Man of Borneo.

In 1896 he fell at the first fence. By now Harry Dyas decided the time had come for Manifesto to be sold, and with this in mind he stabled him with Willie Macauliffe at East Everleigh, near Marlborough, on the grounds that it was easier for a rich English owner, or agent, to view a horse at Marlborough than at Co. Meath.

Dyas made two entries for the 1897 National — Manifesto and Gentle Ida — and offered them as a package at £5000. Luckily for him there was no buyer. Gentle Ida was withdrawn on the eve of the race, and Manifesto won easily by twenty lengths. Two days earlier, Winkfield's Pride, also bred in Co. Meath, had won the Lincoln and the bookmakers experienced one of the worst days in betting history. In February 1898, Harry Dyas finally sold Manifesto. The buyer was Mr Joseph Bulteel, a wealthy stockbroker. The price — £4000.

Now trained by Willie Moore at Weyhill, Manifesto was a week away from the National when disaster struck. Somehow he escaped from his box, jumped the gate of the stable yard, fell and damaged a fetlock joint. His wretched stable lad vanished from the yard and was traced only a month later in another stable working under an assumed name.

Manifesto's second National, in 1899, was an epic. Dyas had also sold Gentle Ida, but still trained her and stated publicly that

Manifesto, who was to carry 12st 7lb, could not possibly concede her a stone. Gentle Ida started favourite, but fell at Valentines. Manifesto took the lead before the second last and to a crescendo of cheering, galloped home to win by five lengths. His jockey, George Williamson, revealed that he had almost fallen at the Canal Turn. After heavy frost, straw was positioned on the landing side and had not been removed. Manifesto landed on it, slipped, and was on the floor. 'I saw one of his legs sticking in the air... the toe of my boot was on the ground, and both irons were gone. I left everything to Manifesto...'

The following year at the age of twelve, Manifesto was saddled with the crippling weight of 12st 13lb (one winces to imagine Jenny Pitman's comments). The public's loyalties were fiercely divided between Manifesto and the Prince of Wales's runner Ambush II. It was one of the great Grand Nationals. Ambush II led over the last, but Manifesto, beautifully ridden by Williamson, came at him on the long run-in. The two horses battled neck and neck to cheering

Big, plain and old-fashioned, Manifesto became a Grand National legend.

the like of which had never been heard before. Finally, 100 yards from the finish, the huge weight and concession of 24lb took its toll on Manifesto, and Ambush II forged away. In the last strides Barsac, receiving 43lb, caught the exhausted Manifesto for third place. Strong men wept over Manifesto's supreme effort; William Allison wrote: 'There are some things about which it is almost sacrilege to write in black and white.'

Manifesto missed the National of 1901, but was to run a further three times. In 1902, at fourteen years, ridden by Ernie Piggott and carrying 12st 8lb, he was third to Shannon Lass (10st 1lb). The following year, under 12st 3lb he finished third to Drumcree, who was receiving a stone, and finally, in 1904, at the age of sixteen, he was last of six finishers behind the New Zealand horse Moifaa. At last it was all over. Nowadays, with the National under attack from the RSPCA, one can only be bemused how over-protective we have become to racehorses.

BIG RACES WON	
Grand National	1897, 1899
Lancashire Chase	1894
Irish Champion Chase	1892
Grand International Chase	1897

MILL HOUSE

IF MILL HOUSE had not been born in the same year as Arkle he would probably now be regarded as one of the three great steeplechasers of all time. Until March 7th, 1964, he seemed possibly the greatest ever. But his defeat by Arkle in that famous Gold Cup was a watershed from which his fortunes never revived.

Foaled 1957
Trained in England

Like Arkle, Mill House was bred in Ireland, by the Lawlors of Naas, Co. Kildare. He was named after Mrs Lawlor's private house, and was reared at the family's famous Osberstown House Hotel, near Naas.

Mill House was sent to old Tom Taaffe to be broken as a three-year-old. Ironically, the nagsman assigned to him was none other than Tom's son Pat who, as Arkle's jockey, was destined to destroy him. Pat schooled Mill House, took him hunting and eventually rode him in his first two races. In his third, Pat was unavailable and Dave Dick, visiting from England, took the mount. Mill House fell, but Dave was deeply impressed. Before long, Jack Doyle, the legendary bloodstock agent, was visiting Taaffe's stables at Rathcoole, with a prospective purchaser. The client was a Mr Bill Gollings, a wealthy advertising man, who trained with Syd Dale at Epsom. Mill House was in a field, muddy and with half of his tail missing, following the attentions of another horse. Mr Gollings was not impressed: 'You've brought me all the way over here to look at this thing?' he complained. 'What is it, anyway? A bloody great hunter?' Nonetheless, Mr Gollings was pursuaded to buy the horse for a rumoured £7500.

After a season with Syd Dale the owner transferred the horse to Fulke Walwyn, whose jockey was the likeable Irishman, Willie Robinson. Pat Taaffe wrote to his old friend: 'You will soon be on the best horse in Britain, and quite possibly the world!' For a while it seemed that Pat Taaffe would be right. The following March, as a six-year-old and after just five steeplechases — in the first of which (from Syd Dale's yard) he had suffered a desperate fall — Mill House won the Gold Cup by twelve lengths.

In November 1963, Mill House had his first meeting with Arkle in the Hennessy Gold Cup. Arkle was barely advanced from the novice stage, but had won all of his six chases. Mill House had twelve stone, Arkle 11st 9lb. The betting was 15-8 Mill House, 5-2 Arkle. Mill House won in brilliant style by eight lengths. Only Pat Taaffe and a few partisans believed that Arkle would have won but for a slip at the last Ditch. Mill House went on to win the King George VI Chase with ease (Arkle stayed in Ireland) and came to Cheltenham with a reputation as the greatest chaser since Golden Miller.

Willie Robinson on Mill House. 'You will soon be on the best horse in England,' wrote his friend Pat Taaffe.

The Gold Cup was not to be his, however. Arkle's victory at the end of the greatest steeplechase of a lifetime, was total and uncompromising. Mill House galloped and jumped to the limit of his ability, but Arkle strode past him with disdain. The course record was demolished by four seconds, and Mill House, his stable, his supporters, were shattered and speechless. Straws were clutched at. 'It didn't help that he had to make his own running...'

Arkle and Mill House met three more times. In the 1964 Hennessy Gold Cup, Arkle carried 12st 7lb and Mill House 12st 4lb. Arkle jumped past him at the twelfth fence and won by ten lengths. Mill House dropped out, dispirited, to finish fourth, beaten twenty-eight lengths. In the 1965 Gold Cup, Arkle now made all the running and won easing up by twenty lengths. Mill House was second.

Their last encounter was in the Gallagher Gold Cup at Sandown in November 1965. Now the weights were Arkle 12st 7lb, Mill House 11st 5lb. David Nicholson was aboard Mill House. After a circuit Arkle pulled his way into the lead, and pricked his ears with majesty as the immense crowd burst spontaneously into applause. It was a magical moment. But Mill House was jumping superbly. At the Railway fences he jumped his way to the front again, and led at the bottom turn by four lengths. A buzz went up from the crowd and David Nicholson recalls: 'I caught a glimpse of Arkle and thought: well old chap, we've got you properly on the stretch. The next moment he was alongside with Pat Taaffe sitting bolt upright... and then he just changed gear. It broke my fellow's heart — all the fight went out of him after that.' Arkle beat Mill House's course record by seventeen seconds that incredible day. Seven weeks later Arkle was to run his last race. But it was too late for Mill House; he was a broken horse. The following March he sustained leg trouble, and thereafter his career was in decline.

There was one last moment of glory at Sandown in April, 1967. Mill House won the Whitbread Gold Cup under a magnificent ride from David Nicholson, struggling past the post so tired that he stopped to a walk just yards further on. The emotion was overwhelming. As the 'Big Horse' stepped down into the Unsaddling Enclosure, the leaves of time fell away. As those who loved him fought back the tears, there were dreams of what might have been.

BIG RACES WON	
Gold Cup	1963
King George VI Chase	1963
Hennessy Gold Cup	1963
Whitbread Gold Cup	1967
Mandarin Handicap Chase	1963, 1965

MONKSFIELD

Foaled 1972
Trained in Ireland

MONKSFIELD WAS THE bravest horse that anyone could expect to see. His exceptional courage and will to win pulled the 1979 Champion Hurdle out of the fire. No matter how severe the driving he never flinched. Yet incredibly he was an entire horse and raced until the age of eight.

The background to the little horse's success is a typical Irish fairy story, marvellously told in Jonathan Powell's book *Monksfield*. He was bred by an astronomy expert called Peter Ryan, who lived in Fulham. On a visit to Dublin, he arranged to meet his brother Arthur, a farmer in Co. Tipperary, at Ballsbridge Sales. Intoxicated by the vibrant atmosphere of the sale ring, but totally ignorant of horses, he decided impulsively to buy a brood mare. The mare he chose was called Regina. Peter Ryan bought her for 1500 guineas. In 1972, at the brothers' third attempt, she was to breed Monksfield.

The undersized Gala Performance colt was bought as a two-year-old for 740 guineas by Des McDonagh, a former amateur rider with a stable of six horses in Co. Meath. That transacton was to change his life. Born and bred in the suburbs of Limerick, McDonagh drifted through various clerical jobs before being offered the post of head man for his father-in-law-to-be Cyril Bryce-Smith, a trainer at Moynalty, Co. Meath. In November 1972 he took out a licence to train.

Monksfield was now owned by a first-time owner in Dr Michael Mangan, a radiologist working in Newfoundland. It was decided to give Monksfield an 'educational' outing on the Flat in October as a two-year-old. Starting at 25-1, and ridden by the unfashionable Ken Coogan, Monksfield staggered everyone by winning by three parts of a length, hard held. Dr Mangan, in Newfoundland, had asked his mother-in-law to bet £10 for him on the Tote. His mother-in-law, on advice, did not place the bet. Monksfield paid 647-1.

Monksfield did not win again on the Flat at two or three years, but became a leading juvenile hurdler. He won his first two hurdle races, a handicap at Navan in March, and at Cheltenham finished second to Peterhof in the Daily Express Triumph Hurdle. The following season he made his first assault on the Champion Hurdle. Ridden by forty-four-year-old Tommy Kinane, and starting at 15-1, he finished a battling second to Night Nurse, ridden by Paddy Broderick, after a mistake at the last. Three weeks later the two horses met again over 2 miles 5½ furlongs at Liverpool. Now in receipt of 6lb and ridden by Dessie Hughes, 'Monkey' ran a dead heat with the Champion Hurdler after one of the most punishing, red-blooded finishes the author has ever seen.

In March 1978, the two heroes were back at Cheltenham. Sadly missing was Paddy Broderick, compelled to retire after a bad fall from the Champion at Kempton on Boxing Day. Also injured was Jonjo O'Neill, replaced by Frank Berry on Sea Pigeon. Tommy Kinane took on Night Nurse a long way from home, and had him beaten at the second last. At the last, Sea Pigeon loomed menacingly, but died in his rider's hands. To tears and emotional Irish cheers, Monksfield stormed up the hill for a famous win. Liverpool was easier this time, and, ridden again by Dessie Hughes (Tommy Kinane was injured), Monkey beat his old rival Night Nurse (Jonjo O'Neill) by two lengths.

The prelude to the 1979 Champion Hurdle was controversial. Tommy Kinane, now aged forty-six, was replaced on Monksfield by Dessie Hughes. Kinane was deeply unhappy and did not hide his feelings. It proved to be one of the finest races ever seen. Monksfield and Sea Pigeon came to the last flight stride for stride

Courage beyond the call ... Monksfield (farside) and Sea Pigeon jump the last hurdle stride for stride in the 1979 Champion Hurdle.

— but Sea Pigeon was cruising and Monkey received three cracks from Dessie Hughes's whip going into the hurdle. The jump conjured by the little horse was staggering. From cantering, Sea Pigeon was suddenly struggling. More and more Dessie Hughes asked, and each time the little horse dug deeper. Incredibly, 100 yards from the finish, he stuck his head in front and seized victory from defeat. It was the greatest display of raw courage ever seen at Cheltenham.

Monkey returned once more, the following year, in a bid to complete the rare Champion Hurdle hat-trick, but this time the cards were stacked against him. The distance of the race was shortened by 200 yards, and the ground on the first day was almost virgin. Now not even Monkey's bottomless courage was enough to repel his old rival Sea Pigeon.

Monksfield retired to stud at the Amgrove Stud, Mountmellick, Co. Laois, the winner of five races on the Flat, and fourteen races over hurdles. For his breeder, owner, trainer and jockeys, he was a once-in-a-lifetime experience.

BIG RACES WON	
Champion Hurdle (twice)	1978-79
Templegate Hurdle (three times)	1977-79
Welsh Champion Hurdle	1979
Irish Benson & Hedges Handicap Hurdle	1976
Huzzar Handicap Hurdle	1976

NIGHT NURSE

NIGHT NURSE and Paddy Broderick were a magical combination, intrinsic to the colourful kaleidoscope of National Hunt racing. Night Nurse, who cost 1300 guineas as a yearling, had a flat-race pedigree, but showed very little ability at two and three. In June, as a three-year-old, wearing blinkers, he struggled home in a 1 mile 1 furlong maiden race at Ripon.

From the time that he jumped his first hurdle, however, he was transformed. As a three-year-old, starting at Market Rasen in August, he won five out of seven races, making all the running in every one of his wins. The following season was sensational. His first big target was the Sweeps Hurdle, which he won by five lengths with the Champion Hurdler Comedy of Errors third. Thereafter, he won the English, Scottish and Welsh Champion Hurdles, once again making every yard on each occasion. At the end of the season he was unbeaten in eight races.

However, the following season Night Nurse met with two defeats before Christmas, which were followed by rumours that all was not well. He came to Cheltenham without having run a race since Boxing Day, and was the subject of wild fluctuations in the market, as many believed that the heavy ground would be against him. Paddy Broderick asserted memorably on television that he was fit to win — and *would* win — and his tough partner did not betray him. Broderick, now aged thirty-seven, enjoyed his finest hour to the full.

The dual champion's next race was in many ways the most memorable — and perhaps the turning-point of his career. Night Nurse was tough, courageous and unquestioning, but the punishment meted out to him and Monksfield in the Templegate Hurdle at Liverpool was not attractive to watch. Night Nurse had taken off a stride early at the third last, and landed on top of the hurdle. It was a desperate mistake, leaving the champion winded, shaken and unbalanced. Broderick drove him straight back into contention, and the two unbelievably brave horses jumped the last two flights head to head, and battled unflinchingly the length of the run-in. Fifty yards from home, Monksfield, under the severest pressure, looked the narrow winner, but right on the line Night Nurse battled back to share the spoils. It was magnificent — but horrific.

At the end of the 1976-77 season, Night Nurse had won eighteen of his twenty-two races over hurdles. But now his career — at least over hurdles — went into decline. The following season he won just one race at Doncaster from ten outings — and needed desperate driving from Jonjo O'Neill to do so. Sadly his old friend 'Brod' had been 'buried' when Night Nurse had fallen at the last flight at

Foaled 1971
Trained in England

Night Nurse and Paddy Broderick — one of jumping's great partnerships, powerfully aggressive at every hurdle.

Kempton on Boxing Day. It was a fall that ended the delightful — but unintelligible — Irishman's career. Nonetheless, Night Nurse started favourite for both the Champion Hurdle and Templegate Hurdle, but Monksfield beat him each time.

Now came the watershed in Night Nurse's career. Many felt that the bold, brave, front-runner was a hurdler through and through, and one that had become prone to make errors. It was suggested that he should retire. However Peter Easterby, his gifted, intuitive, Yorkshire trainer, believed that he could be taught to jump fences. Even more emphatic was 'Brod', who always claimed he would win the Gold Cup. So, at the age of seven, Night Nurse was launched on a steeplechasing career. It began disastrously when he and Jonjo O'Neill parted company at the fourth obstacle he jumped in public, at Market Rasen. A month later Jonjo Broke his arm at Kelso, and that fine rider Ian Watkinson, who started his career in the north with Tommy Robson at Penrith, took over on Night Nurse.

Apart from his memorable race with Silver Buck in the Embassy Premier Chase Final, when Watkinson tried too hard and was unquestionably guilty of excessive use of the whip, it was a hugely successful partnership. Their record was five wins from six races — and by the end of it Night Nurse was established as a top-class steeplechaser. The one horse he could never beat, however, was Silver Buck. In seven meetings, only in the 1981 Gold Cup, when he was second to Little Owl, did Night Nurse beat his great adversary.

At Haydock in November 1979, Jonjo, now back on Night Nurse, felt that he had the measure of Silver Buck going to the last fence in the Edward Hanmer Memorial Chase. But on the run-in, Jonjo felt him go lame and Silver Buck won by a length and a half. Night Nurse was rested for a year, and when he returned to the racecourse, Jonjo was out of action with a broken leg. Apart from his hugely courageous second in the Gold Cup, ridden with liberal use of the whip by Alan Brown, it was a disappointing season.

The following season, with Jonjo back on board, Night Nurse (now eleven) actually started favourite for the Gold Cup, after a magnificent and emotional win in the Mandarin Handicap Chase at Newbury. Jonjo described it later as the greatest thrill that he had ever experienced on a horse. But, in the Gold Cup, ridden on the inside amongst horses, the old horse did not take hold of his bit, and ran well below his form.

Night Nurse ran his last race in the 1982 King George VI Chase. Jonjo had been invited to ride Wayward Lad, the eventual winner, but out of loyalty and affection chose Night Nurse. Night Nurse was unplaced, but Jonjo was determined to share that day with the horse who, next to Arkle and Red Rum, was certainly the most popular jumper since the War. Like Monksfield, he never refused any reasonable demand. Perhaps sometimes he was too brave for his own good.

BIG RACES WON	
(National Hunt)	
Champion Hurdle	1976-77
Sweeps Hurdle	1976
Welsh Champion Hurdle	1976-77
Scottish Champion Hurdle	1976
Templegate Hurdle	1977
(Flat)	
Mandarin Handicap Chase	1982
Buchanan Whisky Gold Cup	1979
Sean Graham Trophy Chase	1979
London & Northern Group Future Champions	
Novices Chase	1979

PENDIL

Foaled 1965
Trained in England

IT IS OBSERVED earlier in this book that Flyingbolt was the best horse never to have won the Gold Cup. Pendil runs him a close second. He was a superb steeplechaser — perhaps the most accurate jumper of fences in the author's lifetime and with any reasonable luck would certainly have won the Gold Cup. At one stage he had won nineteen out of twenty-one steeplechases. The two failures were in the Gold Cup.

Pendil was trained by a permit-holder near Leeds as a three- and four-year-old, and was bought by Fred Winter at the Ascot Sales in June 1969. In his first season with Winter he looked an ordinary horse, whose aspirations were levelled no higher than Fontwell Park. In the Autumn of 1970, however, he showed considerable improvement, and won the Cheltenham Trial Hurdle on the disqualification of Dondieu, with Persian War third. He ended that season carrying 11st 11lb in the Schweppes Gold Trophy, but was unplaced and came back with a 'leg'.

Pendil's first steeplechase at Cheltenham ten months later will always remain vivid in the author's recollection. The race was recorded by BBC TV with the author as commentator. Never can I recall a novice jumping so well at the first attempt. Pendil was a natural. He won by fifteen lengths. 'That horse could win the Gold Cup one day,' I said to my producer. It was so nearly true.

Pendil went through his first season unbeaten, winning the Arkle Challenge Trophy at the festival meeting. He was a medium-sized, beautifully balanced horse who was every inch an athlete. He was the *modern* chaser — far removed from the Manifestos and Jerry Ms of the past. Richard Pitman, his regular jockey, recalls: 'The fitter he became, the more aggressive he was. When he started to goose-step like the German soldiers, you knew that he was ready to win... he would become really *hungry*. As you came to dismount he would turn round and nip your knee. The trick was to lean over his shoulder, and feed him a Polo, then slide off while he was distracted.

Pendil's second season over fences brought him to Cheltenham for the Gold Cup unbeaten in eleven chases. He had won the King George VI Chase by five lengths from The Dikler. The Gold Cup appeared at his mercy ... if he stayed the trip. Pendil jumped superbly and although the pace had been strong, with Charlie Potheen blazing a trail, Pendil jumped into the lead at the third last, and was clear between the last two. Pendil was a shade close to the last and fiddled, but 100 yards up the run-in was still clear. Then two things happened simultaneously. Pendil suddenly seemed to freeze. He shortened his stride; lost his action, and from a racing machine was

transformed into a reluctant beast of burden. At the same time The Dikler started to run. Ron Barry, sensing the opportunity, drove the big chestnut for all he was worth. In the last few strides Pendil recovered himself, and surged forward, but it was too late. The Dikler's momentum carried him past his rival by a short head. (The race had been run in a course record time that existed until Dawn Run's Gold Cup.)

Pendil went through the following season unbeaten until Cheltenham. *Surely* this would be the year.... This time he was 13-8 on, with The Dikler 5-1 and the novice Captain Christy a 7-1 shot. Pendil was cruising at the third last, but Pitman was now determined not to strike the front too soon. As the leaders flew the downhill fence three from home the erratic High Ken crashed to the floor. Seconds earlier Captain Christy and The Dikler had loomed up on Pendil's outside. High Ken lay legs a-tangle, directly in front...there was no way round.... The form book reads simply: 'third and every chance when brought down twentieth.' Captain Christy went on to win by five lengths from The Dikler. It was probably the most disappointing day of Richard Pitman's life.

Pendil (Richard Pitman) jumps the Open Ditch clear of High Ken (Bob Davies) (nearside) and Game Spirit (Terry Biddlecombe) in the 1974 Gold Cup. Disaster is just five fences away.

Pendil began the following season where he had left off but then met with two defeats before breaking down at Kempton the following February. Two seasons later Fred Winter had nursed him back to health and soundness, and after three wins and a creditable second the old horse, now aged twelve, seemed set for a third assault on the Gold Cup. Sadly however, just weeks before the race, he slipped on the roads, damaged his neck and was finally retired ... *almost* the best horse not to have won the Gold Cup.

BIG RACES WON	
King George VI Chase	1972-73
Massey Ferguson Gold Cup	1973
Arkle Challenge Trophy	1972
Welsh Champion Chase	1972
Black and White Whisky Gold Cup	1972
Benson & Hedges Handicap Chase	1972
Newbury Spring Chase	1973

PERSIAN WAR

THE STORY OF PERSIAN WAR is inevitably entwined with the personality of his owner, Mr Henry Alper. Persian War was a truly great hurdler — perhaps the greatest ever. Many people, however, would take the view that Mr Alper was not one of the great owners. Remarkably, Persian War was his first ever runner. Mr Alper played a very direct, personal role in his business as an insurance loss assessor, and he was determined to be directly involved with Persian War. As a result, Persian War had no fewer than five trainers — not to mention his expeditions to France, and for their pains these trainers were barraged by telephone calls at all hours of the day and night. Through all this, Persian War answered every question asked of him with unbelievable courage and determination.

Persian War was bred by Jakie (now Sir John) Astor, and was trained on the Flat by Major Dick Hern. He won over two miles and looked a slow horse. The shrewd Tom Masson bought him for National Hunt racing and saddled him to win his first three races. Henry Alper bought him privately through Brian Swift for £10,000 in January, 1967. Before the end of the season he had won the Victor Ludorum Hurdle and Daily Express Triumph Hurdle. By the following November, Alper and Swift had fallen out. With an impending ban on the movement of animals due to an outbreak of foot-and-mouth disease, Alper arranged for Persian War to go to France without consulting Swift. The outcome was a transfer via France — to the stables of the immensely able and likeable Colin Davies, a former motor racing driver with stables at Chepstow. It was Davies who trained Persian War to win his three Champion Hurdles.

The author well recalls the first occasion that Persian War showed himself to be quite extraordinary. His first spring target in 1968 was the Schweppes Gold Trophy. There was a race at Kempton two weeks earlier called the Lonsdale Handicap Hurdle in which it was traditional for 'Schweppes' horses to have a preparatory race, and, ideally, finish fourth or fifth, without being subjected to a hard race. Persian War ran in the Lonsdale carrying 11st 13lb. He set a terrific gallop and was fifteen lengths clear at half-way in a field of twenty-seven. Over the last he looked punch-drunk, but under desperate driving held on till the last few strides. 'Goodbye Schweppes,' was the immediate thought, but incredibly, two weeks later, he came back fresh as paint to win the Schweppes as a five-year-old carrying 11st 13lb. I was responsible for the BBC Radio commentary and such was the excitement that my voice was little more than a croak in the photo-finish! Jimmy Uttley, Persian War's brilliant jockey, confirmed: 'It was my most thrilling victory.'

Foaled 1963
Trained in England

237

Persian War (Jimmy Uttley) at the course that he made his own. This was his dramatic third and final Champion Hurdle.

A month later Persian War won his first Champion Hurdle. The prelude to his second Champion Hurdle title was an abortive campaign which started with a fall at Worcester where he fractured a femur, and stuttered to its climax with a defeat at 4-1 on at Wincanton. Nonetheless, Davies produced him cherry-ripe on the day.

Even more traumatic was the build-up to his third title. At Alper's insistence, Persian War ran in the Newbury Autumn Cup on firm going on the Flat, as a result of which he was jarred up and lame for over a month. December saw the onset of breathing problems. The vets recommended a soft palate operation, but for the time being owner and trainer decided to tie down his tongue and hope for the best. On Champion Hurdle day, Persian War was without a win for twelve months and known to 'make a noise'. The professionals opposed him and the colourful bookmaker, John Banks, 'stood' him for tens of thousands. His success that day was one of racing's great emotional moments. Winners and losers alike thronged around the Winners' Enclosure to salute a truly great and courageous horse.

It would be nice if the story ended there. It did not. Persian War went from Davies to Arthur Pitt, Dennis Rayson, and finally Jack Gibson. Pitt, to his credit, saddled him to win the Sweeps Hurdle and to finish second in the 1971 Champion Hurdle. Thereafter, the great horse went into progressive decline, throughout which he at least maintained his courage and presence. Henry Alper loved his horse, but his love was blind. As for Persian War, he was the best friend that any man ever had.

BIG RACES WON	
Champion Hurdle (3 times)	1968-70
Sweeps Hurdle	1970
Welsh Champion Hurdle	1969
Schweppes Gold Trophy	1968
Daily Express Triumph Hurdle	1967
Victor Lodorum Hurdle	1967

PRINCE REGENT

Foaled 1935
Trained in Ireland

PRINCE REGENT'S CAREER coincided with the longest European War of modern times. At the outset of the war he was four years old and on the threshold of greatness. At the end of hostilities he was, sadly, on the edge of decline.

Prince Regent was bought as a yearling at Goffs Sales for Mr J.V. Rank, the flour-milling millionaire who was obsessed by the stock of My Prince. Mr Rank had wanted to buy Reynoldstown, also a son of My Prince, who was to win two Grand Nationals, but was deterred by a trainer who was prejudiced against black horses.

After a brief spell in England in the spring of 1939, Prince Regent returned to Ireland to be trained by Tom Dreaper, a sporting farmer at Kilsallaghan, Co. Dublin. Tom Dreaper was a delightful, whimsical countryman with a horseman's instinct and the Irishman's love of a 'proper' day's hunting. His idea of an education for a young horse was to take him out hunting, and jump any available obstacle — regardless of hounds — in either direction. He believed that a horse was not properly schooled until he had 'jumped on top of a bank — and stood there long enough for me to light my pipe!'

Tom Dreaper rode Prince Regent in his three 'bumper' races, the first two of which were strictly 'educational'. In the third, at Naas, he won exceptionally easily. He was the great man's last winning ride, and possibly this accounts, in part, for his extreme affection for the horse. It was not until Arkle had won two Gold Cups that Dreaper conceded that he *might* be a better horse than Prince Regent.

The war restricted Prince Regent's racing career to Ireland for five seasons. Even the resourceful, neutral Irish found it difficult to travel other than by pony and trap, bicycle, or occasionally by train. Horses would be led up to fifteen or twenty miles to the races, or the nearest operational station. Tom Dreaper, whose stables were fifteen miles north of Dublin, would take his horses in convoy to Kingsbridge Station in the capital. One day, at a major crossroads, he asked a policeman on duty to stop the traffic. 'Is Prince Regent there?' asked the Guard. 'He is so,' said Dreaper. 'Right,' said the officer of the law, 'I'll stop the whole lot of traffic, both ways!'

Prince Regent's first major triumph was in the 1942 Irish Grand National. Carrying 12st 7lb and ridden by Tim Hyde, he won by a length from Miss Dorothy Paget's Golden Jack receiving 12lb. It was this race that established him as a great horse. During the next four seasons, Prince Regent never carried less than 12st 7lb in a handicap. The tasks he was set were prodigious, and the opposition strong. With Irish breeders unable to sell their wares because of the war, there was no alternative but to race their best stock.

At last the war came to an end and Prince Regent came to Cheltenham for the 1946 Gold Cup. He won, it seemed easily, by five lengths from Poor Flame and was accorded a hero's welcome. Only Tim Hyde had reservations. 'It took me a moment or two to beat that fellow today,' he said quietly to Tom Dreaper as he unsaddled.

Prince Regent's assault on the Grand National — worth £8805 as against the prize of £1130 of the Gold Cup — was remarkable by any standards. With 12st 5lb to carry, and conceding upwards of two stone to most of his rivals, Prince Regent nonetheless lay up with the pace throughout. 'The Prince' was used to brushing through the insubstantial Irish fences. If he met one wrong he would plough through it. His first attempt at similar tactics with the National fences came as a rude shock. According to Tim Hyde, he made cataclysmic errors at the fourth, at Valentines, and worst of all at the eleventh, the second Open Ditch. Here he stood back, was caught up on top of the fence, and landed at a standstill on

Prince Regent (Tim Hyde), prevented only by Hitler from becoming a steeplechasing legend.

241

all fours. Yet he galloped on, jumping remarkably well until he took the seventeenth fence by the roots. This time he actually fell — but to Tim Hyde's astonishment he regained his footing and galloped on. At last Prince Regent had learned his lesson, and on the second circuit knew what to expect. By the fence after Valentines he had jumped to the front and coming back on the bridle, he jumped the last two fences clear. Tim Hyde could not believe what was happening after mistakes that would have exhausted a normal horse two miles back. Suddenly, on the cruel 494-yard run-in, Prince Regent came to the end of his tether. Another fence to jump might have carried him home, but that awful, gruelling slog and the crippling weight brought him almost to a standstill. Lovely Cottage and Jack Findlay galloped by him and the impossible dream was over.

Prince Regent was the last truly great horse — with the exception of Crisp — to run in the Grand National. Nowadays the Gold Cup has more winning prize money (£55,000 as against £48,000 in the National) and more prestige. In many ways Prince Regent's defeat at Aintree heralded the end of an era.

BIG RACES WON	
Gold Cup	1946
Irish Grand National	1942
Champion Chase	1946
Becher Chase	1947
Baldoyle Chase	1944
Hospitals Chase	1943

RED RUM

Foaled 1965
Trained in England

IT IS INTRINSIC to the British character to hallow the underdog who makes good against all the odds. Red Rum was the ultimate underdog. The story of how he was 'given away' at the Sales, hard raced on the Flat, rejected and maligned, and finally became a legend in the hands of a former taxi-driver, is the stuff of fantasy fiction.

The truth was even stranger. Bred from a 'mad' mare, he was bought for 400 guineas by Tim Molony — the only bidder — at Goffs Yearling Sales. His first owner was Mr Maurice Kingsley, a Manchester manufacturer who was a substantial bettor, and who had a box at Liverpool. Although Red Rum was a May foal — many trainers will not gallop a two-year-old until his second birthday — Molony 'readied' him for the two-year-old selling race at the Grand National meeting. (In those days Liverpool was a mixed meeting.) Red Rum was well backed by his owner and was hard ridden to a dead heat with a filly called Curlicue. By an incredible coincidence, Curlicue had been bred and reared on the same stud as Red Rum, had followed him around the Sale Ring, and been bought for the identical sum of 400 guineas.

Red Rum's first jumping stable was that of Bobby Renton, the octagenarian parson's son, who had trained in Yorkshire for almost fifty years, and had his last ride in public at the age of seventy-five. Renton's greatest triumph was with Freebooter, owned by Mrs Lurline Brotherton, who won the Grand National in 1950. Ever since, he had been on the look-out for another Grand National winner for his main patron. Red Rum's jumping career with Renton was not a success. In the season 1969-70 he ran fourteen times, but did not win. He was riddled with virus, ran in soft going — which he hated — and was ridden by six different jockeys all of whom gave him hard races. Finally he wore blinkers.

Renton retired in 1971 handing over the stable — and Red Rum — to his assistant trainer and former amateur rider, Tommy Stack. Stack's new situation did not last long, as he felt that his riding career was slipping away. He surrendered his licence so as to continue riding, and Anthony Gillam took over. Red Rum, meanwhile, had made a promising start as a steeplechaser, winning three of his first four novices' chases. But soon he reverted to being disappointing and inconsistent. Finally he developed foot problems which were diagnosed as pedalostitis — a bone disease which is often fatal.

So Mrs Brotherton decided to sell him. It is at this point that former taxi-driver and used-car salesman 'Ginger' McCain enters the story. While he was driving, one of McCain's clients was the millionaire retired local businessman, Noel le Mare. McCain would ferry him back from the Prince of Wales Hotel, Southport, on a

'He's done it!' Red Rum (Tommy Stack) makes racing history by becoming the first ever to win three Grand Nationals.

Saturday night and chat to the old man endlessly about racing. Noel le Mare, who started life earning fourpence an hour as a trawlerman in Liverpool, had always harboured an ambition to win the Grand National. McCain's ambition was to become a respected trainer. Endlessly McCain 'nagged' his fare to send him a horse. After one or two miscues, Red Rum became the horse they had both sought. McCain paid 6000 guineas for the Brotherton cast-off — four times the amount he had ever previously paid.

On his first morning at McCain's yard, Red Rum walked through the back streets of Southport to McCain's 'gallops', the Southport sands. As the newcomer trotted on to the beach, McCain's heart stopped. 'My God,' he thought, 'he's lame!' Red Rum stepped through the brine, trotted through the shallows — and walked back perfectly sound. He was never lame again. Any other trainer in England would almost certainly have had a lame horse for life.

The story of Red Rum's five Grand Nationals is now a sporting legend. They made him a major television personality — who could forget his famous walk-on at BBC TV's 'Sports Personality of the

Year' programme? — and one of the highest paid names in the Personal Appearance League. Supermarkets, shows, betting shops, fêtes, have all welcomed 'Rummy' as a fee-earning celebrity. His manners are impeccable; he is long-suffering with children, and indulgent with photographers.

His Grand Nationals are all unforgettable. In 1973 his incredible courage transformed a certain victory for Crisp into a dramatic last-gasp success for the Southport friends — in what was by far the fastest National ever run. In 1974 his second win, carrying twelve stone, lifted him to join the immortals. He was the first dual winner — and the first to win under twelve stone — for thirty-eight years. In 1975 and 1976, L'Escargot and Rag Trade were too good at the weights but, in 1977, he achieved what no horse had ever done in 140 years — win a third Grand National. In a final irony, his jockey was his former trainer, Tommy Stack.

Red Rum is still at Ginger McCain's happy Southport stables, behind what became Britain's best-known second-hand car lot. 1988 sees Red Rum honoured by a life-sized bronze statue at Aintree. Like Rummy, the statue will be an inspiration to anyone who has a dream.

BIG RACES WON	
Grand National	1973, 1974, 1977
Scottish Grand National	1974

REYNOLDSTOWN

Foaled 1927
Trained in England

REYNOLDSTOWN WAS THE first winner of successive Grand Nationals at Aintree since The Colonel sixty-six years earlier. Furthermore, he won two of the most controversial Nationals in the history of the race.

Reynoldstown was owned and trained by Major Noel Furlong, and in 1935 ridden by his son Frank, a subaltern in the 9th Lancers. The family hailed from Co. Cork but now lived at Skeffington Hall, Leicestershire. It was from Ireland too that Reynoldstown was acquired. He was bred by Mr Richard Ball of Reynoldstown, Naul, in Co. Dublin. For a while it seemed likely that the black gelding by My Prince would be bought by Mr J.V. Rank, but one of Mr Rank's trainers persuaded the millionaire against buying a black horse — believing his colour to be 'the mark of Satan'.

Reynoldstown's first Grand National came in the year that Golden Miller started 2-1 favourite, and unseated Gerry Wilson at the eleventh fence. From Bechers on the second circuit, the race became a dual between Thomond II, who had fought out the memorable battle with Golden Miller in the Gold Cup just fifteen days earlier, and Reynoldstown. Reynoldstown took the lead coming back onto the racecourse, but Billy Speck conjured such a magnificent jump from the small but courageous Thomond II at the last fence that the American-owned horse landed in front. But now his exertions took their toll, and Reynoldstown drew away to win by three lengths from Blue Prince, who passed the exhausted Thomond II on the run-in. Reynoldstown, carrying 11st 4lb, was clocked at 9 minutes 20.2 seconds. For many years the course record time was in dispute, as Golden Miller was timed by different individuals at 9 minutes 20.2 seconds and 9 minutes 20.4 seconds the previous year.

Red Rum and Crisp's National put an end to these arguments once and for all. In Reynoldstown's second Grand National he was ridden by Fulke Walwyn — a former brother officer of Frank Furlong's in the 9th Lancers — as even with 12st 2lb, Frank Furlong could no longer do the weight. While 1935 is remembered as the year that Golden Miller did not win, 1936 is most remembered as the year of Davy Jones's incredible misfortune. A tubed horse, and a flat-racing cast-off, Davy Jones was bought a month before the race by Lord Mildmay of Flete for his son, the Hon. Anthony Mildmay, to ride. Davy Jones was unconsidered at 100-1, but the future Lord Mildmay had a memorable ride. Davy Jones made every yard of the running to the second last, jumping from fence to fence, when disaster struck. On landing the buckle of bridle snapped, leaving the reins dangling. At the same time Lord Mildmay had an attack of cramp in his shoulders. Davy Jones came to the last fence

still clear of Reynoldstown, but now with his rider a passenger he ran past the fence, scattering the public. Fulke Walwyn claims to this day that Reynoldstown was closing on Davy Jones, and would have won in any case, but Davy Jones must be looked upon as one of the National's unluckiest losers.

Lord Mildmay died many years later swimming in the sea. It was generally supposed that he suffered an attack of cramp.

Reynoldstown did not run in the National again, and was aimed at the Gold Cup the following year, which was abandoned because of snow. Reynoldstown's second National may have owed something to good fortune, but to have won the race in record time *and* under 12st 2lb entitles the Furlongs' horse to the highest regard.

A family concern. Reynoldstown is flanked by his owner-trainer, Major Noel Furlong and son Frank, who rode him to win the National in 1935.

BIG RACES WON	
Grand National (twice)	1935-36

SEA PIGEON

Foaled 1970
Trained in England

SEA PIGEON WAS an exceptional horse by any standards, and the excellence of his hurdling career has tended to overshadow his remarkable performances on the Flat. It is easy to forget how, as a seven-year-old, he won the Chester Cup in his first flat race for two and a half seasons; how as an eight-year-old he won a valuable handicap with 10st 5lb; how as a nine-year-old he won the Ebor Handicap with a record ten stone. It was after that he proceeded to win two Champion Hurdles!

Sea Pigeon, by Sea Bird II, out of a Round Table mare, was bred to win a Derby. In fact, as a three-year-old, trained by Jeremy Tree, he did run in the Derby finishing seventh. He was also fourth in the Prince of Wales Stakes at Royal Ascot. The following spring, Mr Pat Muldoon, the Edinburgh wine and spirit merchant, bought Sea Pigeon privately from Beckhampton after the dark brown horse had been gelded and turned away. The castration had not been a success and Sea Pigeon was in poor condition for some considerable period.

Sea Pigeon's first National Hunt trainer was Gordon W. Richards, but after he and Muldoon had fallen out over a betting matter, Sea Pigeon was transferred to Peter Easterby's stable. During the next five years he was to become a household name. Sea Pigeon was always a complicated ride and for much of his career needed matters to go entirely his way. He was at his best covered up, ridden well off the pace, and produced at the last possible moment. For most of his career he favoured a sound surface, but his great races with Monksfield in the Champion Hurdle were on soft ground.

Chester was an ideal course for him on the Flat, with its quick turns, short straight and constant distractions. He won two successive Chester Cups, the second under 9st 7lb. But his finest hour on the Flat was in the Ebor Handicap. Ridden by a National Hunt jockey — albeit Jonjo O'Neill with three broken toes! — he beat Donegal Prince (received 35lb) by a short head, after his rider had dropped his hands in the final furlong.

Under National Hunt Rules he seemed doomed to failure in the Champion Hurdle. Although he stayed two-and-a-quarter miles on the Flat, he seemed *not* to stay two miles 200 yards at Cheltenham — especially when the going was soft. To his considerable advantage, the course and distance of the Champion Hurdle were shortened in 1980 and 'The Pigeon' finally won the hurdling crown at the fourth attempt. The following year, at the age of eleven and partnered by John Francome because Jonjo O'Neill had not recovered from a broken leg, he put up the most spectacular performance in the history of the race. Ridden with an artistry that

bordered on the insolent, Francome allowed himself to be led until seventy-five yards from the line, whereupon he shook the reins and Sea Pigeon surged past his rivals with total disdain. It was truly magnificent to behold.

Sea Pigeon and Jonjo O'Neill. If at first you don't succeed ...

There were those who believed to the end that Sea Pigeon was not truly genuine, but the author disagrees. He was simply a horse who liked to arrange things in his own way. Never once did he find a yard for a smack with the whip. In all he won sixteen races on the Flat, and twenty-one under N.H. Rules, winning £277,045. No owner ever had a better servant.

BIG RACES WON	
(Flat)	
Ebor Handicap	1979
Chester Cup	1977-78
Vaux Gold Tankard	1977-78, 1980
Doonside Cup	1980
Duke of Edinburgh Stakes	1972
Tennant Trophy	1979
Bogside Cup	1978
(National Hunt)	
Champion Hurdle	1980-81
Scottish Champion Hurdle	1977-78
Welsh Champion Hurdle	1980
Fighting Fifth Hurdle	1978, 1980
Embassy Handicap Hurdle	1977

SEE YOU THEN

Foaled 1980
Trained in Ireland and England

SEE YOU THEN became in 1987 the fourth horse to have won three Champion Hurdles. But ironically, he was bred more with a view to winning the Derby.

His breeder was the Newmarket trainer Jeremy Hindley, who had inherited the prestigious Ribblesdale Stud at Kirkbymoorside, Yorkshire, from his father, Reg Hindley, the distinguished Three-Day-Event rider. Hindley was breeding with a view to racing and decided to send the stud's beautifully-bred mare, Melodina, back to Royal Palace in 1979. Royal Palace, although sire of the dual Classic winner Dunfermline, had become unfashionable and was reasonably priced.

Sadly, in 1980, Hindley's mother Alycia died, and with estate duties to be paid, the trainer decided to disband the stud. The Royal Palace colt was accordingly sent to the Newmarket October Yearling Sales, and as he liked the horse, Hindley had no compunction in recommending his friends to view him. The author recalls finding Michael Stoute and Guy Harwood in convulsions of laughter in the area of the colt's box. On asking to see the horse, the reason became evident. The powerful bay charged out of his box, sweating profusely, and roaring his head off. Within seconds he had reared up on his hind legs, and made it clear that, like his breeder, he proposed to live life to the full. Hindley had been hoping for a price of around 30,000 guineas, but so badly did the colt continue to behave that the Irish trainer Con Collins, who had trained his own brother Milverton, was able to buy him for 17,000 guineas. Collins quickly eliminated his stallion potential and the Royal Palace gelding — now called See You Then — became a successful second-class handicapper on the Flat as a three-year-old, winning three handicaps in-a-row between 1 mile 2 furlongs and 1 mile 5 furlongs.

It was over hurdles in the autumn that See You Then showed top-class form. In February 1984 he was bought, after lengthy negotiations, by Frank Mahon on behalf of the Stype Wood Stud. After winning at Punchestown in February, he joined the stable of Nick Henderson at Lambourn. See You Then started favourite at 5-2 for the Triumph Hurdle, but, coming from a long way off the pace, was beaten by the 20-1 shot, Northern Game. He then travelled to Italy to win the local equivalent of the Triumph Hurdle, but soon afterwards he fell on the roads, damaged a knee and in July returned to the stud in England to convalesce.

In the autumn he returned to Henderson's yard to be trained for the 1985 Champion Hurdle. After a wide-margin defeat by Browne's Gazette at Kempton on Boxing Day, See You Then came to Cheltenham a 16-1 shot, but won easily by seven lengths. John

Francome, his regular jockey, had been injured in the previous race, so Steve Smith-Eccles picked up a most profitable 'spare' ride. On Francome's retirement, the partnership continued.

Soon afterwards, his training problems began in earnest, and See You Then was blistered and turned out for the summer. The following spring Henderson was only able to give him one race before the Champion Hurdle. It made no difference. He won again in brilliant style, by seven lengths.

In 1987, after further leg trouble, corns, and interruption from bad weather, Henderson despaired of giving him a race before his third Champion Hurdle. Fortunately an opportunity arose at Haydock eleven days before the event, which he won. On Champion Hurdle day he appeared cherry-ripe, but after looking likely to win easily, 'blew up' on the run-in and won by only a length and a half.

His successes reflect immense credit upon his trainer, who was hard-working, resourceful and extremely even-tempered in trying to make his horse fit, under extreme and unreasonable pressure from the popular press. See You Then, for his part, remained an individual of unpredictable and generally unfriendly temperament, having little regard for anyone other than his stable lad, Glyn Foster.

See You Then (Steve Smith-Eccles) jumps the last flight with Gaye Brief (Peter Scudamore) on the way to his second Champion Hurdle.

BIG RACES WON	
Champion Hurdle (3 times)	1985-87

SIR KEN

Foaled 1947
Trained in France and England

WHEREAS THERE ARE those who will always argue the case for Golden Miller against Arkle, as the greatest steeplechaser of all time, there are few who would dispute the status of Sir Ken as the greatest Champion Hurdler.

Sir Ken was bred in France and ran twice over hurdles from the stables of Maurice Adele before Willie Stephenson bought him privately for the equivalent of £750. He ran for the first time over hurdles in England as a four-year-old at Liverpool on Grand National day, 1951. A 'springer' in the market, he won the Lancashire Hurdle by five lengths. Stephenson still owned him at this stage, but after this race passed him onto Mr Maurice Kingsley, the Manchester manufacturer, who was later to own — all too briefly — another great horse who began his career at Liverpool, Red Rum. 'But I didn't get paid until he won his second Champion Hurdle!' claims Willie.

Sir Ken went through his first three seasons in England unbeaten in sixteen hurdle races, including those first two Champion Hurdles. In the first of them his rivals included Hatton's Grace, who had

Sir Ken (Tim Molony) — unbeaten in his first 16 hurdle races in Britain, including two Champion Hurdles.

won the race in the three previous seasons, and National Spirit, the winner in 1947 and 1948. Ridden as always by Tim Molony (and favourite at 3-1) Sir Ken took the lead going to the last flight and beat Noholme by two lengths.

By the following year Sir Ken was considered unbeatable and was made 5-2 on — the shortest-priced favourite in the history of the race. His success was gained readily — again by two lengths — from Galation (Brian Marshall) and Teapot II (Pat Taaffe). Sir Ken finally met with his first hurdles defeat in the first race of his fourth season. Starting at 7-1 on in a conditions hurdle at Uttoxeter in October, he finished third to Impney and Rif II. At last the bubble had burst. It was the first time he had raced on firm going, which did not suit him.

Further defeats followed at Windsor — beaten four lengths by Noholme (receiving 11lb) — and at Kempton, under top weight in a competitive handicap. But back at Cheltenham, starting at 9-4 on, he showed he was still the king by winning his third title. Impney and Galation followed him home.

In 1955, Sir Ken went lame in mid-season and was beaten for the first time at Cheltenham. Clair Soleil, another French-bred, won a first Champion Hurdle for Captain Ryan Price, with Sir Ken fourth. The following season it was decided to try the Triple Champion over fences. The campaign was a considerable success. His four wins from six races included the Cotswold Chase (now Arkle Trophy) at the National Hunt Meeting, and the Mildmay Chase at Liverpool. The 1956-57 season was not so successful. Sir Ken failed to complete in three of his four races, although one of these was the Gold Cup for which he started joint third favourite.

Sir Ken was a grand, slashing type of horse, who was, until 1955, very sound and full of courage. He was owned by a gambler so there were no half-measures when the money was down. His trainer, Willie Stephenson always made sure that he did not go to the races a gallop short. Above all he was a great jumper of hurdles. Willie Stephenson recalls: 'He was a great horse and I've certainly always thought he was the best ever.' At the end of his career he was given to a local farmer, Rodney Ward, to hunt with the Puckeridge Foxhounds. He died in the best possible way — from a heart attack — in harness with hounds running.

BIG RACES WON	
Champion Hurdle (three times)	1952-54
Lancashire Hurdle	1951
Cotswold Chase	1955
Mildmay Chase	1955

TROYTOWN

Foaled 1913
Trained in Ireland

TROYTOWN WAS certainly one of the outstanding winners of the Grand National, if not the greatest of all. He was a power-house of a horse, standing 17hh, with terrific bone, a great shoulder and substantial depth of girth. His jockey at Aintree, the legendary Jack Anthony, probably the finest jockey over the National fences until Brian Marshall, always said that Troytown was the hardest horse that he ever had to ride.

Troytown, by Cyllene's son Zria, was bred by his owner Major Thomas Collins-Gerrard, in Co. Meath. He was given plenty of time to mature, and did not race until he was six. In March 1919, as a novice, he came to Liverpool for the first time and was beaten in the Stanley Chase. Two days later however, he won the Champion Chase. Three months later he travelled to Paris and won the Grand Steeple-Chase.

In 1920 he returned to Aintree, supported by an immense throng of Irishmen, who considered him unbeatable. It was a Grand National that no one present would ever forget. The weather was appalling, with a raging gale and cold slanting rain. The going was heavy. Poethlyn, the hero of 1918 (at Gatwick) and 1919 (when the race returned to Liverpool), was again favourite at 3-1 despite top weight of 12st 7lb. Troytown was second choice at 6-1. Poethlyn fell at the first fence, while Troytown led the field into the driving rain. Always a strong puller with a mouth of iron, Troytown was made almost unrideable, even by Anthony, as the reins slipped through his jockey's gloved hands. Troytown was still pulling his rider's arms out when he jumped the water ten lengths clear with his rivals toiling. Anthony described him afterwards as more like a steam-engine than a horse. At Bechers he jumped so high that his rider described it as like taking off in an express lift. He was almost breathless, but even on the inside, where the drop is deepest, Troytown's remarkable shoulder-power cushioned the impact.

It was at the last Ditch that Troytown made his first and only mistake. Misjudging the take-off in the rain, he slipped and ploughed through the five-foot-high, fir-dressed obstacle, leaving a gaping hole. Almost any other horse would have crashed to the ground, but Troytown, although losing many lengths, found an 'extra leg' and recovered. This catastrophic error left Troytown trailing The Bore, ridden by Harry Brown, but an incredible jump at the third-to-last fence took him from a length down to a length in front. Ears pricked, he jumped the last with the same impetus as he jumped the first and powered his way up the run-in to the roars of the Irish, who mobbed him in the manner of Dawn Run. Jack Anthony was far more exhausted than his tearaway mount and confessed to his

arms being completely numb. Only five of the twenty-four starters completed the gruelling course.

At the age of seven, Troytown was now in his prime, and his sporting owner sent him again to Paris for the Grand Steeple-Chase. This time he had a far from smooth passage in the race, and finished only third. Five days later he was saddled again for the Prix des Drags, but at one of the easiest obstacles on the course, he fell and broke his leg above the knee. Such was his courage and indestructible nature that he struggled to his feet and tried to continue, but collapsed again in a few yards. There was no alternative but to put him down.

He was buried in the animals' cemetery at Asnière, not far from the course, where his name was perpetuated in a headstone. How ironic that sixty-six years later Ireland's greatest mare, Dawn Run, should have perished on the same racecourse.

Troytown was the old-fashioned, late-maturing type of steeplechaser that has sadly become almost extinct. Only Crisp, since the war, has put up a comparable performance at Aintree. He was something special.

Troytown — the 17hh power-house was a handful even for the superb horseman Jack Anthony.

BIG RACES WON	
Grand National	1920
Grand Steeple-Chase de Paris	1919